DATE

JAN -4 2005

GAYLORD

TRENTON PUBLIC LIBRARY

COPY 40

891.7 SETSCHKAREV, Vsevolod
S   *Gogol:* his life and works. Tr. by Robert Kramer
       [New York] N.Y.U. [c.]1965.   264p.   Bibl.
Related   6.00
Books in *1. Gogol', Nikolai Vasil'evich, 1809-1852.*
Catalog   The German edition appeared in 1953.
Under

 Title.   F 66

Gogol: His Life and Works

Gogol:
His Life and Works

By *VSEVOLOD SETCHKAREV*

Translated by Robert Kramer

NEW YORK UNIVERSITY PRESS 1965

© 1965 BY NEW YORK UNIVERSITY
LIBRARY OF CONGRESS CATALOG CARD NUMBER: 65-19518
MANUFACTURED IN THE UNITED STATES OF AMERICA

PREFACE

THIS STUDY of Gogol's life and works is not intended as an original scholarly investigation, but rather as a summary of the previous literary scholarship devoted to Gogol. My purpose has been to examine Gogol primarily as an artist and to elucidate his formal peculiarities. This task could not be performed in its entirety, since all the characteristics of the formal structure of Gogol's works dependent on the Russian language, precisely those which are so important for judging Gogol as a writer, had to be omitted; I was compelled to limit myself to the figures, tropes, and composition, and only refer to sound organization from time to time. In order to make the work more readable, I have not devoted separate sections to Gogol's various literary devices, and instead have discussed them as they occurred in the works. In addition to making the book easier to read, this procedure also has the advantage of revealing more clearly the organic interweaving of form and content.

I have deliberately separated the account of Gogol's life from that of his works, and have largely refrained from pointing out biographically determined elements in his works. Exaggerated biographism, which is irrelevant in judging a work of art, has been given entirely too much attention. The connections between life and literature that are clearly evident will be found by the reader himself; it seemed out of place in a brief study to engage in subtle investigations of such possibilities.

In Gogol's biography, I attribute a decisive significance to his spiritual crisis in Vienna in 1840—much more so than is usual in recent scholarship. Gogol's works seem to me to justify this opinion. His writings before 1840 (everything that established his reputation) had, no doubt, a metaphysical substratum, but only after 1840 does an expressly Church-oriented Christian tendency emerge. There is no question that in the works of his period of artistic creativity from 1829 to 1840, which is all of a piece, Gogol—under the influence of Pushkin and German Romanticism—considered the art for art's sake theory the only true starting point for a philosophy of art. After 1840, he moves away from this position, designating art the servant of religion, and he develops a philosophy of religion that is consistent from the point of view of his new position.

It cannot be emphasized enough that the available translations of Gogol abound in errors and simplifications of text and that they communicate only a very faint idea of what Gogol is really like as an artist. The efforts of foreign critics, based on erroneous translations, are, as also in the case of Dostoyevsky, often worthless.

The transcription of Russian names and words follows the widely accepted pattern and has no claims to scholarly consistency.

I would like to express my gratitude to Dean Franklin L. Ford of Harvard University and to the Clark Fund for making possible this translation from the German, in which language the book had originally appeared in 1953. I am very grateful also to Mr. Robert P. Hughes and Dr. Simon Karlinsky of the University of California, Berkeley, who translated the numerous Gogol quotations from the original Russian and assisted me most effectively in the revision of the final English text.

VSEVOLOD SETCHKAREV

Belmont, Mass.
February, 1965

CONTENTS

PREFACE

Part I Gogol's Life   1

Part II Gogol's Works   93

1. Evenings on a Farm near Dikanka   95
2. Fragments and Arabesques   120
3. Mirgorod   136
4. Two Masterpieces of the Short Form   155
5. Gogol's Theater Pieces   166
6. Dead Souls   182
7. "The Overcoat"   216
8. Gogol's Art after the Crisis   227
9. Selected Passages from Correspondence with Friends   232
10. The Second Part of Dead Souls   247

BIBLIOGRAPHICAL NOTE   257

INDEX   259

Part I
Gogol's Life

THE REPORTS about Gogol's ancestors are confusing and unreliable. The social status of his ancestors was purposely falsified by their descendants in the eighteenth century, and the family relationships were altered, all for the sake of proving that the family was of noble extraction. For, only proof of ancient nobility entitled the landowners of the Ukraine (which did not become part of Russia until 1653) to possession of land and, above all, to possession of "souls," i.e. of serfs, who provided an unpaid work force. The easiest and safest means by which one could make his noble ancestry seem probable was by way of Poland. With forged papers, many a Ukranian landowner sought to establish beyond doubt the connection of his family with the Polish nobility—an action which the authorities obviously did not make too difficult. One branch of Gogol's family unquestionably contained several high Ukrainian officers; in fact, one of them is supposed to have reached the highest position of a hetman,[1] but he had hardly anything to do with Poland. Equally far from being Polish is another line, which derives from a certain Andrey Gogol, who, for some service, is supposed to have been rewarded with landed property by the Polish king John Casimir in the year 1674, which was, strange to say, six years after his discharge from service. Andrey, it is said, was a colonel in Mogilev.

The descendants of this Andrey, who can be considered the

[1] Ukrainian chief.

father of the line from which the author was descended, were, without exception, priests—a fact which speaks strongly against the nobility of the family. In the documents, no family name of these clerical gentlemen is mentioned at all. The great-grandfather of the author, the village priest Demyan, was the first to add to the Polonized first name of his clergyman father Yan, the surname Yanovsky, which was retained by his children. The author's grandfather, Afanasy, and his children called themselves Gogol-Yanovsky. The author himself was the first to drop the second name. Afanasy was also the first member of the family since Andrey who was not a clergyman. Documents bear witness to his entry into the army, where he eventually reached the rank of major. But he also attended a religious seminary; his records contain the observation that he could speak and write Russian, Latin, Polish, German, and Greek. He presumably abandoned his religious vocation at the urging of his father-in-law. As a seminarian, he gave foreign-language lessons to the children of noble families in the surrounding area. This gave him an opportunity to fall in love with one of his pupils, Tatyana Lizogub, the daughter of a distinguished Ukrainian nobleman. According to family tradition, after sending her a declaration of love placed in a nutshell, he carried her off and married her. With their sense of high social position, the parents were at first indignant. (The mother of the bride was descended from old Polish nobility; hence from this side the author has Polish blood.) Finally, they relented, but probably with the stipulation that the husband give up the clerical estate, which was not very highly respected. Thus the poor seminarian Afanasy Yanovsky came to gain possession of land, to enter upon a military career, and presumably also to receive a title of nobility; he gave evidence for the latter by connecting the name Yanovsky with the original Gogol, in which case he was certainly thinking of the unauthenticated and somewhat legendary Andrey. A forged document was not difficult to obtain, and so we find in the peerage book of the province of Kiev under the fifteenth of October, 1792 a notice that the evidence offered by Gogol-Yanovsky as proof of his noble extraction has been found sufficient, after which the entry follows.

The abducted girl—the grandmother of the author—is said

to have possessed an outstanding talent for drawing, which was inherited by her grandson.

For a long time the marriage remained childless until Gogol's father Vasily was born in 1777. He spent his childhood on his father's estate, entered the postal service in a very subordinate position, resigned in a short time, and then went back to live off his income as a small landowner. The most significant event in the life of this dreamy but very cheerful man, who was inclined to the arts and being theatrically gifted even composed Ukrainian comedies himself, was his marriage in 1805 with the fourteen-year-old daughter of a neighboring Ukrainian landowner, Maria Kosyarovskaya. He had known the girl since her earliest childhood and formed a deep attachment to her, which he attributed to divine decree. In a letter to Sergey Aksakov after the death of her husband, Maria Gogol reports that, at the age of fourteen, her husband had a strange vision in church. During the services, the altar gates had opened, and the Mother of God, wearing a purple mantle and a crown, stepped out and addressed him as follows: "You will have to endure many illnesses [as a matter of fact—the writer adds—he did have to go through many illnesses, the last one a fever which persisted two years], but everything will pass; you will recover, marry, and—here is your wife!" With these words she raised her hand, and he saw, sitting on the floor at her feet, a little child, whose features impressed themselves upon his memory. How great was the astonishment of the boy when he recognized the face of the child in the seven-month-old daughter of the neighboring landlord! He spoke to no one about it, but constantly observed the growing girl, playing with her for hours, to the surprise of those around him. And when the same vision appeared to him thirteen years later, and the crowned Virgin stepped from the altar door and pointed to a girl clothed all in white with the words "Here is your bride," he recognized his little friend again and did not hesitate to ask her hand in marriage.

This story is significant: in the Gogol house a firm belief in the direct participation of heavenly powers in the fate of the family prevailed—an essential feature of the intellectual biography of the author. The girl's father, Ivan Kosyarovsky, former postmaster in Kharkov, might have had his doubts, but the decisive voice in the family belonged to his sister Anna; she was married to the brother of a high Russian government official from the Ukraine, Dmitry Troshchinsky, whose influence and riches were of great advantage to the family.

Little Maria was raised at the home of her rich relatives. Somehow her young neighbor succeeded in gaining the favor of her distinguished aunt, who promoted the marriage with the greatest zeal, although the niece was not yet capable of serious love. But the sentimental wooing of the love-stricken youth flattered her exceedingly. Many years later she describes it in her own naive manner. The connection with the house of the great Troshchinsky brought the young husband into contact with a new field of endeavor.

From 1806 to 1814 Troshchinsky lived in retirement on his estate Kibency in the province of Poltava, until he was recalled to the post of Minister of Justice, which he filled for three years. He spent the last period of his life (1829) once again on his estate. When he stayed there, this grandly furnished house, full of paintings, expensive china, bronze, and marble became a center of social life. The distinguished gentleman loved to see guests around him, guests whom he entertained lavishly, and who repaid his hospitality by amusing him. His household, with servants of all ranks, even down to the then popular court fool, resembled the court of a ruling prince. Gogol's father appears to have played the role of majordomo at this court, or in any case of organizer of revels. The house theater was under his management. Here he could display his theatrical abilities, and for this theater he also composed his comedies, which achieved great success, but of which only one remains extant, *The Simpleton, or The Tricks of the Woman Outwitted by the Soldier*. Gogol was very much interested in his father's comedies and used situations from them; his mother later presumed that the son burnt them in Rome by mistake.

But father Gogol did not find his occupation a complete blessing. The role of poor relation in the household of a willful and capricious, although basically good-natured and helpful master was not always easy. Hence he constantly gravitated back to his little estate, Vasilyevka, where, at the side of his young and dearly beloved wife, he could lead a quiet life and manage his 130 souls. The little estate brought in enough so that with sensible management they could live without worry. The father liked to busy himself with the management of the estate, whereas the mother displayed no great talent for it and subsequently brought the estate to the brink of ruin.

Twelve children resulted from the marriage, but only four survived early childhood.

Nikolay Gogol was born on March 20, 1809 in the little town of Sorochincy. Two previous stillbirths had made his parents anxious, so that the eighteen-year-old mother was brought to the house of the best doctor in the district for the delivery. She made a vow that if it should be a boy, she would name him Nikolay, because a wonder-working image of this saint was located in the nearby village of Dikanka. The priest of Dikanka was instructed by the parents to pray ceaselessly for a happy outcome until a request for a mass of thanksgiving would confirm that his prayers had been heard.

At first, the unusually weak child was not thought capable of surviving. At the age of six weeks the infant was brought to his father's estate, Vasilyevka, where he was to spend his childhood. He could not speak until he was three years old, and is supposed to have learned to read by the age of seven. The reports that he wrote poems at the age of five, which caused the noted poet and playwright Vasily Kapnist to prophesy a great career for him, are undoubtedly to be placed in the category of legend. They are based chiefly on the recollections of the mother, who idolized her son and attributed to him the most fantastic accomplishments, such as the invention of the steam engine and the railroad. Again and again in Gogol's letters to his mother, one encounters the request that she praise him less or, better, not speak of him at all.

The recollections of contemporaries picture him as a serious and brooding boy of poor and delicate health. His mother, who was constantly worrying about him, spoiled him a great deal, a fact which may partially explain the strongly egoistic tendency in his character. His dreamy, sickly nature appears clearly in the description of a childhood experience, which his self-styled "soulmate" Alexandra Smirnova recounted according to his own words:

> I was about five years old. I had stayed alone at Vasilyevka. Father and Mother had gone out. Only the old nurse remained with me, but she too had gone off somewhere. Twilight was descending. I squeezed myself into the corner of the divan and listened in the complete silence to the ticking of the pendulum on the old-fashioned wallclock. There was a rushing in my ears, something kept coming upon me, then receding. Would you believe it—at that moment it seemed to me as if the knocking of the pendulum were the knocking of time receding into eternity. Suddenly the faint meowing of a cat broke the oppressive silence. I watched it as it meowed and cautiously crept toward me. I shall never forget how it came over and stretched itself, while the claws in the soft paws scratched faintly on the floor and the green eyes gleamed with an evil light. I was overcome with terror. I climbed on top of the divan and pressed myself against the wall. "Kitty, kitty," I murmured, and, to encourage myself, jumped down from the divan, grabbed the cat, which was very easy to take hold of, and ran into the garden, where I threw it into the pond and kept pushing it out further with a pole when it tried to scramble out. I was afraid, I trembled, and yet at the same time felt some kind of satisfaction, perhaps revenge for the way it had frightened me. But after it had drowned, after the last circles had disappeared from the surface of the water and complete silence and peace prevailed, I was terribly sorry for "kitty," I felt the gnawing of my conscience. It seemed to me as if I had drowned a *person*. I wept dreadfully and only calmed down when my father, to whom I had confessed my deed, soundly thrashed me.

However strange this story sounds and however many romantic embellishments it may contain, it is characteristic of Gogol's early tendency toward the morbid and the horrible; the role which weird cats play in his works gives evidence of the strong impression which this experience had made upon him. No less informative is a letter to his mother from the year 1833, in which he recalls his feelings as a child:

> I recollect that in my childhood I was incapable of any strong feelings; I looked on everything as things made only to please me. I felt no special love for anyone except you, and perhaps I felt it for you only because Nature itself had inspired this

feeling in me. I looked at everything with passionless eyes; I went to church because I was ordered or because I was carried there; but when I stood in church, I perceived nothing but the vestments, the parish priest, and the repulsive bellowing of the deacons. I crossed myself because I saw that everyone else was crossing himself. But once (I remember this occasion very vividly) I asked you to tell me about the Last Judgment, and you told me, a mere child, so well, so clearly, so touchingly of that bliss which men hope to attain for a virtuous life, and you described to me the eternal torments of sinners in such a striking and terrifying manner that it staggered and awakened all my sensibilities, it planted and later developed the loftiest thoughts in me.

A dreamy, withdrawn egoism, which finds world enough in its own imagination, appears best to characterize Gogol as a boy. He was reinforced in this attitude by the death, at the age of nine, of his brother Ivan, who was a year younger and to whom he was very much attached. At the age of nine, Gogol had been sent with him to the high school at Poltava; he lived there in the house of a teacher and wrote sensible, in fact, precocious letters to his parents, in which, among other things, he asked for supplementary tutoring in mathematics.

Perhaps the death of his brother was the immediate occasion which caused his parents to take their oldest son away from the place where their sons had lived together. In Nezhin, a fairly large city in the province of Chernigov, a High School of Advanced Studies was opened. Graduation from this school entitled one to enter upon the career of a government official of medium rank. A boarding school was attached to the institution and the young Gogol was sent here at first at his own cost as a boarding student. After a few months, the influential Troshchinsky managed to arrange for him to be educated at state expense.

In June 1821 Gogol passed the entrance examination with only mediocre grades. He spent the vacation at home and did not fully move into his new quarters until August. He did not find the separation from his parents easy. A letter from August 1821 reads:

Before the vacation I wrote that everything was fine with me here, but now the opposite is true. After the vacation I became so sad, that every blessed day my tears flowed like a stream, and I don't even know why; especially when I think of you, they simply stream down my face. . . . My faithful Simon [an old serf and cook who watched over Gogol] takes such great pains over me, that not a single night passed without him begging me not to cry for you, and he often stayed up with me all night. I already told him to go to sleep, but I just couldn't get him to do it."

Gogol's health was also affected—or did he only hope to arouse the sympathy of his parents, so that he might come home again? "After the arrival in Nezhin," he writes, "the very next day my chest began to hurt. At night my chest hurt so that I could not breathe freely. Toward morning I felt better, but my chest still hurt, and I was afraid that it might be something bad, and then I was so sad, because I was separated from you. But now, thank God, it's all over with, and I am healthy and happy."

Gogol spent seven years at the boarding school. He went home only for the summer vacation and the Christmas holidays. The many recollections of his fellow students and teachers give a rather contradictory picture of his character, since all these memoirs were composed much later, when Gogol was already famous. Some of them attempt to idealize him and to make it seem as if the writer of the memoirs had recognized his genius very early in his career; others are dictated by envy and purposely blacken his character.

Gogol's schoolboy letters to his parents reveal a well-behaved, sensible boy: he reports on the progress of his studies (here he speaks of drawing with special affection), on his pastimes, on his health (which at first left something to be desired; in October 1822, he suffered a severe attack of scarlet fever); and he frequently asks for money for small expenses, such as painting and writing materials and clothing.

During his whole period in school, Gogol was a mediocre student. However, the reason for this does not appear to be a lack of talent, but rather laziness—laziness or distractions; for at the very beginning of his stay in school, his passion for the theater revealed itself, and soon brought him a respected position at the boarding school. At first he did not have such an honored role. He was an extraordinarily ugly, skinny boy, with a transparent complexion and a strikingly long nose. He suffered intensely from scrofula with all its embarrassing side-effects. At school, untidiness—subsequently supplanted by dandyism—was a conspicuous feature of his external appearance, which repelled his comrades. In addition there were his reserved nature, which even amid the wildest revelry concealed the depths of his heart, and his rapid changes of mood alternating between rudeness and deep melancholy. His fellow students called him "the mysterious dwarf."

Once, on returning from a holiday, he brought back a Ukrainian comedy—perhaps written by his father—a performance of which he had attended at Troshchinsky's house theater. He was able to persuade his comrades to put on the play, and soon the whole boarding school was filled with enthusiasm for the theater. Money was collected for costumes and stage properties; Gogol himself painted the scenery; and after a short time they took up more difficult projects.

A letter to his parents from January 22, 1824, reads:

> Send me linen and other supplies for the theater. Our first production will be *Oedipus in Athens*, a tragedy by Ozerov. If possible, have costumes made and send them here—as many as possible, even if only *one*; but it would be better if it were *many*; and at least *a little* money. Each of us already gave what he could, all except me. I'll inform you further of how I'm going to play my role. I want to tell you that I am learning very well, at least as far as my powers allow . . . I think, dearest Papa, if you saw me, you would be sure to say that I have changed for the better, both in morals and in my studies. If you could only see how I draw now! (I am speaking of myself without any vanity.)

The teachers were less enthusiastic. An entry in the class book reads: "The following students received the grade of one [the lowest grade in Russia] in deportment: Yanovsky for uncleanliness, clowning, stubbornness, and disobedience. . . ."

The clowning which had been objected to finally grew into an irresistible theatrical talent. Gogol's gift for playing comedy filled his fellow students with enthusiasm and brought his teachers to despair, the more so since in a few years the weak and sickly child had turned into a happy youth, very much inclined to playing tricks.

Again an extract from the class book:

> "Yanovsky received the appropriate punishment for his bad conduct . . . Yanovsky placed in the corner on account of indecent expressions . . . Yanovsky in the corner for uncleanliness . . . Yanovsky without tea for stubbornness and very extraordinary laziness . . . Yanovsky playing with toys in the religion class—deprived of tea" . . . [etc., etc.]

Physical punishment was extremely rare in the boarding school. But one day Gogol went too far. The gentle director Orlay had to determine a most severe punishment. But Gogol hit upon an unusual way out: as the authorities approached, he played the role of a raving maniac with such perfection, and then feigned a mental illness so well, that instead of being punished he was brought to the infirmary and there given the best of care for several weeks. A stay in the infirmary was, on the whole, very desirable: there one had quiet, one could read in peace—and perhaps even do some writing.

In the letters of the fifteen-year old Gogol one notices a growing interest in literature; gradually literary questions begin to replace the reports of progress in painting.

"You write of a ballad and of Pushkin's *poèma Onegin*; I beg you, couldn't you send them to me? Don't *you* have any verses? Send me these too," he asks his father. At the same time he begins to copy onto the best paper Pushkin's famous verse tales and chapters from *Evgeny Onegin*, and to decorate them with his own drawings. His reading of contemporary sentimental novels shows up in his letters, e.g., when before his departure to spend his vacation at home he writes:

> Already I see in my mind's eye everything that is dear to my heart; I see you, I see my beloved homeland, the quiet river Psel, glimmering through a light veil of mist, which I shall soon throw off when I enjoy my true happiness and forget the sorrows which passed so quickly. A happy minute can repay us for years of grief. [June 13, 1824.]

Gogol's first poetic endeavors were in a lyric vein. We hear of a ballad, "Two Little Fishes," in which he represents himself and his dead brother. There is mention of a tragedy in iambic pentameter, "The Robbers," and of a poem entitled "Russia under the Yoke of the Tartars."

In the spring of 1825, Gogol's father died. The letter which the sixteen-year-old youth sent to his mother, after receiving word of his father's death, is very typical:

> Do not be distressed, oh dearest mom! I have borne this blow with the fortitude of a true Christian. True, at first I was terribly shaken by this news, but I did not let anyone observe that I was saddened. However, when I was alone, I gave myself entirely over to the power of an insane despair. I even wanted to take my life, but God restrained me; and toward evening I observed in myself only a grief that was no longer stormy; but that finally turned into a faint, hardly perceptible melancholy, mixed with a feeling of deep respect for the Almighty. I bless you, holy faith! Only in you do I find the source of consolation and the soothing of my grief. And so now I am peaceful and composed, dearest mommy, although I cannot be happy after having lost the best father, the truest friend, everything precious to my heart. But do I not still possess a sensitive, tender, virtuous mother, who can take the place for me of both father and friend, and everything most dear and most precious? And so I still have you and have not been abandoned by Fate. [April 23, 1825.]

Gogol has been reproached for insincerity and hypocrisy. But even this pathetic letter is undoubtedly genuine; one must not be led astray in one's judgments by literary conventions, which distort and exaggerate feeling and make it appear false. Similarly, many critics of Gogol find it difficult to place themselves in the atmosphere of naive faith from which vantage point Gogol's religious eccentricities lose much of their embarrassing tinge. Gogol never doubted the existence of God, nor the truth of church doctrines; his later psychic torments arose only from doubts about his own merits and from fear of judgment in the next life.

Gogol's health improved as he grew older: "As far as my health is concerned," he wrote to his mother (May 14, 1826), "I can boldly assure you that I have never been in such good condition as I am now: happy and merry." During this period he formed a friendship with an older schoolmate, Gerasim Vysotsky, who, like Gogol, combined romantic daydreams with comic escapades. Many humorous turns in Gogol's early Petersburg works are said to have been taken from Vysotsky. This was probably the only friendship that Gogol had at school. Vysotsky, who suffered from an eye ailment, spent much time in the infirmary behind a protective screen. This infirmary gradually developed into a kind of club, where literature and the events of the day were discussed. There Gogol visited his friend. "My heart," he wrote, "has never inclined to anyone so much as to you. Ever since our first stay here together, we have understood each other, and the follies of men brought us together very soon; together we mocked them and made common plans for our future lives." (January 17, 1827.) Gogol's letters to Vysotsky, after the latter had left school and moved to St. Petersburg, are much freer in tone than the respectful communications to his mother; complaints about the stupidity and narrowness of men, criticism of the teachers, enthusiasm for Nature, and, later, a lively interest in Petersburg fashions succeed one another in his letters. The untidy boy developed into an elegant fop, who could not wait to leave school so as to make a sensation in St. Petersburg. Vysotsky recounts in his memoirs that Gogol had written a rather extensive satire on the citizens of the city of Nezhin under the title "Something about Nezhin, or For Fools no Law is Valid," in which the outstanding people in various classes of society were sharply ridiculed.

From the club conversations there apparently resulted a renewed interest in theatrical productions (again due to Gogol's initiative), which were now organized on a large scale. Gogol wrote to Vysotsky:

> We had a fine time carnival week; we had theater four days in a row, and everyone played excellently. All the visitors present from out of town, experienced people, said that they had never seen such a fine performance in a provincial theater. The sets (changed four times) were masterfully, even magnificently constructed. A beautiful landscape painted on the curtain completed the effect. The lighting of the hall was splendid. Even the music was distinguished; there were only ten of our boys, but they took the place of a large orchestra very well and were situated in the best location, acoustically speaking, in the hall. They played four overtures by Rossini, two by Mozart, one by Weber, one composed by Sevryugin [singing master at the school] and several others. The plays we performed were: *The Minor* by D. Fonvizin, *The Unsuccessful Peacemaker*, a comedy by Knyazhnin, *Das Strandrecht* by Kotzebue and in addition a French play by Florian, and we still were not

satisfied; for Easter we are preparing some more productions. These occupations, however, have distracted me to some extent, and I have forgotten almost all my sadness, but for how long? Lent has come upon us and with it a deadly melancholy. Nothing new or noteworthy has transpired. [March 19, 1827.]

The school authorities took advantage of this enthusiasm for the theater: they required that every performance should include a German or French play in the original language. In this way they hoped to further the knowledge of these languages. Gogol's theatrical talents could now develop to their full extent. All recollections speak unanimously of his excellent performances; he is supposed to have been perfect as a portrayer of comic old women. One of his most brilliant roles was that of Madame Prostakova in *The Minor*, a stupid, tyrannical woman, a crude household despot, yet filled with an all-forgiving, apelike love for her ill-bred son; presumably he also played the role of Harpagon in Molière's *L'Avare*, in which he is said to have succeeded in touching his chin with the tip of his nose in order to attain the true facial expression of avarice. Alongside Gogol, Nestor Kukolnik, who later became briefly famous as a dramatist, played with great success; for the school as a whole housed several artistically talented students.

The theatrical performances, however, were soon interrupted again. Within the staff of teachers, controversies between the liberal and conservative elements had broken out that also affected the students. The younger teachers tried to teach according to new pedagogical manuals, to introduce more liberal methods of education, and to put themselves on a friendly basis with the students. During this period of Nicholas I's gloomy regime, it was easy to represent every independent step as dangerous to the state. Intimations of political untrustworthiness led, after three years of dispute, to the dismissal of the best men.

Gogol had become particularly attached himself to the young instructor Nikolay Belousov, a student of Fichte's disciple Professor Schaad in Kharkov, who lectured with great clarity on the history of philosophy and the system of natural law. The language teachers, on the other hand, had their troubles with Gogol: French he spoke to some extent; things stood badly with Latin; but worst of all with German, although Theodor Singer, the teacher of German, is said to have been a distinguished pedagogue. Singer knew how to interest the students in his subject. Gogol himself spent a great deal of money on Schiller's works in the original—but according to the testimony of a schoolmate, it was only a passing enthusiasm. To his mother he wrote:

> My plan of life is now remarkably strict and exact in every respect; every kopek has its place with me. I refuse myself even the most necessary things, in order to maintain myself in the condition in which I find myself, so that I can satisfy my thirst to see and feel the beautiful. [April 6, 1827.]

One would hardly be wrong to sense here a product of the philosophy of art of German Idealism, which became the prevailing intellectual current in Russia during these years.

Again and again we read in Gogol's letters from this period that he has spent all his money on books. He became supervisor of the student library and watched anxiously over the careful handling of the books. According to one anecdote, he invented special paper gloves which the readers had to put on to prevent grease stains. The library consisted primarily of periodicals from St. Petersburg, whose publications were passionately discussed in student circles. Also works by the students themselves were assembled in school publications, in which Gogol played a lively role. We hear of a periodical *The Star* or *The Meteor*, and of the *Northern Dawn*, which Gogol adorned with his own vignettes, and for which he is said to have produced an historical novel, *The Brothers Tverdislavichi*. The latter was rejected as an inferior work.

As the end of his school days approached, Gogol began to reflect more and more on his future. He did not say a word about a career as a writer. Thoughts of St. Petersburg and an ascent through various posts in the administration occupied his mind. "If I think of anything now," he wrote to his mother,

> it is of my future life. Dreaming or awake, St. Petersburg always hovers before my eyes, and along with it service to the country. Up until now I have been happy; but if happiness consists in being content with one's condition, then it does not quite apply—not entirely—before one enters service, before

one acquires his own permanent position, so to speak. [February 26, 1827.]

The philosophy of one's proper position, which originated with Gogol and grew into a central problem in Dostoyevsky, turns up here for the first time.

From a letter to his uncle Pavel Kosyarovsky (October 3, 1827), we learn how seriously Gogol was concerned with serving the state, being useful, and increasing the well-being of his fellow men:

> Perhaps it will be my lot to live out my whole life in St. Petersburg. I have long since set this as my goal. Since years past, since the very years of uncomprehending childhood, I have burned with inextinguishable zeal to make my life necessary to the welfare of the state. I longed to be of even the slightest use. . . . I went in my mind through all classes, all governmental professions, and stopped at one—at law. I saw that here most of all there was work to do,—that here I can be a benefit, here I would be truly useful to humanity. . . . I have sworn not to lose a minute of my brief life without doing some good. . . . Will my lofty designs be realized? Or will obscurity bury them in its gloomy cloud? In these years I had concealed within me those long-time meditations. Suspicious of everyone, secretive, I did not confide my secret thoughts to anyone, did nothing that could reveal the depth of my soul. For, whom was I to trust anyway, to what purpose was I to speak my mind? Only so that they could make fun of my craziness and look upon me as an ardent dreamer, a hollow person? . . .

We see that under the vain mask of a dandy, definite plans were concealed. These are trains of thought which Gogol never gave up, which determined his whole life, and at a later date, due to their close connection with religion, resulted in a peculiarly practical Weltanschauung. Gogol was justified in asserting that, basically, he never changed. Only a moving mystical experience subsequently superimposed itself upon his old theory of the practical usefulness of the state, which everyone had to serve from his proper position by teaching and example.

Before the final examinations, Gogol expended all his energies in an attempt to attain a reasonably good report card. Certainly his firm belief in his future usefulness for the state must have spurred him on. When he left school in June 1828, his academic achievements were judged to be completely satisfactory. Even though the level of education which he reached at his graduation was not outstanding, it is still a great exaggeration, when the young man, longing to attain great things, described his time at school as "lost years." He enjoyed the Byronic pose of the unrecognized and misunderstood hero, and in a reminiscing letter to his mother he greatly exaggerated the sorrows of his school days:

> I have experienced more grief and troubles than you think; I have purposely taken pains at home to manifest willfulness, caprice, etc., so you would believe that I was little experienced, that I was not overly oppressed by ill will. But I doubt that anyone has ever endured so much ingratitude, injustice, stupid, ridiculous demands, cold contempt, etc. I bore everything without reproach, without grumbling; no one heard my complaints, in fact I even praised those who were responsible for my sorrows. Indeed, I am considered an enigma by everyone; no one has figured me out completely. At home they considered me willful, a sort of unbearable pedant, who thought that he was more clever than everyone else and that he was made different from the rest of mankind. Would you believe that inside I laughed at myself along with you? Here they call me meek, an ideal of mildness and patience. In one place, I am the quietest, most modest and polite person around; in another I am sullen, pensive, unpolished, etc., in a third, talkative and extremely tiresome; on some occasions clever, on others stupid. Only after my real career begins will you learn my true character. [March 1, 1828.]

As literary as all this may sound, Gogol's character on leaving school becomes clearly distinguishable: a young man strongly confident of himself, who felt with certainty that he was called to something beyond the ordinary, who feared mediocrity, but who felt a childlike joy in veiling his true nature in provocative mystery, and even in representing himself as a victim of some sort of persecution. He would reveal his true nature when he would tear himself free from the narrowness of his environment. Dreams, not only of St. Petersburg, but also of foreign countries, floated before his eyes. And even if he should begin as tailor, cook, or housepainter (so he wrote his uncle), he would still attain his goal through patience and persistence. He spoke of all professions except that of an independent writer—perhaps this is a sign that he was thinking most of this very thing, and setting his highest hopes on it—for he already had in his pocket a completed literary effort of quite serious intent.

From July to December 1828, he lived on the family estate with his mother, who had not been able to manage it properly and got into more and more financial difficulties, another reason for him to strive for success and riches. After solving the immediate financial problems through loans, and despite the doubts of his anxious mother, on December 15, 1828, together with his old school comrade and neighbor, Alexander Danilevsky, Gogol departed for St. Petersburg.

The two friends intentionally bypassed Moscow, which lay on the route, so as not to weaken the experience of the new metropolis with impressions from the old. The winter journey was hard on Gogol. He arrived with a bad cold; the city seemed ugly and gloomy to him; he did not get very far with the letters of recommendation that his influential uncle had given him, and the high cost of living brought him to despair. At first he lived with Danilevsky in order to save money, but in spite of this he had far from enough. Above all, his wardrobe was a source of concern. Elegance and originality in clothing were playing an increasingly important role in his life, and so his letters to his mother are full of complaints about his miserable existence and the many joys which he has had to do without. He undoubtedly exaggerated a great deal in order to touch her maternal heart.

At first he appeared to make no great effort towards attaining a post with the government. Loggin Kutuzov, a high official to whom he had a letter of recommendation, was at first ill and unable to receive him; later he made promises which, according to Gogol, he did not keep. It is said that Gogol did not give his letter of recommendation to the Minister of Culture at all. It is clear that he did not want to tie himself down to a permanent position as an official before he had made an attempt to achieve success in the field to which, in the depths of his soul, he felt himself called—literature.

While he consoled his mother, who was waiting with longing for news that her son was solidly established, and pushed the blame for his lack of success onto his protectors, he was secretly contacting literary periodicals. He had success: a leading journal of St. Petersburg, *The Son of the Fatherland*, accepted a poem from his pen, and in the twelfth number of Volume 2, on March 23, 1829, Gogol's first printed work appeared, the poem "Italy."

The verses are conventional and clumsy; the longing for Italy was common to all the Russian romanticists of the 1820's. The great Pushkin had dedicated some wonderful stanzas, glowing with restrained passion, to this fabled land. Gogol imitated him, but he too might have been animated by a genuine yearning; all his life he preserved this love for the nature of a land in which he was to spend his best years. The poem seems like a presentiment of happiness to come. It appeared without the author's name. Anxiously Gogol guarded his incognito; his pride would not endure the impact of a failure. It is not very surprising that the poem passed completely unnoticed.

On April 30, 1829, he wrote to his mother:

> I have changed my apartment. I experienced great need lately, but that is quite unimportant. What harm does it do anyway, to go for a week without dinner? You would not believe how much one spends in St. Petersburg! Although I have denied myself almost all amusements, and no longer dress up as I did at home, although I possess only one decent suit for holidays and for going out, and a dressing gown for everyday, although I don't eat a very luxurious dinner and have quite moderate meals in general, in spite of all this, I still never spend less than 120 rubles a month. In such a situation, how could one help but go around thinking, trying to contrive a way to get some of this vile accursed money; I don't know what in the world could be worse. So, now I've decided. . . . In my next letter, I'll let you know about my success or failure. . . .

But the next letter contained only consoling hopes for the future and requests for money. "Up to now," the fond mother wrote to her cousin Kosyarovsky,

> my Nikolenka still has no position. . . . I had to borrow money again and send it to him. . . . At the end of his letter he consoled me a bit, saying he had some hope, but that he doesn't dare indulge in it and that he regrets not having begun with it earlier because he lost much by this delay, but I don't know what he means. [April 18, 1829.]

How anxious the poor woman must have felt on receiving the following declaration:

> I have been offered a position with a yearly salary of a thousand rubles. In other words, for a sum which would barely cover the yearly cost of my apartment and meals, am I to sell my health and my precious time? And for complete nonsense—what's all this? Every day to have less than two hours' free time, and the rest of the time to be forced to stay at my desk and copy down the ancient babble and the nonsense of the departmental supervisors, etc.? And so I stand on the path of my life, deep in thought, awaiting the outcome of certain expectations. Perhaps in the next few days someone will offer me a more respectable and advantageous position; but I confess: if I should be compelled to spend so much time in a ridiculous occupation there too. . . . In that case, thanks, your humble servant! Finally, my dear, kind, magnanimous mother, I am forced to ask you again for succor. I feel that it must be almost impossible for you at this point, but I will try, by all means, not to burden you again. Just give me a little more time to take root here; then I hope I shall somehow be able to support myself. At the moment I absolutely must have three hundred rubles. [May 22, 1829.]

This time the dark intimation was of no avail:

> I am running all over, trying to arrange my affairs; except for increasing my debts, I am getting no place. I sent the St. Petersburg tax authorities 1450 rubles, which I borrowed from Borkovskaya, then I sold the brass kettle from the brandy distillery and will have a new one made from wood; I have settled with the treasury department for a year, but I still have to send Nikolenka as much as I can; he still has no position. I often get letters from him, and preach to him about morality for pages.

Thus the good mother complained to her cousin. (June 23, 1829.) Her son destroyed these moralizing letters.

Now what was this secret that inspired so much hope? Gogol decided to have printed at his own expense (hence the acute financial needs), naturally under a carefully guarded pseudonym, a longer work which he claimed to have written in 1827. In May 1829 a certain young man gave the St. Petersburg book sellers copies of a small brochure on commission. On the title page was printed: "Gants Kyukhelgarten.[2] Idyll

---

[2] Hans, or perhaps, Heinz, Küchelgarten.

in Scenes by V. Alov [Written in 1827] St. Petersburg, 1829." The preface reads:

> The work here offered would never have seen the light of day, if circumstances which are only of importance to the author had not forced him to publish it. It is a work of the eighteenth year of his youth. Without going into judgments about its merits or defects, which we leave to the enlightened public, we only want to observe that many of the scenes from this idyll unfortunately have not been preserved; presumably they would have better tied together the sections which are now disjointed, and further rounded off the portrayal of the main character. At any rate, we are proud to have helped the public (as far as we were able) become acquainted with the creation of a young talent.

The time of composition of this work must lie between the fall of 1827 and the fall of 1828. There is no doubt that it reproduces to a great extent Gogol's own mood on leaving school, but its expression is determined by a wide variety of literary models. Even the mood itself would not have been such as it was without the influence of Chateaubriand's *René* and Byron's *Childe Harold*, with whom Gogol was certainly familiar. *Weltschmerz* in imitation of literary models was all the rage in Russia at that time. Basically, Gogol loved his native nook, the quiet, unpretentious harmony, the peaceful, vegetating life of its intellectually limited inhabitants, who are happy within their limitations. But he had been touched by the outside world, it drove him forth to great deeds, toward an uncertain destiny, about which he had no illusions. The destruction of the beautiful harmony of such a quiet, patriarchal retreat is the theme of his idyll, which alternates between blank verse and rhymed stanzas. The setting is Germany, in Lünensdorf, two miles from Wismar. Three generations are presented: the old pastor, his daughter Berta and her husband, and their children Luise and Fanny, who spend their lives in untroubled well-being amid surroundings of bountiful Nature. Luise loves the young neighbor Hans Küchelgarten (No doubt Gogol formed the name after that of Pushkin's friend and then already rather well-known writer, Wilhelm Küchelbecker, who had been sent to Siberia for his participation in the Decembrist conspiracy). Hans returns Luise's love, but "the restless wiles of the evil spirit"

Gogol's Life

have confused his soul. Thus, in Gogol's very first work, the devil is assigned a role. Hans has read too much of "Plato, Schiller, Petrarch, Tieck, Aristophanes, and Winckelmann." Another greater and wider world beckons to him. Thus he decides to leave his quiet nook and pursue the beautiful scenes of his imagination. But how the cold, mercenary world disappoints him! He is not a match for it and sadly returns to the faithfully waiting Luise, with whom he resigns himself to the quiet happiness of family life. But will he be able to find it? A thorn remains in his breast; *old* happiness does not come back.

There is no doubt that this first poetic attempt of Gogol's is of little artistic value. The character of the hero is not clearly drawn, and the period of his wanderings is only briefly touched upon, so that his disillusionment remains unfounded. Gogol makes extensive use of the sentimental *Luise* of Johann Heinrich Voss and draws even more extensively upon the classically perfect *Evgeny Onegin* and other works of Pushkin (situations as well as stylistic turns are copied from both authors with pathetic awkwardness); he adds to this the melancholy tone of Zhukovsky, the sentimental romantic predecessor and teacher of Pushkin, brings in realistic expressions from everyday speech, and trims it all with the great pathos of Derzhavin, the baroque ode singer of the time of Catherine II; stereotyped epithets (lily-white arms, heavenly smile, etc.), ugly, unjustified archaisms, awkward neologisms, obvious filler words, and inept images (the rosy hairs of the East) are all to be found in abundance—and yet precisely in this jumble of styles, this mixture of the polished and the unpolished, lie the seeds of the future Gogol. The juxtaposition of high and low language and the mixture of the different genres were to become characteristic features of his personal style. *Gants Kyukhelgarten* taught him perhaps that verse does not lend itself well to such treatment, and Gogol gave up writing it—forever.

Vacillating between hope and fear, he awaited the reactions to his book. The pseudonym enabled him to ask his friends about the poem without embarrassment. They either spoke of it indifferently or did not know of it. Then suddenly the first blow fell. At the end of June, *The Moscow Telegraph*, edited by the well-known journalist Nikolay Polevoy, printed a very ironic review:

> The publisher of this little book says that Mr. Alov's poem was not intended for publication, that reasons important only to the author caused him to change his intent. It would appear to us that he should have had still graver reasons for *not* publishing his idyll.

Then an extremely clumsy verse is quoted to explain the preceding judgment. But the final blow came in July, when the leading St. Petersburg periodical, *The Northern Bee*, published an extremely unfavorable review. Charges of absurdity, awkwardness, bad verse, and general immaturity were directed at the young author, who would have done well to leave the product of the "eighteenth year of his youth" under the bushel, and to wait for riper fruits.

The failure of his first work hit Gogol very hard. *Gants Kyukhelgarten* contains the following verses:

> But when perfidious dreams assail
> With yearning for a fate of splendor,
> And in the soul, no iron will,
> No strength to stand amidst the bustle,—
> Is it not better in quiet retreat
> Across the field of life to travel,
> A family modest to enjoy
> And to ignore the world's excitements?

His own aspirations closely resembled those of Hans, and it seemed that his destiny would be the same. He too was evidently not born to a "fate of splendor."

Gogol's great secret hopes were destroyed and his pride badly damaged. He and his servant ran around all the bookstores in St. Petersburg and gathered up the copies which had not been sold—there were all too many of these. Once home, they burned them. Hence this Gogol first edition belongs among the greatest bibliophile rarities.

How was he to explain to his mother that all his mysterious allusions referred to nothing? St. Petersburg had now become hateful to him. Many of his friends must have known the truth. He wanted to escape—to escape the scene of his disgrace.

With great alacrity Gogol made his decision to leave St.

Petersburg. He thought of emigrating to America, but hardly spoke of it for the time being so as not to commit himself or make himself appear ridiculous. The financial problem was solved in a happy, if not very correct fashion: he received 1800 rubles from his mother to pay an installment on the estate, which was now burdened with mortgages. Quickly making up his mind, he appropriated the money for himself; his efforts to obtain a passport, surprisingly enough, met with no obstacles, and in a few days were successful. But how was he to explain the trip to his mother? How was he to make her accept his arbitrary use of the money? The letter which he wrote shortly before his departure is so amusing that it may be quoted here almost in its entirety:

> Dear Mom, I don't know what feelings you will experience on reading this letter; I know only that you will not be at peace. To speak openly, I have never yet brought you a single bit of joy. Forgive, rare, magnanimous Mother, your son, who is not yet worthy of you. . . . Chiefly to please you, I had decided to seek a position here, at whatever price; but this was not God's pleasure. Misfortune awaited me altogether everywhere, and what is most strange, especially there where I would not have expected it at all. Completely incompetent people without any sponsors attained with ease what I could not attain with the help of mine. Finally . . . what a terrible punishment! For me there has never been anything more poisonous, more cruel in all the world. I can not, I have not the strength to write it . . . Mommy, dearest Mommy! I know, you alone are my true friend. Will you believe it? Even now, when my thoughts are no longer occupied with it, even now at the memory an inexpressible sadness slashes my heart. To you alone can I tell it. . . . You know I was gifted with a steadfastness indeed rare in a young man. . . . Who could have expected such weakness of me? But I saw her . . . no, I shall not name her . . . she is too high for anyone, not only for me. I would call her an angel, but this expression does not fit her.—A deity, lightly clothed with human passion. A countenance whose shattering splendor impresses itself in a moment upon one's heart; eyes which quickly pierce the soul; but their light, that burns, that pierces right through you, no human could bear it. Oh, if you had seen me then! . . . It is true, I was able to conceal myself from everyone, but could I remain hidden from myself? A hellish longing with all possible tortures boiled in this breast of mine. Oh, what a cruel state!

I think, if there is a hell awaiting sinners, it is not so tormenting. No, that was no love . . . at least I have never felt such love. In a burst of frenzy and most fearful spiritual torment, I thirsted and boiled to drink my fill from one glimpse alone. I thirsted after one glimpse . . . to catch one more glimpse of her—this was my only wish, which swelled ever stronger and stronger, with the inexpressible burning of corrosive yearning. I looked around me with dread and discerned my terrible state. Altogether everything in the world was alien to me then, life and death were equally unbearable, and my soul was unable to give itself an account of its own phenomena. I perceived that I had to flee from myself if I wanted to preserve my life, if I wanted to bring but a shadow of peace to my lacerated soul. Touched, I recognized the invisible Hand which takes care of me, and I blessed the path so wondrously assigned me. No, that being that He sent me to rob me of my peace of mind, to destroy my flimsily created world, was no woman. If she were a woman, she would not be able to produce such dreadful, ineffable sensations with all the power of her enchantments. It was a deity created by Him, a part of Him Himself. But for heaven's sake, don't ask her name. She is too high, too high! [June 24, 1829.]

We see that Gogol has pulled out all the stops of poor literary stereotype, and so a fictitious passion for a fictitious woman must serve to justify the departure. Gogol's conscience was also not clear in regard to the money he had falsely taken; hence he enclosed in the letter an official document which transferred to his mother the title to the properties which were to come to him in his inheritance. He swore that he would never burden her again with requests for money, but at the end of the same letter he asked her to send 100 rubles to Danilevsky for a fur coat and some linens which he still supposedly owed him. He gave Lübeck as the destination of his journey, without stating why it had to be Lübeck.

About August 5, 1829, Gogol boarded ship in St. Petersburg and reached Lübeck in six days. He was in a bad mood. If, by chance, he had previously intended to travel farther, the plan was completely abandoned now. In another pathetic letter to his mother, he swore that he could not endure the separation from her:

No, I cannot leave you, my magnanimous friend, my guardian angel! What! For these countless kindnesses, for this love which nothing could repay, am I to bring you new disappointments? I must fill your life with bitter minutes, instead of joy and happy peace! Oh, that is terrible! It tears my heart asunder! [August 13, 1829.]

Self-accusations followed. Why had God given such a coarse covering to a heart that strove for the noble and the good? Why had He clothed the noble essence in a mixture of contradictions, defiance, insolent presumptuousness, and deeply abject humility? Finally, he left the solution of this problem, which human understanding could never attain, to the Creator. Now he claimed that he went to Lübeck to take the waters in Travemünde, which the doctors had prescribed as a treatment for impure blood. His hands and face were supposedly covered with a skin rash; the cure was to last two weeks. Not a word of all this was true. He promised to return soon to St. Petersburg and enter government service, and then, with a bad conscience, entreated his mother to dispose of the properties from his inheritance (which were not hers to dispose of).

We do not know how Gogol spent his month in Lübeck and Travemünde. Evidently he felt so homesick and abandoned that he wanted to return home at any price. To the surprise of his friends, who presumably recalled the dark allusions to his great journey, he arrived back in St. Petersburg on September 22. Here, a terrified letter from his mother reached him. Passionate love, together with the rash and the cure, left her to conclude that he was suffering from venereal disease, a reaction which the son certainly never expected:

> I read with horror your letter of September 6. I was ready for almost anything: well-deserved reproaches, which still would be too mild for me, justifiable indignation, and everything that my thoughtless actions could have called down upon me; only this one thing I could never have expected. How, dear Mom, could you ever think that I fell prey to depravity, that I stood on the lowest step of human degradation! You have resolved to ascribe to me a disease, the mere idea of which has always caused my very thoughts to tremble in horror! How could you believe the son of such angelic parents to be a monster in whom no trace of virtue remained! No, such a thing does not occur in Nature! Here you have my confession: only the proud dreams of youth, which, however, flowed from a pure source, from the sole burning wish to be useful, with-

out being restrained, however, by common sense, have led me too far. But I am ready to answer before the face of God if I have performed even a single feat of depravity, and my morals here were incomparably purer than when I was staying at school and at home. . . . But I can in no way understand how you concluded that I must be suffering from precisely this particular disease. In my letter I don't think I said anything that would particularly point to this disease. I believe I wrote you of the pain in my chest from which I was hardly able to breathe and which, fortunately, has now left me. [Evidently he has completely forgotten the rash.] Oh, if you only knew the terrible state I am in! I haven't slept peacefully a single night, not a single one of my dreams was filled with sweet visions. Everywhere around me hovered the sorrows and cares and anxieties into which I have cast you. Forgive, forgive the unhappy cause of your misfortune!

So ended Gogol's first trip abroad. We shall probably never know for certain whether the failure of *Gants Kyukhelgarten* was the sole occasion for it, or whether there were additional reasons. At any rate, his venturesome spirit had suffered a severe setback.

But Gogol did not yet admit defeat. After his literary failure, he attempted to escape from a compulsory career in the civil service (which he had allegedly longed for so much at first) by way of the theater. There is little reason to doubt that the enthusiasm for the civil service in his school letters is largely camouflage: his pride would not have endured public failure; hence he concealed his true plans from his relatives and diverted their attention with a false lead.

All his friends and contemporaries bear witness to the fact that he possessed a great talent for acting, and yet when he read for a role, the result was a complete fiasco. The reason for this is not completely clear; there are different versions of the story: weak voice, slight build, and the ill will of the examiner, who belonged to the classical school and who demanded exaggerated pathos, whereas Gogol is said to have read simply and without affectation. Gogol's successes at school indicate that his voice was adequate, and his build was completely normal; there remains a final opinion, which has much to recommend it: N. P. Mundt, the secretary to the director, informs us that Gogol's uncertainty and anxiety were the cause of failure.

Gogol's Life

Thus all hopes were shattered, and Gogol was compelled seriously to seek out a position. He could no longer turn to his former protectors: he had too often disappointed them with his negative attitude. And so he hit upon an unusual way out. He went to the influential journalist Faddey Bulgarin, one of the most unpleasant figures in the history of Russian literature. In addition to his journalistic activity, he was an agent of the so-called Third Section of His Majesty's Chancery, an institution that corresponds roughly to the subsequent Soviet secret police. Bulgarin's job was to snoop around literary and journalistic circles and to report expressions of liberal sentiments. His character and the reason for his secure position vis-à-vis the authorities were generally well known. It does not speak well for Gogol that he happened to choose this particular man; but of course Gogol always maintained a favorable attitude toward the Russian autocracy. Bulgarin asserts in his memoirs (published in 1854) and also in a letter (1852) that Gogol introduced himself to him with hymnic verses in his praise—verses which, characteristically, had their intended effect. He obtained a position for Gogol in Section B of the Imperial Chancery itself; what Gogol did there is unknown, but in any case he remained only a very short time and appeared at the office—again according to Bulgarin—only to pick up his small salary.[1]

Gogol's money problems did not let up. The rich Troshchinsky had died. His nephew Andrey, the sole heir, did indeed deposit in the bank the money which Gogol had spent on the senseless journey to Lübeck, and frequently came to his assistance while Gogol himself was still staying in St. Petersburg (until the fall of 1830). But the young man was not satisfied. In his letters to his mother, he enumerated in detail his wardrobe wishes, spoke of the things he had denied himself, assured his mother that he wanted no money from her, and yet in the end finally asked her for some:

> But if it is beyond your means, if you should be thereby forced to deny yourself the necessities, oh, then I will resolve to give

[1] A certain influence of Bulgarin's mediocre novels on some of Gogol's works cannot be denied.

up all the advantages of my position, I will abandon St. Petersburg, where I perhaps could have made my fortune, I shall withdraw somewhere to the provinces, where the cost of living would be less. In short, I shall do everything that anyone could possibly resolve, merely to avoid bringing you any new sorrows and worries! [April 2, 1830.]

In the beginning of the same letter he described the position as "hardly alluring." His mother was touched. She lamented in her letters to Andrey Troshchinsky that her Nikosha had not yet learned how to handle money, but she still sent him what she could. Naturally, one should not imagine the situation to be desperate, for the estate continued to be a source of income; however, she managed things so badly that the burden of debts was constantly growing.

In April 1830, Andrey Troshchinsky secured for his protégé a new post in the ministry. The salary was better, and at first his progress was satisfactory. But soon the requests began anew. His initial zeal soon slackened; the enticements of literature and painting were too strong, and artistic prospects replaced the duties of office in Gogol's life.

In the summer of 1830, Gogol visited the Academy of the Arts, where he came into contact with painters and became familiar with their way of life. In June he wrote to his mother:

> At nine o'clock every morning I go to the office and I remain there till 3:00; at 3:30 I have dinner; after dinner, at 5:00 I go to my class at the Academy of the Arts, where I am studying painting, which I absolutely can't give up—so much the more, since all the means are here to perfect oneself in painting, and they all require nothing more than work and diligence. Through my acquaintance with painters, and in fact with many famous ones, it is possible for me to enjoy means and advantages which are inaccessible to many. . . .

But Gogol had also begun to work on small tales with Ukrainian local color. He had always been interested in the Ukrainian people, their customs, and their history, and he knew them well; the literary fashion of St. Petersburg was at that time just beginning to turn to folklore. Gogol rightly believed that here he could say something new. He asked his mother for appropriate details, whose choice, moreover, indicates that Gogol's circle of themes was already quite firmly established:

Gogol's Life

... don't be angry at me, magnanimous little mother, if I often burden you with requests to send me reports about Little Russia or some such thing. This is in fact my daily bread. Even now I am asking you to collect a few such reports, if you hear a merry anecdote somewhere among the peasants in our village, or in another, or among the landowners. Be so good as to describe the practices and customs, the superstitions. And make inquiries about the olden days with, say, Anna Matveyevna or Agafya Matveyevna (Gogol's aunts): what kind of clothes were worn by the Sotniks, their wives, the Tysyachniks,[3] and they themselves in those days; what kind of fabrics were known in their time, everything with the most detailed detail; what sort of incidents and stories that were comical, amusing, sad, terrifying, occurred in their time. Don't disregard anything, everything has its value for me. . . . [February 2, 1830.]

He also asked his mother to send him old coins and other antiques, for a "magnate," who was a collector of such things, and to whom he wanted to be of service. He also inquired about old manuscripts, family and historical documents.

Now the "magnate" was there only to impress his mother (a tendency which cropped up with Gogol again and again during this period): the person referred to is the journalist, Pavel Svinyin (like Bulgarin, of rather doubtful character), who was in fact a passionate collector of curiosities and also editor of the *Annals of the Fatherland*, a flourishing periodical which, in the February and March editions of 1830, published Gogol's again anonymous tale of the Ukraine, "Bisavryuk, or St. John's Eve, told by the Sexton of the Church of the Intercession."

This work too passed unnoticed, even though it did alert some experts. Gogol did not give up: in the almanac *Northern Flowers*, which appeared in December 1830, edited by Baron Anton Delvig, there is a chapter from a "historical novel" printed with the signature oooo, which is from the pen of Gogol. Baron Anton Delvig, one of Pushkin's closest friends, a noble, highly gifted, intelligent man, himself an above-average poet who wrote good imitations of folk songs and applied antique meters and forms to the Russian language with great skill, gave a new turn to Gogol's life, even though the role

---

[3] Ukrainian military ranks.

which he himself played in it was very brief. He died young in the year 1831. We do not know how his acquaintance with Gogol came about, nor how it proceeded; in any event, Delvig recognized the talent of the young writer. In the first number of his *Literary Gazette*, which was edited in close collaboration with Pushkin (January 1, 1831), appeared a chapter from a Ukrainian tale, "The Terrible Boar," by Gogol, entitled "The Teacher" (signed P. Glechik), and the article "Some Thoughts on the Teaching of Geography to Children" (signed G. Yanov). The fourth issue of the *Literary Gazette* (January 16, 1831) contains the article "Woman," signed for the first time with Gogol's full name; and the seventeenth issue (March 22, 1831) contains a second chapter from "The Terrible Boar." But that was not all. It was undoubtedly Delvig who gave Gogol a letter of recommendation to Vasily Zhukovsky, next to Pushkin the greatest contemporary poet, and also tutor of the crown prince. This led to a friendship which was a decisive influence in Gogol's life. Gogol wrote to Zhukovsky on January 10, 1848:

> I came to you first as a youth who had hardly entered into the great world, while you had already traveled half-way along this path. It was at the Palace of Shepelev. The room no longer exists. But I see it as if it were before me now, all the way down to the smallest piece of furniture, to the tiniest knick-knacks. You gave me your hand, you were immediately so filled with the wish to help your future companion in arms! How benevolently affectionate was your gaze! What had brought the two of us, who were so unequal in years, together? Art. We felt an affinity stronger than blood relationship. Why? Because we both felt the sanctity of Art!

The kindly Zhukovsky, one of the noblest personalities of Russian literature, received Gogol cordially. He recommended him to his friend Peter Pletnev, who enjoyed a certain reputation as critic and poet, but who simultaneously occupied a prominent position in the school system. He was teacher of Russian language and literature to the imperial family and superintendent of the Patriotic Institute, a school for the daughters of high military officers, which stood under the personal protection of the empress. From 1833 until his death in 1865, Pletnev was professor of Russian literature at the University of St. Petersburg. After Pushkin's death he edited the latter's periodical *The Contemporary* and handled both for Pushkin as well as Gogol many purely financial, commercial details connected with the sale of their books. Pletnev espoused Gogol's cause in a touching manner. Since Gogol complained of the burdens of his official duties and felt that they hindered his literary activities, Pletnev secured a position for him which was much less time-consuming. Gogol became teacher of history at the girls' boarding school of which Pletnev was superintendent. The order for this appointment came from the very highest authority on February 9, 1831. A month later Gogol assumed his role as teacher. He wrote with some conceit to his mother:

> The empress has commanded me to lecture at the boarding school for noblemen's daughters which stands under her protection. However, don't think that this means very much. The whole advantage is that I am now somewhat better known, that my lectures are gradually causing people to talk about me, and most important, that I have more free time: instead of painful sitting around whole afternoons, instead of working 42 hours a week, I now only work six hours, moreover, I even get a somewhat better salary; instead of the stupid, senseless work whose futility I always hated, my present work fills my soul with ineffable delight. [April 16, 1831.]

He had left his previous position with a distinguished record, from which we must conclude that he had conscientiously fulfilled his duties. But in the meantime he did not neglect his literary activity: "All my works which are in print today I wrote in St. Petersburg during the very period in which I occupied an official position, when I had no free time amid the bustle and confusion of my job; and the merrier the manner in which I spent the previous evening, the more inspiration I brought home, the fresher was my morning." (September 10, 1839 to Shevyrev.) The "merry" life no doubt refers to his frequent visits to the theater and to the drinking parties with his friends. More than twenty school friends from Nezhin alone were in St. Petersburg at that time.

In addition to the teaching position at the boarding school, Pletnev also secured for the young writer tutoring assignments in distinguished houses, in order to increase his sources of income. The memoirs of Gogol's students, which were written much later, are of doubtful veracity. In any case, Gogol must have avoided the usual routine. His method of teaching seems to have featured lively lectures which emphasized general education rather than a single specialized subject. A mentally retarded boy was also included among his students. With touching patience Gogol endeavored to teach him to read by imitating animal sounds.

But the money was still not enough for him, and the complaining and entreating letters to his mother did not let up.

In May 1831, a very special event in Gogol's life took place. He was introduced to Russia's greatest poet, Alexander Pushkin, whom he admired, even as a boy, above all others. Immediately after his arrival in St. Petersburg two and a half years before, Gogol had run to him. According to the statements of Pavel Annenkov, who allegedly heard it from Gogol himself, the circumstances of the visit were as follows:

> The closer Gogol got to Pushkin's house, the more his shyness overcame him, and finally, by the time he reached the door of his house, it became so strong, that he ran to a café and asked for a glass of liqueur. Strengthened by the drink, he decided to take the fortress by storm; he courageously rang the bell, but in answer to his question "Is the master at home?" the servant replied, "He is sleeping." It was already quite late in the morning. Gogol asked with great sympathy, "He probably worked all night?" "What do you mean 'worked,' " said the servant, "he played cards." Gogol confessed that that was the first blow his schoolboy ideal suffered. Previously he had never been able to visualize Pushkin except as veiled in a cloud of inspiration.

Gogol spent the whole summer of 1831 in Pavlovsk and Tsarskoye Selo in the immediate vicinity of St. Petersburg. Also in Tsarskoye Selo lived Zhukovsky, the recently married Pushkin and his beautiful wife, and the imperial family with the whole court. In St. Petersburg there was a cholera epidemic, and all who could afford to move had fled the city.

During this summer, the first part of *Evenings on the Farm near Dikanka* was printed, and it was published in the beginning of September 1831. The second part followed in the beginning of May 1832.

The *Evenings* opened the way for Gogol into the highest literary circles. He became a frequent visitor of literary salons, and, sponsored by Pushkin, was considered the new hope of Russian literature. Things also went better with him financially. Proudly he wrote to his mother that she had now one mouth less to feed, that in fact he would soon be able to help her and his sisters. Now Gogol himself received visitors. The censor Nikitenko, like Gogol a Ukrainian and an author of very informative memoirs, made the following entry in his diary on April 22, 1832:

> I was at a party at the house of Gogol-Yanovsky, the author of the tales of the beekeeper, Red-haired Panko, which are quite entertaining, especially for a Ukrainian. He is a young man, about 26, of pleasing appearance. However, his face does have a modicum of slyness, which makes one distrust him. At his house I also met up to ten Ukrainians, almost all students from the high school at Nezhin.

At the end of the winter, Gogol was again without money. Perhaps this circumstance contributed to his decision to spend the summer on his family estate. Besides, he had a plan to bring two of his sisters to St. Petersburg and to install them at the boarding school where he worked as teacher.

The trip from St. Petersburg to Moscow was unenjoyable. Gogol caught cold and had to remain in Moscow about fourteen days before his condition permitted him to resume the journey. This stay in Moscow brought him three valuable acquaintances who had a certain influence on his whole life. He became friendly with the historian, author, and editor, Mikhail Pogodin; the writer Sergey Aksakov (subsequently famous as the author of *The Family Chronicle*, one of the most important works of Russian prose), and also with his family; and with the brilliant actor, Mikhail Shchepkin. Gogol's *Evenings* were already being read in Moscow with enthusiasm. Their author was *persona grata* on any social occasion.

On July 8, in a letter to Pogodin, Gogol complained about the bad weather they had had since he started again on his journey. He waited for horses at a post stop and read Richardson's *Clarissa Harlowe*. Concrete indications as to what Gogol is reading are so rare (in sharp contrast with Pushkin) that they are worth noting.

He spent the summer months happily at home, took an active part in the management of the estate, decorated the house with his paintings, and prepared his sisters for the boarding school. More and more during this summer, there were complaints about his health. A stomach ailment tormented him, which neither he nor the doctors could define, but which occupied him a great deal. With great devotion he dedicated himself to the study of the ailment.

The return journey went relatively well. Accompanied by the blessings of his anxious mother, Gogol traveled with his little sisters Elizaveta and Anna. In Moscow there again followed a short stopover with visits to all his new friends. At the end of October Gogol reached St. Petersburg. During this period Gogol had been working on a burlesque tale or scene, "The Washerwoman," which, however, on account of its rather offensive contents (the climax is a quarrel between the washerwoman and a government official about his underdrawers) he either did not complete or destroyed.

During this winter, a cheerful, artistically interested circle of friends formed around Gogol, consisting almost exclusively of old school comrades from Nezhin. Literature and painting (which Gogol did not neglect) were zealously cultivated. Gogol appears to have been the animating spirit of this circle. To his friends he assigned the names of French authors; among them there was a Hugo, a Dumas, a Balzac, a Jules Janin, etc. Joint reading of periodicals, criticism of new publications, literary anecdotes, joint poetic efforts, all of this, spiced with complicated Ukrainian dishes, which Gogol himself prepared—this is the approximate picture of their meetings. Gogol was developing into a real dandy. His manner of dress is described by Annenkov as being rather adventurous. To celebrate his nameday on May 9, for example, he would put on a gaudy necktie, treat his hair with curling irons and pile it up high, and dress up in a short, white, wide-open outer coat with a high waist, so that according to unanimous opinion, he looked very much like a bantam rooster. During this period Gogol enjoyed playing the role of an elegant beau, shaving off his hair so that it might grow more thickly, and in the meantime wearing a wig. But traces of his old unconcern for external things remained. The cotton which he had fastened under his wig is supposed to have stuck out, and behind the beautiful tie, the strings which held together the shirt collar were visible. Dating from this period is the lithograph by Venetsianov which shows an elegant young man with lofty brow, a strikingly long nose, a somewhat ironically shaped mouth, and intelligent eyes.

But in addition to this merry life there was no lack of work. *Mirgorod* and the comedy *The Order of Vladimir, Third Class* were written, the latter soon to be dropped by Gogol because of potential difficulties with the censor. Its hero was to be a government official who sets for his goal in life the attainment of the cross of St. Vladimir, a high decoration with which many privileges and personal nobility were granted. The efforts of the hero to gain this award make up the contents of the comedy. In the end the hero goes mad and imagines that he himself is an order of Vladimir, third class. According to the actor Shchepkin, especially successful was the scene in which the hero sits in front of the mirror, dreams, and imagines that he is already wearing the decoration. Madness had a special interest for Gogol at this time. Annenkov relates that he once met an elderly gentleman at Gogol's who told stories about madmen and the strict, almost logical consistency in the development of their insane ideas; no doubt, the influence of these tales is reflected in *Vladimir* and above all, in "The Diary of a Madman." Gogol generally liked to be told stories; he would retain striking expressions, and note down everything out of the ordinary, in order to use it later in his works.

His creative work gave him trouble. The ingenious tales of the *Mirgorod* cycle were reworked again and again, but nothing new developed. Gogol always placed the greatest demands upon himself. He constantly polished his works and wrote them down many times before he declared them completely ready for print. Even after printing, the work of polishing went on. In his letters from this period Gogol complained of "intellectual constipation," and turned more and more to historical studies. To bring history to life, to make olden times effective in the present (which did not satisfy him) by means of exciting descriptions and vivid characterizations—this appeared to him at times to be his true vocation. He wanted to write a multi-volume history of the Ukraine, but when during his historical studies "the stage of the theater hovers before him, the sound of applause roars around him, mugs peer from the boxes, the gallery, the orchestra, and show their teeth"—then "history goes to the devil."

Gogol also employed this period of failing inspiration for reading. The statements of Annenkov and others about his "lack of education" and deficient knowledge of literature deserve little credence: too many literary reminiscences are found in his works, and his critical essays bear witness to a proficiency which is acquired only by practice. The apparent lack of poetic inspiration is for the most part probably due to the fact that Gogol was about to change his subject matter entirely (Ivan Fedorovich Shponka in the *Evenings* was the first evidence of such a change): "You ask about the *Evenings of Dikanka*," he writes to Pogodin.

> Let the devil take them! I will not publish them [in a second edition]; and even though acquisition of more money would not be superfluous for me, I still can't write for that purpose, or add new fairy tales. I am completely devoid of any talent for schemes for enrichment. I have even forgotten that I was the creator of these *Evenings*, and now you have reminded me of them again. . . . May they be condemned to oblivion until something weighty, great, artful will issue from me. But I persist in my inactivity, in my immobility—I want nothing trivial, I can't think up anything great . . . [February 1, 1833.]

It is striking that Gogol appears to have had no relationships with women, either in his free and easy St. Petersburg years or later. This circumstance has provided psychoanalysts with a great deal of material for strange hypotheses, but it would hardly pay to go into them. As always in such cases, a grain of truth is present, but the attempt to explain the whole body of Gogol's works, his religious upheaval, his illnesses on the basis of sexual inhibitions, is certainly farfetched. His sexual attitudes are usually explained by excessive onanism during his school days; and this is also said to have led to severe psychic depressions, since Gogol saw in it a grievous sin. Gogol himself emphatically denied this assertion at the end of his life. The alleged evidence for it lacks plausibility. It may be that there is something to these claims, but one should guard against exaggerations. In any event it is clear that he did not look upon women as sexual objects. A characteristic letter to his friend A. Danilevsky, who was in love at this time, reads:

> I quite understand the condition of your soul even though, by grace of fate, I have not yet been permitted to experience it. I say "by grace" because this flame would turn me to dust in a moment. I would find for myself no enjoyment in the past; I would strive to transform it to the present, and I myself would become a victim of this effort. And for this very reason I possess, as my salvation, a firm will which twice saved me from the desire to gaze into the abyss. You are fortunate, it is your destiny to partake of the highest good in the world—love; while I . . . but we are falling, I believe, into Byronism. [December 20, 1832.]

Gogol awaited the year 1834 with great expectations. Although he was still wavering between writing a comedy or a historical work, he wanted to accomplish something great. It is astonishing how firmly the sense of being called to exceptional achievements persisted in him from youth, it is no less astonishing that he constantly wavered back and forth in regard to the precise nature of his calling. After his service with the state, he was inclined toward a scholarly career as a professor of history; then the conviction swept over him that a religious mission was his true task; and this feeling did not leave him till his death. In the meantime he believed intermittently in his literary talents; his tremendous literary successes strengthened him in this conviction, but the intermittent appearances of inspiration and the obviously very difficult process of creation caused him to seek constantly a new and different field of endeavor. The religious idea finally gained sufficient strength to engulf the artist in him to a considerable degree.

Toward the end of 1833 the possibility arose of obtaining a professorship in world history in Kiev. His fellow Ukrainian and good friend, Mikhail Maksimovich, who obtained a chair in Russian literary history at the newly-founded University of Kiev, wanted him to move there too, and Gogol, who found the St. Petersburg climate disagreeable, was very enthusiastic. But he was held back in St. Petersburg by debts and publishing interests. He needed great sums of money in order to end his stay in St. Petersburg without financial loss; his faith in his abilities was somewhat exaggerated; above all, Gogol did not see for the moment that he was totally lacking in any scholarly training in history, that interest in it and even extensive reading are not sufficient for a teaching career. Thus he made excessive demands, and despite the intercession of his friends, among them Pushkin himself, he did not obtain the professorship. Gogol had asked for a full professorship in Kiev; when after the fiasco he was offered the position of lecturer in St. Petersburg, he gladly accepted it. This offer, as well as Gogol's whole university career, was made possible only by patronage. Pushkin was friendly at that time with the Minister of Education Uvarov (against whom he later wrote a vicious poetic satire), and he spoke in favor of his protégé. Gogol wrote a "Plan of Instruction in World History" which gained the approval of the minister, and which was printed in the official publication of the ministry (1834), an insignificant piece of sonorous verbiage with a patriotic conclusion (later also published in *Arabesques*). In this way Gogol obtained his appointment.

In the fall of 1834 Gogol gave his first lecture, which was to begin a series on the history of the Middle Ages (published in *Arabesques* under the title "On the Middle Ages"). The lecture hall was filled to capacity, for the students knew and esteemed the author of the *Evenings*; Gogol had prepared his lecture well, and it was a great success. But his subsequent offerings grew worse and worse. Gogol was fundamentally very lazy, that is, he could not work on demand, and so he would either call off the lecture entirely, or cut it short, or recount things which he had just finished copying from books and which he would monotonously read, disregarding the context. Gogol had certainly overestimated his professional competence, but the main reason for his failure was the insurmountable laziness which hindered him in his class preparations. When he was informed that Pushkin and Zhukovsky wanted to attend one of his lectures, he pulled himself together, and the result was the vivid lecture on the Caliph Al-Mamun (published in

Gogol's Life 41

Arabesques), which, although it did not at all fit into the context of the course, showed the lecturer at the peak of his literary art. But then again an abrupt decline followed, and that was the way things were to remain. Among his students, Gogol had a man who was later to become famous—Ivan Turgenev. In his memoirs, the latter wrote:

> I attended Gogol's lectures in 1835 when he was teaching history at St. Petersburg University. To tell the truth, this "teaching" was carried on in a peculiar manner. First of all, Gogol was sure to miss two lectures out of three; secondly, even when he did appear on the rostrum, he didn't speak, but whispered something rather incoherent, showed us little etchings with views of Palestine and other oriental countries, and was extremely embarrassed throughout the whole period. We were all convinced (and we were hardly in error in this regard) that he understood nothing of history and that Mr. Gogol-Yanovsky, our professor (he was so listed in the catalogue), had nothing in common with the writer Gogol, who was well known to us as author of *Evenings on the Farm near Dikanka*. During the final examination in his subject he sat there with a kerchief tied around his head, allegedly because he was suffering from a toothache, with an expression of utter despondency on his face, and didn't open his mouth. Instead of him, Professor I. P. Shulgin questioned the students. As if it were today, I see his lean, long-nosed figure before me, with the two ends of a black silk kerchief sticking up high above his head, looking like ears. Undoubtedly he himself saw very well the whole comedy and the awkwardness of his position; in the same year he handed in his resignation.

This somewhat inaccurate and exaggerated description (in his memoirs, Turgenev tends to overstate his case) still conveys, in general, the correct impression. Gogol had overestimated his energy and failed in the field of scholarship. To his credit it may be said that the condition of his health became worse and worse under the influence of the St. Petersburg climate. In his letters he constantly complained of severe colds; in addition he was plagued by hemorrhoids.

Along with his enforced studies of history and his great plans for historical works (a four-volume history of the Middle Ages, an eight-volume history of the Ukraine), his creative powers broke through again. In January 1835 *Arabesques* was published, a conglomeration of essays on history and geography, literary and aesthetic criticism, fragments of novels he had begun, and three masterworks of the first order: the tales "The Portrait," "Nevsky Prospect," and "The Diary of a Madman." In April 1835 appeared *Mirgorod*, a collection of four stories, three of which reveal Gogol at the peak of his artistic talents. In addition Gogol completed "The Nose," began *The Inspector General*, and worked on *The Marriage*. In view of this tremendous productivity, one may well excuse his failure as a professor.

How soon Gogol lost interest in an academic career is made clear in a letter to Pogodin of December 14, 1834:

> Do you know what it means to find no sympathy, what it means to find no response? I lecture in solitude, in utter solitude at the university here. No one listens to me, I have never noticed anyone who seemed to be struck by a blinding truth. And therefore I am finally giving up all artistic embellishment, not to mention the desire to wake up my sleepy audience. I express myself fragmentarily, look only into the distance, and see everything in the context into which it will be fitted by me within a year. If only one being from among the students understood me! They're a colorless folk—like St. Petersburg!

From a literary point of view, the solemnly greeted year of 1834 had in fact brought a rich harvest—but professionally it was a failure. Although Gogol did not yet give up the professorship for good, in May, 1835 he traveled with a feeling of deep dissatisfaction to his home at Vasilyevka, with the intention of spending the summer, for reasons of health, in the Crimea or the Caucasus. He had only enough money for a short stay in the Crimea, where he "wallows in mineral mud"; the condition of his health improved during the journey. All his life Gogol looked on the process of traveling as the most effective remedy for his ills; this explains his later restless wanderings through Europe. The financial situation of his mother during this period was bad indeed. She had immersed herself in an enterprise that ended in bankruptcy, and a great deal of work and outside help was needed to save the estate from legal seizure.

This time his stay at home did not satisfy Gogol. Dissatisfied with himself, he did not have the energy to pull himself together for a new work: "Subjects and plans have piled up on the journey in tremendous profusion, so that if it were not for the hot summer, much paper and many pens would be used up; but the heat induces frightful laziness, and only a tenth part has been put on paper. . . ." (To Zhukovsky, July 15, 1835.)

On the return trip Gogol stopped for a short time at the house of Maksimovich in Kiev. His stay seems to have been a merry one, although in his memoirs Maksimovich is subsequently inclined to date the "radical change" in Gogol from this period, and to trace it back to the influence of the "Russian Jerusalem." Here is further proof of the danger in relying on recollections about great men, written down at a later date. Gogol was still the irresistibly comic companion and drinking partner, who himself was able to remain in dead earnest and thereby to increase the effects of his jokes, but who meanwhile, in spite of all the merriment, kept at a distance from his friends and maintained his own little domain. Characteristic is an anecdote from a later period, when Gogol wanted to test out his *Inspector General*. While traveling to Moscow with two friends, he sent one of them ahead with the instructions to mention in passing at all post stations that an inspector general was following him incognito. Gogol, whose travel passport gave "adjunct-professor" as his profession, was thought to be an adjutant of his majesty by the well-meaning and anxious station superintendents at the mail coach stations, and since he played his role so brilliantly and asked apparently innocent but yet embarrassing questions and requested to see various institutions, the journey proceeded very smoothly and comfortably, something extremely unusual for Russia at that time.

Gogol spent several weeks in Moscow. Here, at a gathering in the house of Pogodin, he read the first version of *The Marriage*, under the title *The Suitors*. All judgments of the quality of his delivery are ecstatic. His talent in this area indeed appears to have been tremendous. The actor Shchepkin advised young actors to apprentice themselves to Gogol. About his reading of *The Suitors*, Pogodin reports:

> Gogol read as hardly anyone else knows how to read. It was the peak of astounding perfection. I can even say the following: As splendidly as his comedies were performed, or more precisely, as admirably as many of the roles were interpreted, they never

made the same impression on me as they did in his readings. Once at a large gathering at my house in 1834 or 1835, he read his *The Marriage*. When he came to the suitor's declaration of love to his intended—"In which church were you last Sunday? What flower do you love most?"—interrupted three times by silence, he expressed this silence so well, it appeared so clearly in his face, in his eyes that the whole audience literally doubled over with laughter, while he kept silent as if nothing had happened and only let his eyes wander.

Pogodin is not suspect of any bias in favor of Gogol, so that we can place considerable trust in his judgment. Gogol recited with the same success at the house of the former Minister of Justice and renowned author of fables, Ivan Dmitriev.

Gogol did not look forward to St. Petersburg. His failure as a professor gave the servile official journal, directed by the extremely unpleasant Bulgarin, occasion for crude ridicule, which also extended to his newly published works (*Arabesques*, *Mirgorod*). Everything in them served as a target for ridicule; the novelty, the absolute originality of these works were not noticed, and even the broad public concerned themselves, basically, only with the obvious humor; they overlooked all the profound aspects and stamped Gogol irrevocably as the amusing author of merry humorous sketches. Then came a bright moment for Gogol: an extremely favorable article in the *Telescope* by the subsequently famous critic, Vissarion Belinsky. Gogol was here unreservedly proclaimed the coming great writer. Although Belinsky, as usual, completely overlooked Gogol's true greatness and judged his works by social and "realistic" criteria, both of which have little application to Gogol; and although, in addition, the meaning of his statements suffered greatly from his customary torrent of words, there were still many favorable epithets; and just then, Belinsky was beginning to make a big name for himself as a critic. Thus, somewhat comforted, Gogol arrived again at St. Petersburg on September 1, 1835.

He had so neglected his teaching and so prolonged his leave of absence without permission that he found his position already occupied by someone else. The university salary was his only source of income, but even this would not be available much longer—of this Gogol felt very sure. Thus he turned to Pushkin and asked him to give him an idea (according to other versions,

Gogol stole the idea) so that he could immediately begin writing a comedy for the purpose of strengthening his financial resources. Pushkin is said to have generously given over to him the plot of *The Inspector General,* which already lay before him in a rough draft; and in two months there developed from this the most famous Russian comedy. Gogol was in a hurry, for the university no longer offered him any sense of pleasure or satisfaction. In December 1835 he gave his last lecture.

> I thumbed my nose at the university, and in a month I'll be a free cossack again. Unrecognized, I mounted the rostrum, and unrecognized I shall depart it. But in this year and a half, the years of my disgrace (for according to the consensus of opinion, I got into the wrong business), in this year and a half I have learned a great deal and incorporated it into the treasure chambers of my soul. No more childish ideas, not the limited sphere of my previous knowledge, but lofty ideas filled with truth and terrifying grandeur stirred me. Peace be with you, my heavenly guests, which brought me divine moments in my cramped quarters so close to the attic! No one knows you, I'll let you sink again to the bottom of my soul until your reawakening; when you will burst out again with even greater strength, then will the shameless impudence of the learned ignoramus, the learned and unlearned mob, this ever-agreeing public, etc., then will they no longer be able to resist. I speak to you alone about it; I will tell it to no other; they will call me a braggart and nothing more. Away, away with it! [December 6, 1835 to Pogodin.]

The winter of 1835–1836 was devoted to inspired, feverish work on *The Inspector General,* and then to its staging. As always, Gogol read the comedy aloud to perfection; Zhukovsky and Pushkin were enthusiastic, and when the censor flatly refused to permit a performance, Zhukovsky, energetically supported by the distinguished literary critic Prince Vyazemsky, a friend of Pushkin's, and by the influential courtier and talented composer Count Vielgorsky (Schumann called him "a dilettante of genius"), turned directly to the Czar. Vielgorsky read the comedy aloud at the palace. The Czar himself examined the manuscript and authorization for performance was granted by royal command. Now the censor too found that the piece contained nothing dangerous. Gogol was in a very good mood. Even though he always maintained a reserve in deeply personal questions, as all his friends complain, he still lets his irresistible humor overflow in abundance. "The audience choked, had fits, crept on all fours in an attack of hysterical laughter." Thus an eye-witness describes the effect which Gogol achieved in the telling of a Ukrainian anecdote. He was the great attraction at Zhukovsky's literary "Saturdays." Here he read with the greatest success "The Nose," which Pogodin had previously rejected.

In the end of February, the rehearsals for *The Inspector General* began at the St. Petersburg State Theater, which Gogol tried to influence, for this kind of comedy was completely new to the actors and to the director. It fitted neither into the canon of the neoclassical comedy of Molière nor into the current type of vaudeville which dominated the stage at that time. The lifelike quality of the characters, which were not actually lifelike, but had all the outward signs of life and were not meant to be overplayed, brought the whole company to their wits' end. Only the great actor Sosnitsky, like Shchepkin in Moscow, was enthusiastic and immediately struck the right tone. All the rest exaggerated and, to Gogol's horror, fell into the style of a farce and tried to dazzle the audience with cheap effects. An actor described the figure of the author himself behind the scenes, as he excited the merriment of the company:

> Of medium height, blond, with a huge wig, wearing gold-rimmed spectacles on his long, birdlike nose, with squinting little eyes, and firmly compressed, as if bit-together, lips. The green frock coat with long tails and little mother-of-pearl buttons, brown trousers, and the high top-hat which Gogol took off with a jerk one moment, while digging his fingers into his wig, and which in the next moment he turned around in his hands—all of this gave his figure the appearance of a caricature.

Gogol's suggestions were seldom followed, and there was no dress rehearsal, so that he went to the premiere with a sense of foreboding. On the surface it went off splendidly. The theater was filled to overflowing, the whole aristocracy of St. Petersburg, and many cabinet ministers were present. At the last moment Czar Nicholas I appeared in person. The success was overwhelming. The audience laughed and applauded. They called tumultuously for the author, but he did not appear. On leaving his box, the Czar is said to have remarked: "Well, that's quite a little piece! Everyone got theirs, and I most of all!" The anecdote in itself is not very probable: Nicholas was very sparing in his self-criticism. Nevertheless, he officially ordered all civil service heads to attend a performance of the play. The subsequent performances were always sold out, but the enthusiasm was not universal. According to the report of Annenkov, even at the premiere a sense of disapproval spread among the audience. The topical nature of the play—political bribery, shocking corruption in the civil service, self-assurance of petty people in important positions who were able to tyrannize those around them without fear of punishment—all these phenomena peculiar to an absolutistic state suddenly stood so vividly before the audience that the salvos of laughter were followed by an oppressive silence. The dignitaries involved were furious. They considered the author a malicious slanderer. How was it possible that this play which shook the "foundation" of the state was allowed to be performed? "All want to be more monarchical than the emperor" writes the witty Prince Vyazemsky,

> and all are angry that the performance of this comedy was allowed, which by the way, was a brilliant and complete success on the stage, though not a success in the sense of gaining universal approval. It is incredible what stupid opinions you hear about it, especially in higher social circles! "As if there were such a city in Russia!" "How is it possible not to present one decent, honorable man? As if there aren't any in Russia!"

People tried to emphasize the elements of farce interpolated by the actors, and even to attack the piece from an artistic standpoint, but the only ones who cried out were those who felt themselves implicated, and the great majority among the public were very favorably inclined toward *The Inspector General*.

Gogol's reaction is interesting. He clung to the unfavorable judgment with a veritable passion. He came back to life, as it were, when he imagined himself persecuted, even threatened. "They are all against me," he wrote to Shchepkin (April 29, 1836),

> the older and honorable officials shout that for me nothing is sacred, since I dared to speak thus about public officials; the policemen are against me, the merchants are against me, the

literary people are against me. They abuse me and go to the play; the fourth performance is already sold out. . . . I see now what it means to be a writer of comedies. The smallest trace of truth, and they are up in arms against you, and not just one person, but whole classes. I can imagine what would have happened if I had portrayed something from St. Petersburg life, which I know more and better now than provincial life. It is annoying for one who loves men with brotherly love, to see them turn against him.

He turns down the request of his Moscow friends to come to Moscow and be present at the staging of his comedy.

I feel that Moscow can offer me no peace now, and I wouldn't like to go there in the restless state that I am in now. I am going abroad, and there I'll try to get rid of the sadness which my compatriots cause me. The present-day author, the author of comedies, the author concerned with morals must live far from his homeland. A prophet is without glory in his own country. Even if I am not disconcerted by the fact that now, as a matter of fact, all classes are against me, still it is somehow sad and painful when you see your own compatriots whom you still love from the heart unjustly prejudiced against you, when you see how falsely and how wrongly they interpret everything. [May 10, 1836 to Pogodin.]

Gogol's letters from this period are full of such complaints; they were scarcely justified by reality, but he obviously enjoyed them. "Everything that happened to me, it was all salutary for me. All the insults, all the unpleasantness were sent to me by divine providence for my education, and today I feel that it is not an earthly will that directs my path. This path must be necessary for me." (May 15, 1836 to Pogodin.)

The religious tendency in Gogol appeared here for the first time. The effect of *The Inspector General* on the public proved to him that through his writings he could teach and influence men. From this moment on he began to reflect on the purpose of his words and to choose them on the basis of their effect. All his major works were already in the budding stage at this time. After them Gogol wrote nothing more of significance. After *The Inspector General* the way was paved for the turn to religion. It satisfied his deepest nature to stride forward on the path preordained by God, in spite of all temptations, in spite of all dangers. His mind was made up—he was determined to go into "exile," to gain distance, to collect his thoughts. If his words could cause such a resonance, if his speech is listened to in such a manner, must he not become clearly conscious of what he is to say and how he is to say it? He wanted to look at Russia from a distance, a distance that would clarify his thoughts about his vocation. On July 6, 1836, together with his friend Danilevsky, Gogol went abroad.

After a stormy and unpleasant voyage on a steamer with machinery that constantly broke down, Gogol arrived after a week and a half journey in Travemünde and traveled by way of Lübeck to Hamburg. He described his impressions in a humorous letter to his sisters in St. Petersburg:

> I was in the theater which is played in the garden in the open air. An extraordinary crowd of Germans comes to see it, and the German women come here with all their housework, and all of them, without exception, knit stockings throughout the whole performance. . . . Once when I went for a walk on the outskirts of the city, I caught sight of a rather large and splendidly illuminated building. The music and the great crowd of people caused me to go inside. The hall was of a tremendous size, many chandeliers, and a great deal of light, but I was amazed at the fact that the dancers were dressed sloppily, each one wore what he felt like wearing. They were dancing the waltz. But you've never seen such a waltz in your whole life: One turns his lady to one side, the other to the other; many simply hold hands and do not even turn, but stare at each other like billy goats and spring about the room, without paying any attention to see if it is done in time or not. Later I found out that this was the famous sailors' ball.

From Hamburg he went by way of Bremen, Münster (whose Gothic churches delighted him), and Düsseldorf to Aachen. Here he remained several days, contracted a slight throat infection, and therefore found the whole city repugnant. His companion Danilevsky traveled to Paris while Gogol journeyed up the Rhine by steamer, which brought him to Mainz. The many scenic landscapes wearied him. He was happy to be in Frankfurt, where he especially enjoyed the opera, for in almost every city Gogol sought out the theater. His destination was Switzerland, but in Baden-Baden he met old acquaintances from St. Petersburg: the Balabin family, whose youngest daughter Maria was his pupil, and the family of Prince Repnin, who were related to the Balabins by marriage. All her life the young Varvara Repnina remained a fervent admirer of Gogol; her fragmentary recollections of him have been preserved. He was so well received, surrounded by so much veneration, that he gladly stopped there. The three days which he wanted to spend in Baden-Baden grew into four weeks. Gogol was friendly and open; he read from his works, as always to perfection, and enjoyed the lovely town and its environs. He did not leave Baden-Baden until the middle of August. He saw Basel, Berne, and Lausanne, and found none of them particularly pleasing. In Geneva his stay was longer. Two memorable sights especially impressed him: the Alps and the Gothic churches. In Gogol's letters architecture always plays a prominent role. He read a great deal, read through all of Molière and Walter Scott, went on trips, e.g. to Ferney, where he reveled in reminiscences of Voltaire, and went on mountain-climbing expeditions (for example, he climbed Mont Blanc), but his work proceeded badly. He complained of laziness and indisposition, and finally attributed his ill health to the Geneva climate, and moved to Vevey, where he spent a splendid autumn. His state of mind improved because he could write again; he began working on *Dead Souls* and made progress. But in the long run, Vevey was also too cold. He wanted to go to Italy, but a cholera epidemic was raging there, and the frightened Gogol decided instead to visit Danilevsky in Paris. Here he spent the winter of 1836–1837. He was not happy until he found a room with a good stove. His sensitivity to cold began to grow more and more intense. Work on the new book, *Dead Souls*, took up almost all of his time: "The 'dead' flow along gaily," he wrote to Zhukovsky,

> more briskly and confidently than in Vevey, and altogether it seems to me I am in Russia; everything I see before me is ours: our landowners, our civil servants, our officers, our peasants, our huts—in a word, Orthodox Russia in its entirety. It even seems funny to me, when I think that I am writing *Dead Souls* in Paris. Another Leviathan is being planned. A sacred shudder of anticipation runs through me in advance when I think about it; do I sense something from it? I shall partake of divine moments . . . but right now I am entirely

immersed in *Dead Souls*. My task is hugely immense and I shall not complete it soon. Many new classes and the most varied gentlemen will rise up against me. But what am I to do? It is my destiny to be at odds with my compatriots. Patience. Someone invisible is prescribing my way with a mighty staff. I know that my name after me will be more fortunate than I am and the descendants of these very compatriots, perhaps with eyes moist with tears, will pronounce their reconciliation with my spirit. [November 12, 1836.]

Gogol did not take much part in Parisian life. He was glad that he could work, and the Parisians, with their interest in politics and the transitory events of the day seemed superficial to him. "Everyone here is more excited about Spanish affairs than about his own." But this was of no interest to the artist. However, the city made a great impression on him. He seldom missed an opera or theater performance; Molière especially impressed him in the Théâtre Français. He learned French almost perfectly.

An old casual acquaintance was renewed and deepened. In Paris he met Alexandra Smirnova, a famous beauty, lively, clever, and well educated, the friend of Pushkin, Zhukovsky, Lermontov, and Vyazemsky, who lived with a rich diplomat in an unhappy marriage. After several years, one of Gogol's most genuine friendships was to develop from this acquaintance. The memoirs of Madame Smirnova are a valuable source for Gogol's biography. In Paris Gogol also became acquainted with the very important Polish poet, Adam Mickiewicz, with whom he shared many opinions, especially in politics.

The report of Pushkin's death in the beginning of March 1837 struck Gogol like a thunderbolt. Paris, his work, his life were made loathsome to him. He was transformed, lost all vitality, all vigor; he quickly made up his mind to leave and sought distraction in an exhausting journey to Rome by land and sea. But he could not get rid of the thought that his idol was no longer alive. His first letter from Rome (to Pletnev) reads:

> Worse news could not possibly have come from Russia. All enjoyment in my life, all my greatest enjoyment has disappeared with him. I undertook nothing without his advice, I didn't write a line without seeing his face before me. What

> will he say, what comments will he make, what will he laugh about, to what will he give his imperishable and eternal approval—all of this occupied my mind and animated my powers. A mysterious trembling of satisfaction not to be tasted on earth embraced my soul . . . God! my present work, inspired by him, his creation . . . I have not the strength to continue it. Several times I have taken hold of my pen, and the pen fell from my hands. [March 16, 1837.]

Or later:

> My life, my highest bliss died with him. The bright moments of my life were moments of creation. When I created, I saw only Pushkin before me. All the blows struck at me meant nothing to me; I spat at the disdainful mob; dear to me was his eternal and irrefutable word. I didn't undertake anything, I didn't write anything without his advice. Everything that is good in me, I owe it all to him. Even my present work is his creation. He made me swear that I would write, and I didn't write a line without his form appearing before my eyes. I was glad at the thought how satisfied he would be, I guessed what would please him, and that was my highest and first reward. Now no reward is waiting for me! What is my work? What now is my life? . . . [March 30, 1837 to Pogodin.]

But little by little Italy and Rome took effect. Gogol was enthusiastic: "It is as warm here as if it were summer," he wrote in April 1837 to Danilevsky, "and the sky looks all silver. . . . The sun is further and greater and plunges it more vividly in its brilliance." The Italian countryside reminded him of the Ukraine; the eternal city cast a new spell that he had never felt before.

> When I entered Rome, I at first could give no clear account of it to myself: it appeared small to me; but the longer I know it, the larger it appears to me, the buildings seem more immense, the views more lovely, the sky better; and pictures, ruins and antiquities suffice for a whole lifetime. You fall in love with Rome slowly, gradually, but then for your whole life. In brief, all of Europe is there for viewing, but Italy for living!

Only lack of funds and the mysterious stomach ailment somewhat darkened the bliss. He asked Zhukovsky to apply to the Czar for financial support, but the situation was not desperate, since he had many Russian friends in Rome, especially painters. He was in splendid spirits; he was witty, original, and well-liked. Soon the Italian summer became too hot, and in spite of a lack of funds, Gogol traveled to Baden-Baden, where he expected a cure for his hemorrhoids from the waters. He hardly arrived before he was tortured by a longing for Rome: "He who was once in heaven will not want to return to earth." (July 16, 1837.) "My heart longs for Rome, for my Italy. I can hardly wait for the month to pass which I must spend at the waters here." (July 21, 1837.)

A rainy Rhine journey took him to Frankfurt; then he went south again to Geneva, where he spent almost two months in the company of Danilevsky and Mickiewicz. By the end of October he was again in Rome and again very happy.

> Oh, if you only knew with what joy I left Switzerland and flew to my dearest, to my lovely one, to my Italy! She is mine! No one in the world will take her from me. I was born here. Russia, St. Petersburg, snows, the scoundrels, the office, the rostrum, the theater—that was all a dream. . . . I am joyous. My soul is bright. I labor and rush my work to completion. Life! Life! Still more life!

Thus he wrote to Zhukovsky (October 30th, 1837), who had been able to inform him that the Czar had granted him a rather large sum.

The winter of 1837–1838 was all bathed in light. "I was never so happy, so content with life. My apartment is entirely in the sun: Strada Felice Nr. 126, ultimo piano." (February 2, 1838, to Danilevsky.) The work on *Dead Souls* proceeded very well. On many days he retired to his apartment and wrote; otherwise he enjoyed life with his Russian painters, while amazing them with his curious dress and his appetite (in spite of the stomach ailment); he was an habitué of several restaurants and a fastidious gourmet.

He could not see enough of Rome; the churches filled him with enthusiasm. "Only in Rome does one really pray; elsewhere one just acts as if he were praying." St. Peter's and the Colosseum crop up again and again in his letters; other churches are also mentioned and sometimes enthusiastically described. This was perhaps the happiest time in Gogol's life.

This winter was interrupted by a merry intermezzo. Gogol

became acquainted with the rich Catholic convert, Princess Zinaida Volkonskaya, who fanatically adhered to her new faith. She was surrounded by Polish priests, whose task it was to gain supporters for a newly founded Polish order with its seat in Paris, and who dedicated themselves with particular passion to the work of conversion. What a triumph it would be to lead the famous Russian author to the true faith! The sly Gogol acted as if he were going along with their endeavors. The reports of the priests to Paris sounded very confident, until the princess left Rome. Immediately Gogol broke off all relations with them, and nothing more was heard of his Catholic sympathies. But in Russia the rumor had already become widespread that Gogol had been converted, and half-ironically and half-emphatically, he had to calm his horrified mother. No doubt Gogol pretended to be interested in order to insure the favor of the rich princess; it is wrong to construe from this interlude mystical inclinations allegedly already present, as many scholars have tried to do.

Gogol's complaints returned with the rainy spring: "My life would be the most poetic in the world, if a handful of prose had not interfered: This prose is my bad health!" It had an unfavorable effect upon his capacity for work. His head was heavy as if in a cloud. He wanted to have his hair shaved off in order to get it free. Again he thought of traveling. All his life, Gogol's literary inspiration was subject to strange fluctuations. Periods of creativity alternated with periods of complete sterility, during which he suffered terribly. His almost ten-year agony is to be attributed, to a great extent, to the periodic breakdowns of his literary productivity. No doubt this breakdown of inspiration was closely connected with his real or imagined physical ailments. He almost always thought that he was ill. He distrusted his stomach (in the beginning, probably without particular reason), observed it anxiously, and reported his impressions to his friends without imposing any restraint upon his eating habits, for from all sides his gastronomic understanding and even his culinary skill are praised.

Gogol spent the summer of 1838 in Naples, whose sea climate was supposed to help him get over the summer heat. An aversion to creative work tortured him constantly. Great ideas ran through his head, but he thought that he was too ill to give them concrete form. In addition, new financial problems developed. He asked Pogodin for a loan, which his Moscow friend gave him without hesitation. In Naples there was no lack of Russian acquaintances. In a very amusing manner, Princess Repnina describes how Gogol worried about his health: it was as if his friends were living in his stomach, so vivid were the descriptions of his physical sensations.

After a short stay in Paris, where he wanted to help Danilevsky, who was taken sick (Gogol never missed a chance to travel), Gogol returned again to Rome in October 1838. In Paris he had always felt very well. With ironic longing he recalled the Paris "cathedrals" (meaning the great restaurants), which made him forget the Roman (real) cathedrals.

> With the zeal of a newcomer I wanted to throw myself into the arts and to rush off and to re-inspect diligently all the Roman wonders; but in my stomach sits some sort of devil, who prevents me from seeing anything in the proper light, and now reminds me of lunch, now of breakfast—in short, of all sinful impulses, in spite of the holiness of the place, of the splendid sun, of the splendid days. . . . [No date; to Danilevsky.]

Such passages in his letters indicate, moreover, that the final turn to religion, which many scholars place in the year 1836, had by no means taken place yet. Such trifling with sacred matters would be impossible later.

The winter of 1838–1839 was rich in events. In December, Gogol became acquainted with the great painter Alexander Ivanov, who was working on his subsequently famous picture, "Christ Appears to the People." In the same month, the Russian crown prince, Alexander II, came to Rome, and with him Zhukovsky. Pogodin followed soon after.

> I no longer think of my health at all: Really, it bores me. Besides, I am so delighted now by Zhukovsky's arrival that this is the only thought in my head.—Our meeting was very touching. The first name that we mentioned was Pushkin. Even today his brow becomes clouded with grief when he thinks of this loss. We spent almost the entire day looking at Rome together, from morning till night, with the exception of the days on which he has to go through the same procedure with the heir apparent. [January 18, 1839 to Princess Repnina.]

Rome always filled Gogol with renewed enthusiasm. With Zhukovsky (a skilled draftsman, as was Gogol himself) he toured Rome and its environs; many of Zhukovsky's sketches from this period have been preserved. When Pogodin arrived in the beginning of March, Gogol again had the pleasure of acting as guide through his beloved Rome, although the unpolished, sly businessman could not take the place of the kind, sensitive Zhukovsky, who departed at almost the same time. Gogol found particular pleasure in surprising visitors with unexpected views. He would go by the most roundabout way to show off a beautiful building from the most favorable side.

In the spring of 1839, a tragedy occured which severely shook Gogol's psyche and which prepared the way for the subsequent turn to religion: Gogol experienced death at close quarters. Count Iosif Vielgorsky, the twenty-three-year-old school companion of the heir apparent, an extremely gifted, dreamy youth, was ill with tuberculosis. He had to leave the retinue of the prince on his tour of Europe and arrived in Rome in November 1838, seeking a cure. Gogol became acquainted with him soon thereafter. A deep and stormy friendship developed. But the condition of the patient was hopeless, and he died in June 1839, literally in Gogol's arms. With touching devotion Gogol attended the mortally ill youth. Night after night he sat by his bed, waiting at his beck and call. Gogol cared for the patient with a genuine fervor. The entries in his diary entitled "Nights at the Villa" speak a romantically ardent language of friendship.

> They were sweet and torturous, these sleepless nights. Gravely ill, he sat in a deep arm-chair. I beside him. Sleep was not to touch my eyes. It was so sweet for me to sit beside him, to look at him. For two nights already we had addressed each other in the familiar form. How much closer I felt to him since then! He sat there, always so gentle, quiet, resigned. God! with what joy, with what jubilation would I take his illness upon myself, and if my death could give him back his health, with what readiness would I abandon myself to it!

In every entry, in spite of obvious literary elaboration, we get a sense of genuine feeling and honest compassion. "I am much too occupied now with my sick Vielgorsky; night after night I sit by him without sleeping, trying to catch his every gesture. There are sacred duties of friendship, and I must now fulfill them. But it is strange—I feel no weariness at all, and my health has by no means worsened. Even my face does not bear any sign of exhaustion. . . . Sweet and sad are my present minutes. . . ." Something new was beginning to appear in Gogol. He who previously always conducted himself quite egotistically now forgot himself completely. Or is it the lack of inspiration, the inability to work, for which Gogol is trying to make excuses in a respectable manner? Or both reasons? Who can say? In any case, it is striking that even here in the face of death there is no mention of God. "Nights at the Villa" contains no religious emphasis at all, an attitude which would be unthinkable at a later time.

Gogol took it upon himself to conduct the unhappy father of Vielgorsky to Marseilles, where the rest of the family was waiting; on the ship he met the French literary critic, Sainte-Beuve, who later praised the clear, clever conversation of Gogol with its abundance of striking observations.

In the beginning of June, he is again in Rome, but not for long. His sisters had come of age and had to leave the boarding school in St. Petersburg. For better or for worse, Gogol has to undertake the task of providing them with lodgings and of taking care of their needs. In addition to this he would like to make arrangements for a new edition of his works. Traveling was his passion. He felt better physically when he was traveling, and he could work. One might think that Gogol abhorred above all the pressure of being obliged to work; his inspiration left him immediately at the thought that he would now have to work; while he was traveling he felt free of this obligation; he really did not need to work—and so he was again capable of it and felt content and healthy. Gogol traveled by way of Munich, which made a great impression on him, to Marienbad, where he met Pogodin. They planned to make the trip home together. Gogol took advantage of the opportunity for a brief cure at the resort; in Marienbad he got to know the distinguished poet Nikolay Yazykov, who was later to become a close friend.

From Marienbad he traveled to Vienna, where he again had to wait for Pogodin. This time his hopes for the beneficial results of traveling did not entirely materialize, because he did not really want to return to Russia and was in a depressed frame of mind. He was desperate because he could not work: "It's hard to find oneself an old man at an age which, properly, still belongs to youth, terrible to come upon ashes instead of flames inside oneself and to be conscious of failing inspiration." (September 5, 1839.) In a bad mood, he roamed through the streets of Vienna bored and annoyed. "All of Vienna is gay, even the local Germans are gay, but their gaiety, as is well known, is dull; they drink beer, sit under the chestnut trees at wooden tables—that's all there is to it. The work I have begun is not progressing, and yet I feel that it could grow into something very fine." (September 10, 1839.) The reference here is to a drama about Ukrainian life, *The Shaved-off Mustache*, which was never completed. Finally Pogodin arrived, and reluctantly, concerned about his health, bothered by a lack of funds, Gogol left his sunny south. On September 26, 1839, he arrived in Moscow.

We are well informed of the period in Russia from September 1839 to June 1840, thanks to the memoirs of Sergey Aksakov. Aksakov was perhaps a bit inclined to favorable exaggerations but he was a good observer, and his genuine love for Gogol sharpened his powers of observation.

> Gogol's external appearance had changed so much that it would be quite possible not to recognize him at all. No trace of the former smoothly-shaven and (with the exception of the high combed forelock) cropped dandy in a fashionable frock coat. Beautiful, thick blond hair reached almost to his shoulders; a handsome mustache made the transformation complete; all his features had acquired a completely different significance; in his eyes, especially when he spoke, goodness, cheerfulness, and love toward all were expressed; but when he was silent or became immersed in contemplation, then they immediately acquired a serious turn toward something not external. A cloaklike coat took the place of the frock coat, which Gogol only wore when he could not avoid it; Gogol's whole figure had become much more dignified in the coat. In those days he often joked, and his jokes, which are almost impossible to reproduce, were so original and amusing that all his listeners were seized with uncontrollable laughter; but he himself always joked without smiling.

Gogol's Life

Gogol was greeted with enthusiasm by the Slavophile circles. Invitations piled up; but again and again they were accompanied by the question whether he had brought anything back from abroad—a question which, to an increasing degree, caused Gogol to react in an almost pathological manner. The fear that his inspiration would leave him, that he would not be able to write any more, pursued him continuously. There is no doubt that his subsequent turn to religion was prepared by these fears, and to a great extent determined by them. The "incapable" poet wanted to gain acceptance as a prophet. At this time there was still no trace of any special religiosity.

Due to the enthusiasm of those around him on the one hand, and through his own inner insecurity on the other, Gogol became moody and made a very unfavorable impression on strangers, especially as a pampered guest of the Aksakovs. He annoyed the public at large at the performance of *The Inspector General* which was expressly put on in his honor. Attending half-hidden in a box, he did not put in an appearance on the stage, but, in spite of thunderous cries for the author, sneaked unnoticed from his box, practically on all fours, and hurried home. It is striking that close acquaintances spoke of Gogol's openness, cheerfulness, and friendliness, while people who met him for the first time or just once described him as reserved, sullen, and arrogant. Among the latter group is the critic Belinsky, whose expansive nature was tempered by Gogol's ironic coolness.

Gogol was afraid that his anxious mother would hurry to Moscow to see her son. But he wanted to handle his sisters' affairs alone, and he therefore dated his letters to his mother from Trieste and Vienna while he had already been living in Moscow for a considerable length of time, so that she might not learn of his presence. It seems farfetched to me to see in this bit of trickery proof of Gogol's insincerity, as do many of his biographers. Gogol stayed a month in Moscow and then traveled to St. Petersburg with Aksakov, who wanted to have his youngest son admitted into the St. Petersburg Corps of Pages. Gogol was happy to see his school friend Prokopovich again, his patron Pletnev, and above all Zhukovsky, with whom he stayed in the Winter Palace. But the St. Petersburg climate and, above all, the terrible cold brought him to the brink of despair. The provisions for his sisters were taken care of with the financial help of Aksakov, but the return trip was delayed because Gogol wanted to travel with the Aksakovs, whose affairs kept running into new difficulties.

In spite of or perhaps because of this uncertainty of his position, since there was no immediate pressure on him to work, Gogol worked diligently. He continued writing *Dead Souls*. Aksakov reports that he wanted to visit Gogol one day, but it was explained to him that Gogol was not at home, and so he spent two pleasant hours with Gogol's host, Zhukovsky.

> Finally I took leave of my gracious host and said I would come back to find out if Gogol, with whom I had to speak, had returned. "Gogol hasn't gone out at all," replied Zhukovsky. "He's at home and writing. But now it's time for him to go for a walk. Come along!" And he led me through the inner rooms to Gogol's study, quietly unlocked the door and opened it. Before me stood Gogol in the following fantastic get-up: in place of boots—long Russian woolen stockings, which reached above the knee; instead of a jacket—a velvet spencer over a flannel camisole, with a large, bright-colored scarf wrapped around his neck and a raspberry-colored, velvet kokoshnik, embroidered in gold, on his head, quite similar to the headdress of Finnish tribeswomen. Gogol was busy writing, buried in his work, and we had obviously disturbed him. He looked at us for a long time without seeing, as Zhukovsky put it, but was not at all embarrassed about his costume. . . ."

This is practically the only time we ever hear of the manner in which Gogol worked; he anxiously shielded his work from profane eyes; the strange attire seems to have served as a stimulant for him, in the manner of Schiller's rotten apples. We also find allusions to this elsewhere. Andrey Bely makes this the cardinal point of his bold and ingenious theories.

Finally, in the middle of December, Aksakov, Gogol, and his two sisters departed. The two girls had become completely estranged from the world in the seclusion of the boarding school, were afraid of everything, were embarrassed without reason, quarreled—in brief, Gogol had his troubles with them; but in spite of everything, he was a loving, fatherly brother, who knew how to combine mildness with strictness. He felt himself responsible for the welfare of the family, was saddened by the ruin of the family estate, did not have much confidence in his mother, and wanted at least to control the future of his sisters. "I was in St. Petersburg and have brought back my sisters," he writes to Danilevsky, "they will live in Moscow; I will get them lodgings somewhere, perhaps with one of my acquaintances, so long as they do not know and do not see their own home, where they would be completely ruined. You know that my dear Mama looks and does not see, that she does not at all what she imagines she is doing, and on the assumption of making them happy, will make them unhappy, only to place the whole responsibility on God and to say that what happened was the will of God." (December 29, 1839.) This manner of speaking about trust in God would not be possible for Gogol at a later time.

In Moscow a lively social life began again. Encouraged by universal admiration, Gogol read from his works—fragments of new comedies and finally also the first six chapters of *Dead Souls*, which he always delayed reading until the requests were overwhelming. Friends and foes alike could not find words to express their praise of his brilliant skill in reading aloud. In addition, the memoirs of his contemporaries constantly praise his culinary abilities and his gastronomic sensitivity. In the preparation of Italian macaroni, for example, he was a virtuoso. But—things were going too well for him. He had plenty of free time in which he could work—and was unable to do so. On the one hand he enjoyed the admiration displayed by all around him —on the other, he was afraid, as ever, that the inspiration could leave him, that he would be a disappointment. A feeling of inner unrest set in, and along with it the observation of imaginary illnesses, which developed into real ones due to the constant nervous strain. Gogol's life was again marked by a trembling fear about his literary abilities—perhaps he felt that his particular province was rather limited, even though he attained the highest measure of perfection in it.

Gogol was dissatisfied and longed for change, for travel, for Rome. But financial means were lacking. In spite of his fame, his works were not selling very well, and Gogol rejected an extremely unpromising offer for publication from the St. Petersburg wholesale book dealer and publisher, Smirdin. Zhukovsky again came to the rescue in his moment of need; with the support of the heir apparent, he advanced Gogol 4,000 rubles so that another stay in Italy was assured in the near future. Several weeks before his departure, his mother arrived in Moscow with his youngest sister, Olga. In spite of all his joy at seeing them again, he was drawn irresistibly back to work. One of his sisters, Elizaveta, was taken in by a friendly Moscow family; his mother departed with the other two. On May 9, his nameday, in the garden of his friend Pogodin, with whom he was then staying, Gogol gave a magnificent literary dinner at which Lermontov and other prominent persons were present. A few weeks later, accompanied by his friends to a point far outside of Moscow, he journeyed by way of Warsaw to Vienna, with the intention of traveling from there on to Rome.

When he arrived in Vienna, Gogol sensed a return of his creative powers, which filled him with enthusiasm and renewed confidence. In addition to his work on *Dead Souls*, he was also busy with the revision of *Taras Bulba*, wrote the famous "The Overcoat," and set to work again on *The Shaved-off Mustache*. He was under the impression that Marienbad waters, taken in Vienna, would be highly beneficial to his health, and decided to remain there a while, even though the "Germans" annoyed him with their gaiety.

But the nervous tension which accompanied this period of creativity suddenly turned into a nervous ailment—a very serious illness, which brought Gogol to the edge of the grave and which represented the decisive turning point in his life. Its symptoms were: agonizing restlessness, shortness of breath, stomach complaints, and complete apathy. When Gogol believed with absolute certainty that he was going to die, he had a vision, which he discussed with no one except the Russian businessman Botkin, who, as a compatriot in Vienna, took care of him with great devotion. However, there are intimations of it in Gogol's letters, and Aksakov too reports that he heard of it. We know nothing of the nature of the supernatural phenomenon, but Gogol's decisive turn to religion was evident from this time on, a turn which determined the last twelve years of his life. His new, deep, mystical faith drew its unshakable strength and

Gogol's Life

certainty from this mysterious vision; from now on, Gogol felt himself as one chosen, on whom a grace was bestowed; he felt renewed certainty about his calling as teacher and his role as prophet. Art as such was no longer the chief purpose of his existence; it was only the means to open the blind eyes of mankind to the one eternal truth. He to whom God has granted genius bears a tremendous responsibility. Gogol finished writing the first part of *Dead Souls* as he had started. Then he began to wrestle with the problem of the purposeful nature of religious art. As a religious thinker he succeeded in creating a remarkably closed system. Gogol the artist received a fatal wound in Vienna.

After Vienna, Gogol's mystic, religious frame of mind grew steadily more intense. He held fast to his new faith with absolute certainty, which enabled him to act not only as writer (a role which caused him constant worry about his inspiration), but also as teacher and prophet. When Gogol believed he was dying, he had himself placed in the post coach and driven in the direction of Italy, so as not "to have to die among the Germans." He suddenly began to recover in an astonishing manner. In Venice he was already almost completely recovered, even though his frame of mind continued to be gloomy. Rome itself no longer had the same effect:

> Neither Rome, nor the sky, nor all that should have enchanted me, nothing now has any influence on me. I don't see them, I don't feel them . . . I look upon myself with anxiety. I started on my journey so bravely, so briskly, to create, to work. Now . . . O God! how much my friends have sacrificed for me . . . when shall I return it all! And I had believed that this year already I would finish the work which, with one stroke, would take from me this burden which lies on my unscrupulous conscience. What lies ahead of me? . . . [October 17, 1840 to Pogodin.]

Again the worry about the work, the feeling that he had to create something quickly, which tortured and paralyzed him. Gogol could only work when he was not compelled to work. In this regard, we should observe the manner in which he bubbled over with creative energy when he occupied a secure position in St. Petersburg, and the way he suffered increasing torment as an independent writer.

Slowly he began to regain his confidence. He worked on the first part of *Dead Souls*, made corrections in what he had already written, had new ideas, and prepared the first volume for publication. In Rome he again associated with Russian painters, who had a high regard for him as critic and teacher. He stood up for them in a touching manner and secured commissions for them from the nobility. Thus the winter of 1840–1841 passed. In the spring he dreamed again of traveling, but his financial situation was dismal. He asked his Moscow friends for help—for now he was certain that he could return everything to them.

> A wonderful work is completing and perfecting itself in my soul and not infrequently now are my eyes filled with tears of gratitude. I see clearly here the sacred will of God: such an inspiration does not originate from a mere human being; he could never think up such a subject! Oh, three more years with such refreshing moments! . . . [March 5, 1841 to Aksakov.]

He wanted to return again to Moscow. His friends were to meet him and accompany him back, for he now contained a valuable treasure.

> People must cherish me now not for my sake, no! They will not be performing a worthless task. They will be bringing back an earthen vase. Of course this vase is now full of cracks, rather old, and barely holds together; but in this vase now a treasure lies enclosed; consequently, one must take care of it. [March 5, 1841 to Aksakov.]

Completely engrossed in his work, he firmly rejected the request of his practical-minded friend Pogodin to write something short for his journal. Finally, however, he had to give in; this is probably the reason why the planned novel *Annunciata* remained uncompleted. At the end of 1841 Gogol revamped the beginning, which had been written in 1839, and the fragment, entitled "Rome," was printed in the periodical *The Muscovite* (No. 3). After this, Gogol no longer concerned himself with it. He had a horror of journals, since they demanded short-order work, which he was not capable of producing.

On the whole, however, the summer of 1841 flowed by rather pleasantly and calmly, for *Dead Souls* was progressing very well. Pavel Annenkov, Gogol's acquaintance from St. Petersburg, spent a few months in Rome. He lived in a room next to Gogol's, made a fair copy of *Dead Souls* from Gogol's dictation, and has left us very informative recollections of this period. The intimate connection between Gogol's inspiration and his frame of mind is here confirmed anew. Gogol dictated the famous Plyushkin chapter:

> Never had the pathos of Gogol's dictation reached such heights, at which he nevertheless maintained all his artistic naturalness, as in this section. Gogol even arose from his chair (one could see that the nature described by him was at this very moment floating before his eyes) and accompanied the dictation with a proud, almost imperious gesture. After the completion of this astonishing sixth chapter, I was very excited, put down the pen and said frankly: "Nikolay Vasilyevich, I consider this chapter a work of genius." Gogol rolled the little notebook from which he had been dictating into a tight ring, and spoke with a thin, hardly perceptible voice: "Believe me, the others are no worse." But he immediately continued in a raised voice: "You know we still have time till *cenare*; let us look at the gardens of Sallust, which you do not yet know, and we can also drop in at the Villa Ludovisi." From his radiant expression and from the proposal itself, one could conclude that the impressions of the dictation had put him into a merry frame of mind. This became even more evident on the way. Gogol had taken along his umbrella just in case, and hardly had we turned into an empty alley to the left of the Palazzo Barberini, when he began to sing a swashbuckling Ukrainian song, finally broke into a dance and performed such feats in the air with the umbrella that hardly two minutes went by before only the handle was left in his hand while the rest of the umbrella went flying off. He quickly picked up the broken part and continued his song. . . .

Amusing anecdotes which give evidence of Gogol's merry moods, his rather free joking conversations with the waiters in the restaurants in which he was a finicky patron, his newly revived enthusiasm for Rome, for the Italians—all this bears witness to the high spirits of the happy writer.

But the mystic vision of Vienna was not forgotten. God sent him the good fortune of being able to write, and he wanted to proclaim God's glory. Now the plan ripened to make *Dead Souls* into a great poem in honor of God. The dark first part was to be followed by new, bright parts.

He would proclaim salvation to men and teach them the

way to it. Should the poet in him die, the prophet too has worth, perhaps even a higher worth. This is a dangerous proposition for the true artist, which Gogol basically did not find convincing. Gogol's spiritual torment became more and more critical. A letter to Danilevsky is typical. (August 7, 1841.)

> As pleasant as it was for me to receive your letter, I found it painful reading. From its idly dragging lines speak melancholy and boredom. You have not yet taken hold of the rudder of your life; it is still drifting away vainly and aimlessly, for the slumbering helmsman is dreaming of other things. . . . Look around you and rub your eyes: The best there is is around you, as it is everywhere around Man and as only the wise man alone recognizes it, often too late. Do you still fail to see how much higher the sphere of action in Semerenki [Danilevsky's estate] can be than any prominent and worthless official life, with all its conveniences and splendid comfort, etc., etc. . . . But hear this: you must now listen to my word, for my word has a double power over you, and woe to him, whoever he may be, who does not listen to my word. For the time being let everything go, everything which stirs your thoughts at times in moments of indolence, however enticingly and pleasantly it may stir them. Submit and busy yourself for a year, only a year with your estate. A year! And this year will be eternally memorable in your life. I swear it will begin the dawn of your happiness. Fulfill, therefore, without grumbling and resistance, this request of mine. Not for you alone,—you will be doing me a great, great service. Do not try to find out what this service is: you will not be able to recognize it, but when the time comes, you will thank Divine Providence, which gave you the opportunity to do me a service; for the greatest good in the world is the opportunity to be able to perform a service, and that is the first service that I ask of you—not for the sake of just anything: you know yourself that I have never done anything for you, but rather for the sake of my love for you, which is capable of bringing about a great, great deal. Oh, believe my words! From now on my word is clothed with the highest power. Everything can disappoint, deceive, betray, but my word will not betray.

Along with the high spirits resulting from the renewed ability to work ran the gradual maturing of a tightly constructed theological-philosophical system which rested on the firm basis of a mystical experience. As long as the artistic inspiration was there, it remained primary and suppressed the religious feeling, but a slackening of the former was immediately accompanied by

Gogol's Life

a surge of religious spirit, which becomes apparent in letters like the above.

The first volume of *Dead Souls* was finished. Gogol wanted to see about its printing himself and to carry on personally the probable war with the censors. At the end of August he left Rome, visited Zhukovsky (who in April 1841, at the age of fifty-eight had married the eighteen-year-old daughter of the painter Gerhard von Reutern) in Frankfurt, lived for a short time in Hanau, where a deep friendship grew out of a meeting with the poet Yazykov, in whom he found a follower and admirer, and traveled by way of Dresden and St. Petersburg to Moscow. From Dresden he wrote to his new friend, who was in doubt as to whether he should follow him to Moscow:

> No, Moscow with its noise and its obtrusiveness is not to frighten you any more; you must now remember that I am waiting for you there and that you are coming home, and not as a guest. . . . Oh, believe in my words! . . . I can say nothing more to you but: believe in my words. There is something wonderful and incomprehensible. . . . But the sobbing and weeping of a most deeply inspired and grateful soul have prevented me from ever expressing it completely. . . . And my lips would become dumb. No human thought can possibly imagine the hundredth part of that infinite love which God has ready for man! That is all. From now on, your gaze should be brightly and confidently directed upward: for this, our encounter was needed. And if at our parting, as we shook hands, no spark of my spiritual strength passed through my hands into your soul, then you, therefore, do not love me. And if sometime you are overcome with boredom and if, in thinking of me, you are incapable of overcoming it, then you, therefore, do not love me. And if a sudden illness overwhelms you and your spirit becomes downcast, then you, therefore, do not love me. . . . But I am praying, praying fervently in the depth of my soul at this very moment that it may not happen to you, and that dark doubts about me fly away from you, and that as often as possible the same brightness may prevail in your soul as has enveloped me at this moment . . . [September 27, 1841.]

The friends in Russia were to find a new Gogol.

Gogol's stay in Moscow from October 1841 till June 1842 was filled with worries about the printing of *Dead Souls*. The censorship caused difficulties, and Gogol suffered terribly from them. At first the Moscow Censorship Committee forbade the whole book. Those who had to make the decision were intimidated, for the secret police habitually found allusions, supposedly directed against absolutism or against the Orthodox religion, in every harmless passage. Both author and censor would be punished; the history of Russian literature in the nineteenth century is full of grotesque episodes of this sort. *Dead Souls* is also an example of this. Immediately, the title met with objections: the soul is immortal, said the chairman of the committee, hence, the author was attacking fundamental doctrines of the church. When the true sense of the title was understood, the affair became even more complicated, for it was now clear that this was an attack against serfdom; at that time it was even more dangerous to attack the latter. The low price which Chichikov paid per soul was also attacked: it was said to degrade Man. Finally, they even went so far as to see an allusion to the Czar in the episode of a landowner who went bankrupt by building a large house in Moscow; for the Czar was just in the process of erecting a palace in Moscow. All of this in Gogol, when nothing was further from his mind than liberal ideas! In brief, the book was banned. Gogol was deeply shaken. His labor of years was to be wasted. Desperately he plunged himself into the struggle. He sent his manuscript to the St. Petersburg Censorship Committee, mobilized all his high-ranking and influential friends, wrote them moving letters, even composed a letter to the Czar, who once before, on the occasion of *The Inspector General*, had come to his aid; and he was finally successful. His friends went to work zealously in his behalf, and in February he received the news that St. Petersburg had agreed in principle to the printing, provided that "The Story of Captain Kopeykin" be omitted. Instead, Gogol revised this chapter so that nothing in it could possibly be interpreted as unfriendly to the government. The printing was begun in April, but the period of waiting and uncertainty had too depressing an effect on Gogol. Russia had become distasteful to him. He longed again for Rome. His health was again seriously affected. He was unable to work as long as he knew of nothing that he could be certain of; his mystical experience in Vienna rose up again before him, and the religious spirit gained new strength. "I was ill, very ill," he wrote to Maria Balabina in February 1842, and even today I am still sick within. My illness expresses itself in terrible attacks such as I've never experienced before, but that state seemed most terrible to me which reminded me of my terrible illness in Vienna, and especially when I felt that excitement rising to my heart which transformed every image which floated by in my thoughts into a giant, and which caused every insignificant pleasant feeling to turn into such a terrible joy as the nature of Man cannot bear, and which transformed every dark mood into grief, heavy, torturing grief —and these were followed by fainting spells; finally, a complete state of somnambulism. And even then it had to be, that in addition to all this, when my illness was already unbearable even without this, still more troubles were added, which would have been shattering even for a healthy person. How much self-control I had to develop in order to hold out! And I did hold out; I am pulling myself together as best I can; even go out, don't complain, and let no one see that I am ill, although it often, too often seems unbearable to me. . . .

Also the relationship with his host was noticeably deteriorating, and this strengthened in him the desire to leave Russia. Pogodin demanded contributions for his journal. Gogol could not and would not give them. The businessman Pogodin had no understanding of this. This situation finally became unbearable. Sergey Aksakov describes Gogol's stay in Moscow in detail. Gogol was frequently a guest at Aksakov's house. Father and sons (Ivan and Konstantin), as exponents of the Slavophile movement, sought to win Gogol over to the "Russian idea" with all the means at their disposal. The fact that Gogol wanted to travel abroad again grieved them very much. Gogol partially agreed with their ideas, but with him the accent lay much more heavily on God than on Russia. In Gogol's thinking, Russia never played the messianic role which fanatical Slavophiles, above all Aksakov's sons, allotted to her. Gogol frequently found it embarrassing to be proclaimed an exponent and prophet of an ideology with which he did not entirely agree. On the other hand, he did not want to offend his passionate friends. His vacillating from side to side was frequently interpreted as insincerity and egotism. The many amusing anecdotes which Aksakov tells about his unreliability and peculiar conduct are frequently explained by this dilemma. At any rate, Gogol associated primarily with Slavophile circles; his acquaintance with Khomyakov, the brilliant dialectical "philosopher" of the Slavophiles, was strengthened; his religious inclinations found expression in his relations with the clergy. Worth mentioning is his acquaintance with Nadezhda Sheremeteva, an extraordinarily pious and charitable old lady, whose touching letters to Gogol and his friendly answers prove how genuine Gogol's faith really was. He called her his spiritual mother and sometimes sent her money to distribute among the poor.

Gogol decided to make *Dead Souls* into a great epic on the purification of Man, in the manner of Dante, to which the first part represented only a kind of entrance hall. He began to worry again about inspiration, and the less artistically inspired he felt, the greater he felt a sense of religion. Aksakov reports that Gogol came to him one evening with transfigured countenance and said that something had taken place for which he had waited a long time. Since his arrival in Russia, Gogol had been waiting for someone to bless him with an ikon, and this had now been done by Bishop Innocent, a preacher famous at that time. Now he could reveal his long cherished decision: he was leaving Russia in order to make a pilgrimage to the Holy Sepulchre. Aksakov looked on Gogol's religious development with great misgivings. He attributed them to nervous hypertension and feared for Gogol the artist with good reason. The mystical revelation was not accessible to the author of *The Family Chronicle*, and the transformation in Vienna he could not understand.

Gogol wrote to Madame Smirnova:

All my literary friends had gotten to know me at a time when I was still the former man, and even then they did not know me very well. . . . Since the time when I left Russia, a great change has taken place in me. My soul occupied all of me, and I saw only too clearly that without directing my soul to its highest perfection I would not have the power to develop even one of my talents, and that without this spiritual education all of my efforts will be temporarily brilliant, but vain in essence. . . . On my arrival in Russia, all my literary friends received me with open arms. Each of them was busy with some literary affair or other, one with a journal, another with something else; each was completely wrapped up in some favorite idea, and when he found in others opponents to his opinion, he waited for me like a Messiah, convinced of the fact that I would share his thoughts and ideas and that I would support them and defend them against others; each assumed this as a first condition and act of friendship, without thinking (in all innocence) that these demands were not only nonsensical but even inhuman. It was impossible for me to sacrifice my time and my labor to support their favorite ideas, first, because I did not entirely agree with them, and second, because I somehow had to maintain my miserable existence, and I could not afford to sacrifice my articles to them by sending them to their journals, but had to print them separately as new and fresh in order to gain some income from them. They overlooked all these trifles. They interpreted my coldness toward their literary interests as coldness toward themselves. In their thoughts they didn't hesitate to make me into an egotist, to whom the common welfare was worth nothing, and to whom only his own literary fame was dear. . . . The misunderstandings went as far as such insulting suspicions; such crude blows were directed and moreover against such fine and sensitive strings, of whose existence those who struck the blows could have not the slightest idea, so that my whole soul was tortured and tormented, and I suffered too much. [No date.]

On May 21, the first copies of *Dead Souls* were ready. With all the means at his disposal, Gogol again endeavored to leave Russia. He left the editing of his works, which he had planned, to his St. Petersburg friend Prokopovich and at the end of May traveled by way of St. Petersburg to Germany.

From May 1842 until April 1848, Gogol lived abroad. His old conviction that travel was beneficial for his health never let him stay long in one place. Also he constantly needed company and conversation. But since he felt free only with close friends, he would hurry off to the places where he knew he could find them. On these occasions distance was of no concern.

After a short stay in Bad Gastein, he traveled to Rome, where he spent the winter of 1842-1843. His letters are full of questions about the public reaction to *Dead Souls*. He incessantly begged his friends to inform him of all criticisms, even the most inane. This desire to hear criticism, which at times seems like a mania and which became still more extreme with Gogol's next work, *Selected Passages From Correspondence with Friends*, is explained by Gogol's longing to purify his soul and lead it to perfection. Even the most inadequate criticism can contain a spark of truth, can throw light on the character of the author whose ego is reflected, perhaps unconsciously, in the work. One must search everywhere for these bright lights in order to attain the ideal to which criticism no longer can be applied.

Gogol lived in Rome with the seriously ill Yazykov, for whom he cared with great devotion; perhaps even *too* great devotion. In spite of the similarity of their religious attitudes, little disagreements seem to have cropped up. But Gogol found a splendid substitute in his old acquaintance Alexandra Smirnova, who after a very frivolous youth felt inclined toward an even more intensely exalted mysticism. Gogol acted as her guide in Rome. In her memoirs Madame Smirnova tells of the enthusiasm with which Gogol conducted her around the city, and she admires his detailed knowledge and his deep understanding of the art and architecture of the Eternal City. Every tour ended at St. Peter's. "And so it must be," said Gogol. "You can never get tired of looking at St. Peter's even though its façade resembles a chest of drawers." Otherwise his enthusiasm was directed, above all, toward Raphael and Michelangelo's Moses, which he knew how to show to his friends with great dramatic effect. Only when they had reached a certain position in San Pietro in Vincoli were his companions permitted to look to the right, and then the famous statue loomed up in all its grandeur before them.

Financial worries compelled Gogol to turn again to his Moscow friends. Filled with a sense of the importance of his work on the second part of *Dead Souls*, he asked them to relieve him of all day-to-day financial concerns for three years. They were to deal with his works as with their own and to guarantee him only 6000 rubles—a proposal which caused his friends the greatest embarrassment, since a short time before, much to their consternation, he had transferred the editing of his works to Prokopovich in St. Petersburg, and ready cash was not at hand. But they did what they could, especially Aksakov.

Gogol's former gaiety had disappeared. Although even now he still met with the Russian painters, he was withdrawn and silent—obviously he was again suffering from the fear of losing his creative powers. In the summer he traveled around in

Germany. Bad Ems, Baden-Baden, Frankfurt and Düsseldorf were the stops, depending on where Zhukovsky or Madame Smirnova were staying.

Gogol did not make much progress with his writing—he believed that a new work would be produced only when he had been spiritually purified and matured. For this he needed peace of mind and financial security. "I know," he wrote to Pletnev, "that later I shall work more extensively and even more quickly, but I won't reach that point for some time yet. My works are so closely bound-up with my own spiritual education, and I have such a great inner process of self-education to go through that there is no hope that my works will be published in the near future." (October 4, 1843.)

He spent the winter of 1843–1844 in Nice. Madame Smirnova was there, with the writer Count Sollogub, his wife Sofia, née Vielgorskaya, and Countess Vielgorskaya with her second son and her youngest daughter, Anna. All of these ladies were religiously oriented, and for them Gogol was a prophet to be listened to with respect. Gogol does not appear to have been completely indifferent toward Madame Smirnova. Ivan Aksakov reports that she once told Gogol directly he was in love with her, at which Gogol, however, became very angry. Similar rumors were also current in Russia, as we can see from the letters of Madame Sheremeteva to Gogol. Anna Vielgorskaya, whom Gogol seriously wanted to marry, will be discussed below.

Once more gay and amusing on the outside, Gogol suffered from his inability to continue his work. "I keep on working as best I can," he wrote to Zhukovsky, "but still not as much and not with the same success as I would like. But however, with God's help,—and I feel it,—my work will certainly progress more quickly later, because now I am still at the difficult, boring part. Every hour and every minute I have to force myself, and without forcing myself almost nothing is to be accomplished." (December 8, 1844.) He advised Count Sollogub to write every day, even though it was very hard to do so. Every day one should take his pen in his hand and force himself to express his thoughts on paper.

An anecdote related by Madame Smirnova is characteristic of Gogol. One day he was in a good mood and let himself be persuaded to read aloud from the second part of *Dead Souls*. In the middle of his reading, a storm broke. Gogol was deeply shaken, trembled from head to toe, and after the storm was afraid to go home alone. Later he confessed that he had recognized the voice of God in the storm, forbidding him to read his unfinished work.

The awareness of having to produce something great and the inability to do so tortured Gogol more and more, and as always when he found his artistic powers at a low ebb, his didactic religiosity became more evident. During this period he wrote a letter to Sergey Aksakov in which he explained in detail how and when the latter was to read Thomas a Kempis. This provoked a kindly but pointed reaction on the part of Aksakov, who three months later wrote to him:

> My friend, I did not doubt for a moment the sincerity of your convictions or your desire to do good for your friends, but I must confess that I am dissatisfied with these convictions and especially with the forms in which you express them. I even fear them. I am 53 years old, I had already read Thomas a Kempis before you were even born. . . . I condemn no beliefs and no one's beliefs if only they are sincere; but at the same time I shall very certainly not adopt any of these beliefs . . . and suddenly, as if I were a boy, you assign me the reading of Thomas a Kempis, without the slightest knowledge of my beliefs, and besides, in what form? At an appointed time, after coffee and with division by chapters as in a school assignment. It is both comical and annoying at the same time. . . . Also in your earlier letters many words have been a source of concern for me. I fear mysticism like fire, and it certainly seems to me that it is somehow showing through in you. I cannot stand any moralizing, nor anything that looks like faith in talismans. You are moving on the razor's edge. I tremble lest the artist come to grief!

Gogol provoked this reaction in almost all his friends. This is due not so much to the "what" of his demands as to the "how." The elevated, didactic tone provoked them to opposition, a circumstance which contributed so much to the fiasco of the *Correspondence*.

In March 1844 Gogol traveled by way of Strasbourg, Darmstadt, and Baden-Baden to visit Zhukovsky in Frankfurt; this was not exactly a pleasure for Zhukovsky's young wife, for the gloomy, sickly Gogol had a depressing effect on her. Strange attacks, fainting spells, and feelings of weakness increased. Since the Sollogubs were staying in Ostende, Gogol traveled there in July, and the sea baths seemed to help him. In October he was again with Zhukovsky in Frankfurt, where he wanted to spend the winter of 1844–1845. But he again felt the need to travel. In January he traveled to Paris to meet Vielgorsky and Count Alexander Tolstoy, a new friend. The Parisian climate did not agree with him. In March he returned to Frankfurt; the condition of his health was becoming catastrophic; he believed he was dying and suffered from terrible depressions. The nature of Gogol's illness has never been definitely established; it has been thought to be malaria, which, combined with strained nerves, periodically exerted its debilitating effect due to psychic overexcitement. On March 28 Gogol wrote to Tolstoy:

> I shall not conceal that the symptoms of my illness have frightened me: in addition to an unusual loss of weight—pains in my entire body. My body suffered from terrible chills; neither day nor night was I able to find anything to warm me. My face is yellow, while my hands became swollen and black; they were turned to ice which nothing could warm, so that their touch frightened even me. . . .

And to Madame Smirnova:

> For a long time now, God has taken from me the ability to create. I have tortured myself, forced myself to write, suffered severe pains when I saw my impotence, and several times already I have even brought on the illness from such constraint and was unable to produce anything, and everything came out forced and inferior, and many, many times I was seized with sadness, indeed, almost with despair for this reason. . . . Certainly, God knows best whether the illness causes this condition in me or whether the illness develops just because I forced myself to put my mind into the state necessary for creative work; in any case I thought of my cure only in this sense, not that the suffering would become less, but that the life-giving moments of creating and being able to have the creation become word would return again to my soul.

This letter (April 2, 1845) touches on the very core of Gogol's suffering, from which he would eventually perish.

The summer of 1845 was taken up with the search for the

nature of his illness and for methods of curing it. In Bad Homburg, Karlsbad, Berlin, and Dresden, Gogol had himself examined by medical authorities, among others the famous Dr. Carus; but they all came to different conclusions and recommended different remedies. He finally traveled to Gräfenberg, where the cold-water cure of Priessnitz appeared to bring him relief. But he felt alone there, did not complete the cure, and in October arrived again in Rome. During this summer Gogol burned almost everything that he had written of the second part of *Dead Souls*, probably influenced by the depressed state of his health. He remained in Rome during the winter of 1845–1846; but the city no longer exerted its former beneficial effect. Illness, melancholy, boredom, and inner emptiness torture him, even though in letters he speaks of happy moments which enable him to work and which compensate for all his suffering. Not until May 1846 did Gogol leave Rome to return to Gräfenberg. But first he decided to "drop by" Paris, where Alexander Tolstoy was staying. By chance he met Annenkov there, who writes in his memoirs:

> Gogol has aged, but he has acquired a special kind of beauty, which one cannot define better than to characterize it as the beauty of a thinking person. His face has become paler and thinner; deep, torturous mental labor has impressed upon it the clear stamp of exhaustion and weariness, but his over-all expression appeared to me to be somehow brighter and calmer than formerly. It was the face of a philosopher. As formerly, it was overshadowed by long, thick hair that reached to his shoulders, in which frame, Gogol's eyes not only had not lost their brilliance, but, so it seemed to me, were filled with even more fire and expressiveness.

From Paris Gogol traveled to Gräfenberg, this time without finding relief, and then back by way of Schwalbach, where Zhukovsky was staying, to Ostende. In October he was in Frankfurt, in November in Rome and Naples. During these months he was working with feverish industry on a new work: *Selected Passages from Correspondence with Friends*. Since the second volume of *Dead Souls* was still not progressing very well, Gogol turned with renewed energy to religion. A harmonious religio-philosophical system had matured within him. Now it was time to express it in words. In this work he found strength and consolation. He believed that men would become better if he showed them how it could be done. Everything that he had written previously now seemed pale in the face of this achievement. He eagerly urged Pletnev to hurry with the printing: it was important, important for him and important for the world. In addition he wrote a stage piece intended to explain the meaning of *The Inspector General* ("The Dénouement of *The Inspector General*"), which gives the comedy a moralizing, allegorical interpretation: the town of the plot is our soul; the Inspector General, the awakened conscience, the bad officials, our passions, etc., an interpretation which was certainly far from Gogol's mind when he wrote the play. This tasteless and artistically impossible scene was supposed to be performed on the occasion of the stage jubilee of the famous actor Shchepkin, who was to be crowned with a wreath by his colleagues at the end. Both the theatre management and the actor himself rejected Gogol's demands. The printed version of *The Inspector General*, with this scene, was to be sold for the benefit of the poor, who were to be selected by a board determined by Gogol, consisting of his influential friends in St. Petersburg and Moscow. Gogol also wanted the proceeds from the edition of his collected works to be put to the same charitable use. This money was to be used to help poor students. This request, expressed in a letter full of pathos and urgency, was carried out by his friends, but reluctantly and incompletely—for Gogol had debts. The purpose of this step, in Gogol's eyes, was self-castigation, but ascetic desires at the expense of others were not likely to be understood.

Gogol spent the winter of 1846-1847 in Naples again. Since the completion of his last work, a wonderful sense of peace filled his soul. The condition of his health improved. Here too he saw a divine reward. On December 31, 1846, his book was published in St. Petersburg. The effect was explosive, but touched only the literary circles close to Gogol. The book did not sell well: the public wanted to laugh and found it strange, to say the least, that the merry Gogol suddenly had serious, "boring" things to say.

Gogol's circle of friends split into two camps. His pious female followers, Pletnev, and, to a considerable degree, the

Slavophile Professor Shevyrev were enthusiastic. Gogol, the teacher, had spoken something decisive. (One must admit that if one grants Gogol the right to teach, then the book contains a great deal of worthwhile material.) But most were indignant. The liberal circles saw in the book a terrible betrayal of the cause of social progress, an apology for absolutism; they accused Gogol of impure motives, base flattery, and servility. At that time the critic Belinsky spoke the loudest. As a typical product of his time, he was simply not capable of comprehending that there could be things which stand higher than social questions, or in any case, stand on a very different plane. In his reviews he examined only the social position Gogol had taken, and sharply rejected what he found. His famous letter to Gogol, copies of which circulated in Russia, shows with great clarity that he had not at all understood what Gogol's concern was. This is not to say that the pretentiously pious ladies who gushed over Gogol understood this either. Praise from them was a doubtful matter. But there is no doubt that Gogol had a great deal to say, that he had managed to construct a system that went to the heart of the matter, and that he was also able to give it a valid literary form. Only a very few people grasped the true meaning of his book. Aksakov rejected the work because he heard in it (rightly so) mystical notes which he considered fatal for Gogol as an artist. He was annoyed about Gogol's attacks on Pogodin; he saw in them insane presumptuousness and hateful flattery—all objections which could be raised only by someone who was incapable of appreciating a genuine mystical experience. Gogol was very sincere in his letters. There is no question of any dishonesty here. His mistake was perhaps only that he judged others by himself in too dictatorial a manner, that he did not realize that there were people to whom his knowledge was completely inaccessible, and that he wanted to force on them with too much urgency conclusions for which they were simply unprepared. This overestimation of his friends also reveals itself in the fact that he asked them to describe Russian types for him, since he did not live in Russia and needed the latest Russian milieu for his books. For example, he asks Madame Smirnova, whose husband had become governor of Kaluga, to describe provincial types: "The Salon Lion," "The Misunderstood

Wife," "The Honest Bribetaker," etc. were to be the titles of these detailed characterizations. Madame Smirnova as well as the other friends of whom he made the same request complied only partially, a fact which he attributed to laziness and unfriendliness, without realizing how difficult, indeed, for many, how impossible the task was which appeared so easy to him. The press reviews of Gogol's book were almost all unfavorable. As was always the case in Russia, people began to jeer, not only at the work, but also at the person of the author.

Gogol felt deeply hurt. His hope of being able to improve and convert people was disappointed. He stood disgraced and derided. Gogol acted in accordance with his basic attitude: he viewed this fiasco as a test. Without abandoning any of his beliefs, he admitted that he had struck the wrong note, that he had been too proud and arrogant. He accepted with Christian humility the slap in the face that they gave him, compared himself to Khlestakov, and was ashamed. But deep down he felt himself in the right. He welcomed with open arms the great number of favorable and unfavorable letters which he received. The perfection of his ego, on which he was working, was easier in the mirror of this criticism. But nevertheless the shock was great. His health did not stop deteriorating until he was able to convince himself that his work on the whole was of value after all.

Summer again brought its usual period of wandering. In May he traveled to Paris to visit Tolstoy; from there to Frankfurt, Baden-Baden, Ems, and Ostende; and in November he returned again by way of Nice and Rome to Naples.

One gets the impression that the failure of his book strengthened Gogol and that it placed him on a new, higher level. He found his equilibrium in the fact that the storm of indignation was not able to shake him in his deepest beliefs. He had found solid ground. "What a treasure of knowledge and wit, and along with it what goodness, what constant, well-balanced benevolence"—this is the impression he made on a Russian (V. A. Mukhanov) in Paris at that time. He saw himself and the disposition of his soul clearly; he analyzed his psyche sharply and uncompromisingly. A characteristic letter to Sergey Aksakov reads:

> I loved you much less than you loved me. I was (so it seems to me) always in the position of loving everyone in general because I was not capable of feeling hatred toward anyone; but I was able to love someone in particular above others only from reasons of self-advantage. If someone brought me substantial benefits and my mind was enriched through him, if he caused me to make new observations in him or in other people, in brief, if somehow through him the scope of my knowledge was broadened, then I indeed loved this person, though he may have been less worthy of love than another, though he might also love me less. What to do? You see what a creature Man is: his first concern is his own welfare. [December 12, 1848.]

Through sharp self-analysis Gogol progressed more and more in the purifying of his soul. His *Correspondence* helped him take a great step forward in his work on his inner self; he believed that a stimulating effect upon his artistic creativity would result from the inner certainty which he had now gained. He believed he would succeed in casting his religious experience into an artistically perfect form. But he had to learn that genuine art does not bow down even before religion. Whenever Gogol was writing well he was inclined to consider the contents harmful; if the contents corresponded to his inner will, the artistic form was lacking, without the divine spark. He was eventually to be destroyed by this conflict.

Basically, Gogol no longer felt the urge to make the pilgrimage to the Holy Land. He had hoped for companions from his circle of friends, but they all disappointed him. However, he had spoken too much of the pilgrimage. It was now too late to turn back. In January 1848, he boarded a boat in Naples. The journey began with terrible seasickness, which tormented him till Malta, but then all went smoothly. In Beirut, Gogol lived with his schoolmate from Nezhin, Basili, who was Russian consul-general there and who personally accompanied Gogol through Syria to Jerusalem. But Gogol's letters reveal that the great experience he expected failed to materialize:

> What can my sluggish impressions convey to you? I saw this land as though in a dream. We got up before dawn and mounted our mules and horses, accompanied by guides both on foot and mounted; in single file the long procession moved

on through the small desert on the seashore or through the shallow water, so that on one side the sea washed the horses' hooves with its flat waves, while on the other side lay sandy plains and the white slabs of the higher ground, covered with low-lying shrubbery; at noon—a well, a water receptacle faced with slabs in the shadow of two or three olive or sycamore trees. Here a half-hour rest and again the journey, until on the evening horizon, which is no longer blue, but colored copper by the setting sun, five or six palm trees appear and along with them a little town that jutted out sharply against the rainbow-colored mist and that looked picturesque from a distance, but wretched up close—some Sidon or Tyre. And such is the road to Jerusalem. . . . Somewhere in Samaria I plucked a wild flower, somewhere in Galilee another. In Nazareth I sat around for two days because it rained heavily, and forgot that I was sitting in Nazareth, as if this were happening in Russia at a post coach station. [February 28, 1850 to Zhukovsky.]

Gogol received communion in the Church of the Holy Sepulchre and was able to hear mass from a very advantageous position beside the grave of Jesus. "I no longer remember whether I prayed or not," he writes to Zhukovsky.

I think I was only glad that I had a place which was so suitable for prayer and which was conducive to prayer; but I properly didn't have time to pray. So it seems to me. The liturgy flew by so quickly, it seemed to me, that even winged prayers were not capable of keeping pace with it. I barely had time to recover my senses, when I stood before the chalice, which the priest had brought out from the sepulchre in order to give unworthy me communion. [April 6, 1848.]

Gogol left Jerusalem dissatisfied. His inner firmness needed no strengthening at this time, even though he himself attributed his condition to a hardening of the heart. At the end of April 1848 Gogol traveled to Beirut, where he spent some time as guest of Basili, and then returned by ship to Russia. He landed at Odessa. He had not been in Russia in almost six years. He was not destined to leave again.

After a quarantine, which every new arrival from the orient had to undergo, Gogol traveled from Odessa to visit his mother on the family estate, Vasilyevka. His introspective nature disappointed his family. He himself suffered from it: "My mother and my sisters presumably were delighted to the *nec plus ultra* by my arrival, but we cold males do not melt so quickly. A feeling of an inexplicable sadness can be closer to us than anything else," he wrote to Danilevsky. (May 16, 1848.)

Gogol's contemporaries often accused him of arrogance and lack of feeling. His correspondence should correct this impression. Uncertainty and laziness often made Gogol seem arrogant. Large gatherings, new faces, above all, persons to whom he knew he was to be shown off—all this had a chilling effect upon him. He retreated within himself and was simply not able to act naturally. So also at home when outbursts of joy were expected of him. He stayed at home all summer, aside from small excursions to Poltava and Kiev. He did not work much and suffered from the heat. His old joy in gardening reappeared: he had avenues laid out and was interested in the botanical collection of his youngest sister. His dealings with the serfs were in the style of the *Correspondence*: he exhorted them to diligent work for the sake of the kingdom of heaven, rewarded the assiduous, and scolded the idle.

In the end of August he traveled to Moscow and immediately on to St. Petersburg. "Gogol has arrived here," writes Pletnev, ". . . he looks very healthy, even stouter than he has ever been. His appearance, fastidious to the point of elegance, does not resemble the author of the *Correspondence*. He doesn't say anything about the condition of his spirit." [To Grot, September 22, 1848.]

Gogol visited his friends, above all the Vielgorskys. Closer ties were now beginning to develop between him and the youngest, Countess Anna.

In the middle of October Gogol returned to Moscow. At first he stayed with Pogodin, with whom a half reconciliation had been made; then he moved to the house of Count A. P. Tolstoy, who placed several rooms at his disposal. The work on the second part of *Dead Souls* progressed very well. At social gatherings he was the center of attention. Everyone wished to see him, and he suffered from this. Very frequently he was with Aksakov again, who observed him lovingly and joyfully perceived a rise in his spirits. Basically, Aksakov was not at all glad to see Gogol move in with the pious mystic Tolstoy, and when in the spring of 1849 Gogol again began to suffer from a nervous disorder, Aksakov attributed it to Tolstoy's influence. In order to get to know the Russian countryside for his writings, Gogol wanted to take a trip through Russia, to visit little towns and villages, to talk with the people, and to see for himself their life and doings. His friend Madame Smirnova offered him the first opportunity to do this, when she invited him to visit her in Kaluga and on her estate in the same province, where he spent the summer working diligently. He took this life with his friends as a matter of course. On the occasion of a gift of books to Anna Vielgorskaya he writes her: "I am richer than you and have more opportunity for acquiring books, precisely because I have no other sort of expenses. I pay no one for my room and board. Today I live with one, tomorrow with another. I shall come and stay with you too without paying a kopek for it." (July 30, 1849.)

Gogol spent the whole summer of 1849 with friends on their country estates. In August he was with Aksakov in Abramovo near Moscow, where he read aloud the first chapter of the second volume of *Dead Souls*. Aksakov tells of his feelings on this occasion:

> I cannot express what took place in all of us. I was completely annihilated. Not joy, but fear that I would hear something that was unworthy of the earlier Gogol so embarrassed me that I became confused. . . . From the very first pages I saw that Gogol's talent was not lost, and went into complete ecstasy.

From this point on we frequently hear that Gogol read aloud to his closest friends chapters from the second part of *Dead Souls*, and the enthusiasm was unanimous. Parts of the first chapter of the fragment which has been preserved, which are still written completely in the style of the first part, are actually brilliant. Only in the description of positive characters, which he attempted later, does Gogol fall down. It will probably never be definitely established to what extent the versions read aloud agree with the fragment that has been preserved.

During the winter 1849–1850 Gogol lived in Moscow. "Gogol is very gay; consequently he is working," writes Alexey Khomyakov in a letter. The work was really progressing splendidly.

It seemed as if I had spent only an hour at work, no more; I look at the clock—already it's dinnertime.... The whole work, i.e., I mean the end of *Dead Souls*, is still not near completion. Almost all the chapters have been planned and even sketched out, but no more than *sketched out*; only two or three have been properly written, and that's all. I don't even know if one can produce a proper artistic work quickly. [To Pletnev, January 21, 1850.]

In the spring a creative crisis again ensued, and immediately affected his health. Gogol complained of nervous disorders and suffered from depression. The only love episode in Gogol's life took place during this period. From the very first moment, Gogol had found the Countess Anna Vielgorskaya very pleasing. As early as 1847 he wrote to Pletnev: "I particularly advise you to get acquainted with Anna Mikhailovna Vielgorskaya. She possesses something that I know of in no other woman: not an analytical mind, but the higher power to reason; but one does not get to know her at once: she lives completely within herself." The young countess was very much of a religious frame of mind. She listened with respect to Gogol's teachings and exhortations. From literary questions, they proceeded to philosophical problems. Gogol's letters to her contain instructions for a pious life, such as Gogol loved to impart. He thought that he found in her an especially strong and genuine response. We do not know to what extent this was really the case. It appears certain that Gogol proposed marriage to her, although through the mediation of a third party; and that the family, proud of their nobility and taken aback at the idea of such a marriage, rejected his proposal. A letter from Gogol to Anna, the meaning of which is not quite clear to us today, strongly confirms in its allusions the conjectures expressed above. After this letter all connections with the Vielgorskys cease.

The summer brought Gogol renewed improvement, and at the same time his desire to travel was revived. In June he departed again for the Ukraine. His old friend Maksimovich, whose estate was located near Vasilyevka, accompanied him. On the way Gogol did not fail to visit the monasteries for pious devotions. The famous monastery Optina Pustyn, where he stayed for a short time, made a particular impression on him. In the seclusion from the world and happy contentment of

Gogol's Life

the monks, Gogol saw the ideal of Christian living fulfilled. There he read the works of the church father, Isaac the Syrian, which moved him deeply and caused him (in a marginal note in his copy of *Dead Souls*) to again sharply reject all his earlier works, an attitude which is frequently expressed in his letters.

The stay in Vasilyevka passed uneventfully. Gogol decided to spend the winter in Odessa, from whose milder climate he expected a beneficial effect. It was so expensive abroad, and one also detected there the "stench of political events": in this way Gogol describes the after-effects of the revolutions of 1848, which he strongly opposed. He was also drawn to Odessa by the presence of the pietist and mystic Alexander Sturdza, whom Gogol had met earlier in Rome and whose religious attitude was basically identical. In addition several former acquaintances from Moscow and St. Petersburg lived there.

The winter of 1850–1851 in Odessa was a pleasant time for Gogol. He worked, read the church fathers, especially Basil the Great, studied modern Greek, because he was playing with the idea of traveling to Greece, and engaged in a lively social life with his friends. A circle of admirers gathered around him at lunch in his favorite restaurant; he was invited by the highest Odessa aristocracy but turned down almost everything, and instead visited the friends to whom he had become accustomed. He often attended the Italian Opera of Odessa, took part in the staging of plays at the theatre, and read aloud to the actors *The School for Wives* by Molière and his own *Servants' Room*.

An elderly maiden lady, not identifiable today, lived with the family of Prince Repnin, whom Gogol often visited. In her enthusiasm for Gogol, she registered his activities and his utterances in her diary and thus preserved for us many an interesting character trait from this period; however, the sentimental ornamentation and the very naive form of description produce a disturbing effect. She also reports of Gogol's brilliant skill in reading aloud, for example from the *Odyssey*, whose vividness he admired, in Zhukovsky's translation, and from Molière. Gogol is said to have represented the despair of the old lover in *The School for Wives* so genuinely and so powerfully that the final reply of Agnès was felt to be out of place.

The writer even supposes that Gogol had been inspired to this lifelike reading by his own experience. His other readings consist mainly of sermons and excerpts from the church fathers. We hear of the great enthusiasm with which he read a sermon of Filaret's to the ladies. When he read from Basil the Great, he is said to have communicated his own conviction directly to the audience. With holy awe he read the prophet Jeremiah and the story of Jacob. Daily he read to himself a chapter from the Bible in Old Church Slavonic, Latin, Greek, and English.

There is little doubt that in this relatively peaceful time in Odessa Gogol did a great deal of work on the second part of *Dead Souls*. The thoughts of death that we hear of in accounts of friends from this period could only spur him on to further work. He wanted to calm his fear of God's judgment by means of his work; it was to serve the glory of God. In the middle of April, rather calm and in tolerably good health, accompanied by the blessings of his friends, Gogol left Odessa and returned by way of Vasilyevka to Moscow.

During the final nine months before his death Gogol alternated between periods when he could work and periods of depression. The accounts of this period are contradictory. In some, Gogol is described as gay and completely recovered; in others there is talk of fear of people and deep melancholy. Perhaps it is best to give credence to both versions. Gogol's mood was determined by the progress he made in his work. Since he increasingly felt his creativity to be a gift from God, a great task which God had assigned him vis-à-vis mankind, he was compelled to look on unproductive periods of time as withdrawals of God's grace. But the work was now particularly difficult, for he felt himself obliged to create according to God's plan, i.e., to propagate the religious weltanschauung. The period of his free, unbiased art was now definitely over. If, nevertheless, the second volume of *Dead Souls* was a great work of art (as several listeners, e.g., Aksakov, Arnoldi, and Madame Smirnova report), this is easily explained by Gogol's tremendous creative powers, which broke through again and again. Only the testimony of Aksakov, however, seems really reliable to me, and he presumably heard only the first chapter; the others probably paid more attention to the ideas expressed than to the artistic merits of the book. The periods of depression had an unfavorable effect on Gogol's health. Nervous disorders shook his whole body. He asked himself whether he was on the right path, whether he had correctly understood God's will. He was tortured with doubt and indecision; he would gladly have left decisions to God's decree. Thus after hesitating for a long time, he had decided to travel home to his sister's wedding. But he got only as far as Kaluga; there he became slightly ill. He visited the Optina Pustyn and asked a monk for advice in regard to the continuation or interruption of his journey. He came back four times to explain his doubts to the monk, until the pious man finally lost his patience. Gogol returned to Moscow, but the unpleasant awareness of not having fulfilled his obligations toward his family remained in his heart.

In spite of these vacillations, one should not conceive of Gogol as a sick and dying man. When he was able to work again, his spirits soared; he was talkative and looked good. Turgenev gives a very vivid description of his external appearance after visiting him on October 20, 1851:

> I peered at his features more closely. His blond hair that fell straight down from the temples, as is customary with the cossacks, still had kept the color of youth, but had already become noticeably thin; as before, one could easily recognize his intelligence from his prominent smooth, white forehead. At times his small brown eyes flashed with merriment—really merriment, and not just irony; but on the whole their look seemed tired. The long, pointed nose imparted a sly and foxlike quality to Gogol's face; his soft puffy lips beneath his clipped mustache also made an unfavorable impression; in their indefinite outlines, at least it seemed so to me, the shady side of his character was expressed:—when he spoke, they opened in an unpleasant manner and revealed a row of bad teeth; the small chin vanished amid the wide black velvet cravat. Gogol's bearing and his movements did not have anything professorial about them, but rather something schoolmasterish—something that reminded one of teachers from provincial secondary schools. "What a clever, and strange, and sick creature you are!" one thought involuntarily when one looked at him.

Since 1847 Gogol had been carrying on a correspondence with a priest of the Church at Rzhev, Matthew Konstantinovsky. Count A. P. Tolstoy had called Gogol's attention to this clergyman as an extremely pious and strict Orthodox believer, and recommended that he turn to him in all doubtful questions. In Moscow they met in person for the first time; several other meetings followed. There is no doubt that in the last years of his life Gogol listened very much to Matthew's opinions and that he saw in him the incarnation of the firm, unreflecting, childlike faith in the dogma of the Orthodox church. In earlier Gogol scholarship, Konstantinovsky is described as Gogol's evil genius, who through his fanatical intolerance finally forced Gogol to religious mania, condemned his art as contrary to God's will, and ultimately, after the burning of *Dead Souls*, was largely responsible for his death in a state of complete insanity. Konstantin Mochulsky in his book *Gogol's Spiritual Path* has tried to shake this thesis, which had congealed into a mechanically repeated cliché. But his attempts to make Matthew into a harmless, friendly country priest are not successful, and one must admit that Matthew's destructive influence on Gogol's art has been hardly exaggerated. Matthew was an uneducated, fanatical believer who impressed Gogol by his uncompromising attitude. Certainly that did not at all prevent him from differing with Matthew in his opinions about art, and from arguing with him; still Mochulsky does not proceed quite properly in compiling the testimonies which are supposed to bear witness to Matthew's harmlessness; he avoids quoting the following account of the priest:

> The indestructibility of his faith expressed itself in many downright improbable examples. Once in the summer he went on business matters to the town of Torzhok, and on the way was taken seriously ill, perhaps even with cholera. At this time the parish church in Torzhok was being renovated, and unexpectedly the grave of St. Yulianiya was discovered under the altar. Godfearing people immediately hurried to the holy spot and drew out all the water that filled the grave, believing it possessed curative powers. When Father Matthew, disregarding his illness, arrived at the spot, only lumps of sticky, stinking muck were to be found at the bottom of the grave. Without hesitating, Father Matthew climbed down, reverently gathered together these remains, ate them . . . and recovered entirely.

Such reports, together with accounts of his intolerance and severity toward the members of his congregation are not likely to prove Matthew's harmlessness. In addition there is a letter from the later Chief Procurator of the Holy Synod, Terty Filippov, a very intolerant, fanatical man, who writes to a monk of the Optina monastery:

> "Father Matthew did not leave the region of the miraculous for a moment and loved to assign an extraordinary significance to completely ordinary events. My own soul has experienced the harmful effect of this mental trait of his; the superstition into which he would fall would also cling to my mind, and it required efforts to free my soul from this enslavement."

It is clear how destructive such a spiritual orientation must have been for Gogol, who himself was inclined to see symbolic meanings in all things.

Without a doubt, Matthew was a strong personality and an above-average priest (his rhetorically brilliant sermons were highly praised), but it is just as certain that his outlook was very narrow, and that his sincere and honest faith bordered on blind fanaticism and permitted no deviation from dogma. As an artist, Gogol must have been hurt by his influence, even though Matthew did not describe artistic creation as "Satan's work" or forbid Gogol to engage in it, as has been asserted. Gogol's nervous system had become so sensitive as a result of his creative crises that one can well imagine how harmful the influence of such crude power upon it must have been; in any case, one can hardly deny that Gogol's association with the narrow-minded priest prepared the way for his eventual collapse. His last visit in February 1852, appears to have made a shattering impression on Gogol. It is reported that Matthew demanded that Gogol renounce Pushkin as a sinner and pagan; he required the most extreme abstinence in regard to food for the greater glory of God; he painted the hereafter and death in the gloomiest colors, as just reward for the sins in this world. Once after one such tirade Gogol said to him: "Enough! Stop, I can't listen any longer, it's too terrible!" The last meeting ended on a sour note because Gogol opposed many of the priest's demands. But after his departure new doubts arose. In a letter, Gogol asked him for pardon and then carried out just the demand that was most harmful—the abstinence from food—so literally that it became a decisive factor in his death.

Another circumstance also played an important role. The wife of the Slavophile Khomyakov, sister of the deceased poet Yazykov, died after a short but severe illness. Gogol often used to visit at Khomyakov's house, and this death made a terrible impression on him. He tried to work, but the work was meant to be religion: "What am I to tell you about myself?" he writes Zhukovsky on February 2, 1852. "I am still sitting at the same thing, I am busy with the same thing. Pray for me so that my work might become truthful and conscientious and so that I might be found to some extent worthy of singing a hymn to divine beauty."

We do not know the immediate occasion that brought about Gogol's final decision to die. The death of Madame Khomyakova and Matthew's visit took effect together. We hear that in his last days Gogol periodically experienced moments when he was afraid of death. It seems as if he wanted to speed up his death in order to get this experience over with once and for all, and to bring about rapidly that which had to be. He died because he now wanted to die. After the priest's visit on February 6, Gogol stopped eating almost entirely. It was the beginning of Lent. Gogol wanted to do more than the Church prescribed. He spent hours in prayer. His shattered nerves were damaged more and more by his bodily weakness. On the night of February 11–12, Gogol burned everything of the second part of *Dead Souls* that he had written in the last years. We cannot determine whether he really wanted to burn his work. The possibility of a mistake on his part is not to be excluded. On the day before, Gogol asked his host, Count A. P. Tolstoy, to take his papers and to submit them after his death to the spiritual censorship of the Moscow Metropolitan Filaret. Tolstoy refused so as not to increase Gogol's morbid frame of mind. After the burning, Gogol summoned him and said weeping: "Look what I have done! I only wanted to burn certain things that should have been burned a long time ago, and I burned everything! How strong the Evil One is—he caused me to do that. . . ." It is quite possible that Gogol had really made an error, which now completely crushed him. He wanted death. When Khomyakov tried to console him over the death of his own wife, Gogol replied: "One has to die sometime, and I am ready and shall die. . . ." "They should leave me in peace; I know that I must die," he said a week before his death. Involuntarily one thinks here of the death of the two old people in "Old-World Landowners," which, like the death of the author, results from the belief that one has to die now.

Dr. Tarasenkov, who was one of those who treated Gogol, declares decisively that his refusal to eat could not be attributed to loss of appetite. He was organically healthy, but firmly resolved to die.

> His facial expression had not changed at all; it was just as peaceful and just as gloomy as before; neither anger nor bitterness, neither astonishment nor doubt were even suggested. He looked like a man for whom all questions were answered, all feelings silent, all words vain, and for whom any wavering was impossible once the decision had been made.

"Leave me, I am content," he replied to all attempts of his friends to get him to want to live again. Even the intervention of the Metropolitan Filaret, who called upon Gogol in the name of the Church to give up his fasting, brought no results. Gogol remained firm. One is almost tempted to think of the reappearance of a mystical vision.

When his strength finally left him and he was obliged to lie down, a council of doctors was summoned. The weak, defenseless man was now treated as if he were mentally incompetent. The tortures that were inflicted on him were cruel and senseless. They placed him in a bath of clear broth, poured spirits over him, stuck leeches on his nose, and covered him with hot loaves of bread. Gogol groaned and yelled. Finally he lost consciousness. He was tormented with hallucinatory dreams —the results of a nervous fever. Again and again he asked to drink. "A ladder, faster, give me a ladder . . ."—these are said to have been his last comprehensible, feverish words. On the morning of February 21, 1852, Gogol died.

His estate consisted of items of clothing and books, which were sold or given away without anyone taking the trouble to catalogue the author's library. All the intellectuals of Moscow were present at his funeral. On his tombstone is inscribed: "Through my bitter word I shall laugh," an incorrect translation of Jer. 20: 8 (Septuagint).

Part II

Gogol's Works

1 · Evenings on a Farm near Dikanka

EVENINGS ON A FARM NEAR DIKANKA is a collection of stories allegedly edited by the beekeeper Red-haired Panko of Dikanka.

In the preface, the beekeeper declares that he has heard so many beautiful things from various storytellers on winter evenings that in spite of all the dangers involved, he is venturing into the literary world. The first part contains the following stories: "The Fair at Sorochincy," "St. John's Eve," "The May Night or the Drowned Woman," and "The Lost Letter"; the second also contains a preface and the following stories: "Christmas Eve," "The Terrible Vengeance," "Ivan Fedorovich Shponka and his Aunt," and "The Enchanted Spot."

Gogol succeeds in synthesizing two completely opposing tendencies: he combines rough comedy composed of elements from the Ukrainian puppet theater, the Ukrainian folk-anecdote, and the Ukrainian folksong with a peculiar, metaphysically tinted imagination largely based on German Romanticism. The combination of an ominous, supernatural spirit world and realistically detailed pictures of Ukrainian life gives his tales a bizarre, exotic flavor, which is to be found only in Gogol. Gogol also attempts to intensify this coloring lexically by frequently employing Ukrainian dialect words; in fact, to aid in their understanding, he even attached a small explanatory glossary to the preface.

The theme is the intrusion of evil, irrational powers into plain, everyday life. The brilliant surface of the beautiful world is deceptive; love, dancing, and cheerfulness are transitory and extremely variable; at any moment the devil is ready to appear where one least expects him. And woe to the person who follows the devil's enticements of his own free will; he is lost beyond help—no turning back, no repentance can save him now, even the church and the monastery are powerless. All rejoicing is frozen in this dark, lurking subterranean world, and hopeless grief lies at the end of radiant life.

The beginning of "The Fair at Sorochincy" is resplendent:

> How intoxicating, how splendid is a summer day in Little Russia! How exhaustingly hot are the hours when noon glitters in stillness and heat and the blue immeasurable ocean, sloping over the earth like a voluptuous dome, seemingly falls asleep, completely immersed in languor, enclosing and pressing the beautiful one in his ethereal embrace! Not a cloud in the sky. In the field not a word. Everything as if dead; only above, in the depths of the sky the lark is quivering and silvery songs fly over airy steps down to the adoring earth; in addition the cry of the gull or the ringing voice of the quail re-echoes now and then from the steppes. Idle and thoughtless like aimlessly strolling people, cloud-touching oaks stand, and dazzling flashes of sunbeams ignite whole picturesque masses of leaves, while they cover others with shadows dark as night from which gold bursts forth only in strong winds. Emeralds, topazes, rubies, and sapphires of ethereal insects fall in a shower over bright-colored vegetable gardens shaded by stately sunflowers. Gray haystacks and golden sheaves of grain are encamped in the field and wander about in its immensity. Bent by the weight of the fruit, the broad branches of the cherry trees, plum trees, apple trees, and pear trees; the sky, the river—its clear mirror—in its green, proudly raised frame . . . how full of voluptuousness and languor the summer is in Little Russia!

From this fantasy on the theme of Nature—a good example of Gogol's Nature pathos—we proceed to the action of the story. It is a noisy and merry one. Gypsies help the handsome peasant boy Grytsko outwit the stupid, goodnatured peasant Solopy and especially his wicked, wanton wife Khivrya so that he can finally marry the beautiful Paraska, Khivrya's stepdaughter. But a sinister story about the devil serves as the means for perpetrating the trick. According to an old folk legend, the devil walks about on earth in the shape of a pig and searches

Evenings on a Farm near Dikanka

for pieces of his red shirt. He had sold the shirt to get money for drink, and subsequently it brought misfortune to all its owners until a furious peasant hacked it to pieces with an axe. The effect is uncanny when, in broad daylight, in the middle of the noisy, crowded market place (vividly described by Gogol with onomatopoetic assonances and hyperbolic cumulations) the horror breaks loose. The beginning of the story about the devil not only causes ignorant Solopy's hair to stand on end, but even the reader is taken aback—however, Gogol breaks off here and goes over to the love episode.

As night falls the fear grows even more intense. But Gogol presents all the diabolical goings-on amid the atmosphere of a farce—sharp contrast is the effect he aims for and achieves. The interrupted scene with the priest's son at Khivrya's house bears all the marks of a traditional folk play with the theme of the hidden lover (real similarity can even be pointed out between this episode and a comedy written by Gogol's father), but it runs into the now complete devil story, which, interrupted by comical expressions of fear from the listeners, produces a weird tension.

At the climactic moment, in the middle of a word, the window is shattered: "The panes flew out with a crash and a terrible pig snout pushed its way through the window and let its eyes wander around the room as if it were asking: 'What are you doing here, good people?'" So it goes in the world: into the midst of a peaceful room comes the evil power from the beyond —here the pig is another trick on the part of the gypsy, whose description (Chapter 5), to be sure, compared with the evil sorcerer from "The Terrible Vengeance," bears some disturbing traits; but how about the pig that steals the petition of Ivan Nikiforovich (*Mirgorod*), and how about the pig snouts that the mayor sees in *The Inspector General*? What were merely simple everyday matters suddenly appear different. Why? . . . And now farce and fear follow in rapid succession, and no matter how often one insists that only ignorant peasants are affected with this fear, it is still somehow more than that—it is contagious. And the author invents comparisons in comic scenes which are really very odd: when Solopy falls down as he is fleeing from the supposed devil, we read: "Here his consciousness flew from him, and he remained dumb and motionless in the middle of the road like a dreadful dweller of a narrow coffin." Gogol does not say "like a corpse," and it is just such unusual figures of speech that reveal the double basis of the whole and produce its bizarre ring.

The gypsy is triumphant, the couple is united, even though the furious stepmother scolds, and all dance and shout with joy. But strange—this dance in which all take part, has, precisely because *all* take part, something sinister about it; what sort of power is it that takes control of everyone when the musician's bow touches the strings? Where does it come from? The motif of the questionable nature of art (developed in detail in "The Portrait") is touched upon. An "inexplicable feeling" would seize the viewer,

> but an even stranger, an even more enigmatic feeling would be awakened in the depths of the soul on seeing the old women on whose worn faces wafted the indifference of the grave, as they bounced around there among the new laughing, lively humanity. Carefree ones! Even without childlike joy, without a spark of sympathy, whom drunkenness alone enabled to perform something like human actions, as the mechanic does with his lifeless automaton, they waggled their intoxicated heads, danced about in imitation of the merry crowd without even glancing at the young couple.

One should note the unusual apostrophe with an adjective used as substantive after the model of the Homeric νήπιοι, which skillfully changes the tone and transforms it into something pathetic.

But just what is the point of all this, in the context of an apparently traditional "happy end" of a merry village tale? Just as the sound of the violin sadly fades away into the night, so too in the end man remains alone.

> In its own echo this sound hears already sadness and a desert, and it listens wildly to this echo. Do not the companions of stormy, free youth also lose themselves in the world in the same way, each individually, one after another, and do they not finally leave their brother of old alone? It is tedious for him who has been left behind! And his heart becomes heavy and sad, and there is no remedy for it!

So ends this gay, merry, bright-colored story that took place on a brilliant summer day, and yet everything turned out so well, and the lovers are united.

In the first tale, despite all the menace, the evil power and its effects in the human world have a relatively natural explanation; while in "St. John's Eve" it triumphs and no longer has anything to do with the natural order of things.

This story had been published in 1830 under the title of "Bisavryuk," but the editor P. Svinyin had so "improved" Gogol's style that the latter was hardly able to recognize his own work. The comical special preface alludes to this.

An old mythic theme reappears here: in order to gain power and riches one must shed innocent blood. But the riches acquired by evil means do not last and finally bring destruction upon their owner.

The poor farm hand Petrus and the beautiful Pidorka, daughter of a rich peasant, are in love with one another. The father is concerned only with money and chases the farm hand away when he catches the two of them by surprise as they are kissing. The Evil One, who is now called Basavryuk and who goes around the village in the guise of a sinister eccentric, approaches the desperate Petrus. The devil is willing to get him money for "just one deed," and Petrus is "ready for anything," even though he knows with whom he is dealing.

Once a year, on St. John's eve, ferns, are said to blossom, but only for a very short time. If someone succeeds in plucking the fiery red blossom at midnight, it will show him the place where a treasure lies buried in the earth. Tomorrow is St. John's day, and at midnight Petrus and Basavryuk are in the forest. A horrible "Wolf's Glen Scene" follows (perhaps indeed influenced by reminiscences of *Der Freischütz*); parallels to the Witches' Kitchen in Goethe's *Faust* also suggest themselves— the whole is a mad witches' revel and full of incantatory magic. Petrus plucks the blossom and finds the treasure, but as he tries to grasp it, the six-year-old brother of his beloved is suddenly standing there before him, and the old forest witch demands that he first cut off the child's head. After some hesitation he does what she demands, intoxicated by the brilliance of the jewels that gleam up at him from the now transparent earth, and then flees from the triumphant howling of the Evil Ones. After a heavy sleep, he awakens in his hut and finds sacks of gold at his feet. But he has lost his memory; he is no longer able to remember anything, and when Pidorka tells him that her little brother has been carried off by gypsies, it makes no impression on him. Now there is nothing more standing in the way of the wedding. But Petrus is not happy. He racks his brain to remember, and is seized with depression and fits of madness. Nothing helps, and the desperate Pidorka finally summons the forest witch, who is able to cure people with her spells. Exactly a year has passed—and when Petrus sees the witch again, he suddenly remembers everything. He and his gold go up in flames and only a pile of ashes and broken potsherds are left. What was accomplished by the lovely Pidorka's entering the cloister? what was accomplished by the priest's sprinkling all the houses with holy water?—the devil even today haunts the village, the village that on the surface looks so quiet and peaceful.

This horrible story is allegedly told by the sexton of the village church at ———. Due to the narrator's unusual manner of speaking, the tone does not always correspond to the dramatic nature of the situation; horror and humor follow close upon one another. Thus the narrator constantly refers to the aunt of his late grandfather, who supposedly has lived through it all herself. The tragic nature of the conclusion (Pidorka as a nun in the cloister in Kiev) is mitigated by the subsequent reports of the manner in which the devil continues to appear; these reports, products of wine-heated minds, are both sinister and comical. But the last scene—the flocks of crows flying off into the sky with wild cries—leaves behind a gloomy impression.

Amorous conversations and nature descriptions are absent from this story; the manner in which Gogol makes use of folksong materials—early attempts which come to full bloom in "The Terrible Vengeance"—is shown, for example, in the scene where the unfortunate Pidorka tells little Ivas to bring a message to her beloved:

> Ivas my dear, Ivas my darling. Run to Petrus, my golden child, like an arrow from a bow, tell him all: I would love his brown eyes, I would kiss his dear white face, but my fate will not have

it so. More than one towel have I drenched with my burning tears. I am sick and heavy at heart. And my own father is my enemy; he wants to force me to marry the detested Polack. Tell him that they are already preparing for the wedding, but there will be no music at our wedding; deacons will chant instead of lutes and pipes. I shall not walk to the dance with my bridegroom; they will carry me. Dark, dark will be my house! Of maple wood, and instead of a chimney, a cross will stand upon the roof.

Petrus' answer sounds similar; thus in the intertwining of these folksong-colored intonations and figures of romantic excess of horror with crass realism and the colorful superstitions of the Ukrainian people lies the peculiar charm of Gogol's style.

In the third tale "The May Night or the Drowned Woman," the accent again lies on the comical—i.e. the ending is happy, but the sad legend framed by the action casts its dark shadows on it.

Once again Gogol uses the double-composition technique: he tells two stories which intertwine at the end. The three types of style employed in "St. John's Eve" are worked out here much more clearly. Ukrainian folksong is emotionally intensified and threatens to turn into an operatic aria, just as the fantasia on the theme of the Ukrainian night gleams with dangerously ornate baroque tones; this time the romantic element in the legend has a melancholy undertone and is clearly marked off from the action of the story by narration and dream; the coarse-comic element is broadly worked out and clearly reveals that Gogol's abilities are greatest in this area. Levko, the son of the village mayor, loves the beautiful seventeen-year-old girl Ganna, but his old, tyrannical, and very narrow-minded father is also pursuing her. At their nocturnal rendezvous, Levko tells his young beloved an old legend: an abandoned, decaying house stands by the lake outside of the village (the two see it shimmering in the moonlight); once a rich cossack lived there with his beautiful daughter, whom he loved dearly. But when he brought home his second wife, his love for his daughter came to an end, for his beautiful young wife was a witch. She hated her stepdaughter and gained complete control over her husband so that the poor, tormented girl drowned herself in the lake. There she became queen of the water nymphs, and one day, together with her playmates, she dragged the evil stepmother into the lake in order to whip her there. But the latter quickly transformed herself into a water nymph, and the poor queen was no longer able to recognize her among the rest of her band. She compels everyone whom she meets by the shore to guess which is the right one, but no one has picked her out yet. Levko realizes what his father is up to and arranges a wild nocturnal spook show with the village boys to irritate the old lecher. But after this he has even less of a chance to win Ganna. Exhausted, he falls asleep by the shore of the lake. The water nymphs rise up and, lo and behold, Levko guesses—in a dream or awake?—which one is the evil witch. As a reward, the queen of the water nymphs arranges things so that the father can't help letting his son marry Ganna. Thus all ends well, and yet the turning point is so strange, that one believes all the good in the story to be but a dream; and only the radiance of the Ukrainian night, which serves as the frame for all these events, makes them acceptable.

It is nowhere clearer than in this tale that Gogol's Ukraine is not the real Ukraine. Proceeding from realities, he creates a fantasy world; but the real details of Ukrainian folk life are so skillfully distributed, and the artistic power of the presentation is so great, that one completely believes in a reality that does not at all exist.

In the Dikanka stories, two generations stand in almost complete contrast to one another. The old people are representatives of crude reality—as individuals, they are splendid people, full of vitality—here represented by the village mayor and the distiller, the peasant Kalenik and the "female relative" of the mayor; in their totality, however, they form a completely unreal assemblage, whose connections with life, work, source of income, and religion remain completely unclear—only their attitude toward the devil is clearly outlined—for an inescapable superstition rules all of them.

In sharp contrast to this generation are the young people, who are real neither as individuals nor in their totality. Levko and Ganna love one another and go into raptures—and do nothing else. They are ideal characters, and would be lifeless if their flowery, peculiar, and exotic style of speaking did not give their existence an authenticity of another sort: poetic authenticity of a rounded character, growing out of itself according to definite laws.

> Ganna, honey! You're sleeping or you don't want to come out to me. You're probably afraid that someone could see us, or maybe you don't want to expose your white little face to the cold. Don't be afraid—there's no one here! The evening is warm. But even if someone should show himself, then I'll cover you with my coat, wind my sash around you, shield you with my arms, and no one will see us. But if a cold breeze should come blowing by, then I'll press you closer to my heart, warm you with my kisses, stick your white little feet into my cap. My heart, my dear little fish, my string of pearls! Look out here for a moment. Just stick your white little hand out the window . . .

The conversations of the lovers concerning the stars and Jacob's ladder are just as unrealistic as the prose serenade of the peasant lad Levko quoted above, and yet they affect us through the touching naiveté of the ornamental diction; embedded in the festively sparkling nature description with the "thunder of the Ukrainian nightingale" and the play on all the registers of rhetoric, the whole acquires a suprarealistic validity. It is of course a dangerous game, and often Gogol is bordering on *Kitsch*—but he always manages to glide past it safely—as Tchaikovsky often does in his music. In the legend, reality and chaos again lie frighteningly close together; the horrible cat whose paw is cut off by the poor stepdaughter, and the stepmother who comes out of her room on the third day with a bandaged hand are symbolic of this. Levko's dream is quite beautiful when he sees the crumbling house reflected new and shining in the lake; delicate, as if woven from silver moonlight, is the dance of the water nymphs; touching are the pleas of the queen of the water nymphs. From the authenticity of the folksong, Gogol draws a warmheartedness which is otherwise lacking in him, and which he later loses entirely.

It is already lacking here, for example, in the case of the drunken Kalenik, who represents a transition to realism. The narrow-minded, one-eyed village mayor, who fears no one but the "female relative" who handles his financial affairs (Gogol's ambiguous allusions to the nature of this relationship are refined in later works), and the fat, superstitious distiller with the smoking pipe, who tells the fearful story of the corpse on the chimney with a dumpling in its teeth—these characters are genuine and convincing.

Through skillful repetition of little gestures and peculiar comparisons, Gogol describes his types. The mayor, for example, hears only what he wants to hear, and otherwise plays deaf; and here is the description of the distiller:

> Under the icons in the place of honor sat the guest—a rather small, round little man, with small, ever-laughing eyes in which, so it seemed, the enjoyment stood written with which he smoked his short little pipe; while he smoked, he was constantly spitting and pressing down with his finger on the tobacco that had turned into ashes and that kept dropping out of the pipe. The clouds of smoke around him kept increasing rapidly, veiling him in gray-blue mist. It looked as if the broad chimney of some distillery or other had become bored with sitting on its roof, as if it had decided to take a little walk, and as if it had come to sit sedately at the table in the house of the village mayor. Beneath his nose, a rather short and thick mustache protruded; but it shimmered so indistinctly through the tobacco atmosphere, that it looked like a mouse that the distiller had caught and now held in his mouth, thus undermining the house cat's monopoly.

Gogol describes the distiller's laughter in the following manner: "After these words, the little eyes of the distiller vanished; in place of them, rays extended up to his ears; his whole body began to quiver with laughter and the merry lips let go of the smoking pipe for a moment." The smallest details, each in itself, serve as striking symbols for each man, although their totality often produces a very unreal man, more like a marionette without a soul. The manner of speaking and the reactions of these people within their very limited circle, which they consider so great, already foreshadow the technique of *Dead Souls*.

The last story of the first part, "The Lost Letter," ends happily, even though a real witches' sabbath is unleashed. It ends well because the hero—the grandfather of the narrator—is just too naive and in complete innocence has his heart in the right place. It is a splendid device on the part of the narrator to make the grandfather in his younger days the hero of the story: he is constantly designated as grandfather, while his actions are not at all grandfatherly—this contrast produces the desired comic effect. This grandfather is supposed to bring a letter from the hetman [1] to the Empress. He sews it into his cap and starts on his way. In the next city there is a fair. Everywhere there is something to drink. And an upright young cossack who has a lot of stories to tell joins the party. But he becomes sad when night falls. He has sold his soul to the devil, and today the time is up. His merry drinking companions want to keep watch in order to drive away the devil when he comes to fetch him. But little by little, they all fall asleep, even the grandfather—and when he awakens, the cossack, his horse, and his cap have vanished. What should he do? The proprietor of the inn, who resembles Basavryuk, shows him the way. At night in the forest there is a witches' sabbath—there he is to try to get back his cap. His walk into the forest, his experiences with the witches, and his card-playing for the cap are a precious conglomeration of weirdness and comedy. In brief—he gets back his cap because he hits upon the idea of making the sign of the cross over the cards, and thus he wins against the witches. But they give him a steed so fiery that on riding it he loses his sight and hearing, and he wakes up all bloody on the roof of his house. And behold! His wife too seems to be dreaming: she is astride a bench, bouncing up and down. He wakens her —her dream too was very strange. Was the whole thing only a dream after an overly energetic farewell celebration, or was it reality? Gogol purposely tells the story in such a way that indications of one and the other are both present, and in the end one understands nothing but the fact that the story was very suspenseful and that the grandfather is a full, living character. Gogol achieves the first effect through the skillful employment of folk legends, which he intertwines and transposes with great ingenuity; he accomplishes the second through his artistic power. The grandfather now starts out again and sees such wonders around the Empress in the capital as can be told of only in the far-off Ukraine. In the next story, which begins the second part, we hear further details about this.

"Christmas Eve" is noteworthy especially from the point

---

[1] Ukrainian chief (cf. p. 3).

of view of structure. It consists of fifteen sections of varying length, joined together in the manner of a mosaic, which describe the destinies of the main characters on that night. The arrangement of these sections furthers the development of the plot, which is presented very briefly and concisely, even though the jumping from one subject to another skillfully conceals this fact. Again, Gogol achieves his effect by combining opposites, this time not only in style but also in composition. The main characters are the devil, the pious blacksmith and painter Vakula, the smith's mother, Solokha, who is a witch, the beautiful Oksana, and her father, Chub.

Realistic and fantastic elements are blended here completely as a matter of course, as if there were no dividing line between them at all. Vakula's mother, after stealing stars from the firmament and disappearing into the chimney of her house, "crept out of the oven, took off the warm sheepskin, set herself to rights, and no one would be able to realize that just a minute before she had been riding on the broom."

The devil is also very real. The fact that he pilfers the moon in order to prevent old Chub from going out in the dark, and in this way spoiling the rendezvous of the lovely Oksana and the pious smith Vakula, whom he hates—this fact is certainly "lawless," but not impossible.

The smith loves Oksana. She is coquettish and superficial, and only teases him. Her father, Chub, is courting Vakula's mother, Solokha, and she is not averse to marrying the rich cossack, but at the moment he is far from being her only lover, as he believes.

On this night, the last on which he is able to act on earth before the great holiday, the devil does everything wrong. He himself comes for his lovers' tryst with Solokha; and in order to avoid gossip, he is hidden in a sack, just like the other candidates for the witch's love, who are arriving one after another on account of the snowstorm that he released in the wrong place.

The haughty Oksana demands slippers from the smith as beautiful as those the Empress wears, and Vakula, who manages to trap the devil in the sack, forces him to carry him to the Empress in St. Petersburg. The undertaking succeeds, and for

Evenings on a Farm near Dikanka

the only time in the whole cycle, the devil is completely an object of ridicule. The smith gets his Oksana, who has been chastened by her fear for him; he paints a picture for the church, which portrays the devil in a none too flattering manner.

On the night before Christmas, it is the custom among the Ukrainian village youth to go from house to house and with song and dance to beg for little gifts of food, which are collected in large sacks and then distributed. This is what makes the night that Gogol describes so animated and provides the background for the complications. The high-spirited youths in the snow-covered, moonlit village, the genuine lover's pangs of the smith, the devil's wiles, Chub's stupid, tyrannical complacency, Oksana's coquetry, the witch's intrigues, the sinister Patsyuk (again a successor of Basavryuk) and his self-propelled dumplings, Solokha's sedate lovers, and finally brilliant St. Petersburg and the fairy-tale palace of the Empress—all of this combines to form a picture of brilliant color that is scarcely to be surpassed, and in which every detail gleams like a polished gem. There is an abundance of these details, and each is of a different sort.

The devil's gallantries with Solokha in the sky move Gogol to a digression on Man's passion for imitation and to a sigh over the vanity of the world. Even the repulsive devil walks the paths of love. "But the most annoying is that he probably imagines himself wonderfully handsome, while as a figure—one is ashamed to look at him!" Is this not the prototype of Gogol's characters who think they are so many things they are not?

The scene with the succession of lovers at Solokha's house is a very original version of an essentially traditional farce scene. The manner, for example, in which the deacon introduces his declarations of love is so laden with sensuality and at the same time so comical that one would have to search a long time to find an equivalent in the history of literature.

> Here he came closer to her, coughed slightly, smiled, and with his long fingers touched her full, bare arm, and spoke with an air that expressed both slyness and self-satisfaction: "And what do you have here, my sublime Solokha?" And after he had spoken in this way, he jumped back a little. "What do you mean?—What? That's my arm, Osip Nikiforovich," answered

Solokha. "Hmm, your arm, heh, heh," said the deacon, who was heartily content with this beginning, and took a little walk around the room. "And what do you have here, dearest Solokha?" he said with the same air, as he approached her again, clasped her lightly around the neck, and jumped back in the same manner as before. "As if you don't see it, Osip Nikiforovich," answered Solokha, "It's my neck, and on my neck a coin necklace!" "Hmm, and on your neck a coin necklace, heh, heh," and the deacon again walked around the room rubbing his hands. "And what do you have here, incomparable Solokha?" It is not known what the lecherous deacon would have touched with his fingers now, for suddenly a knock was heard at the door and the voice of the cossack Chub.

The ride on the devil to St. Petersburg and the reception of the Empress are a precious mixture of historical fact and impossibilities. Gogol's imagination in regard to the ride is amazing.

Everything could be seen; and one could even observe a sorcerer sitting in a pot flying past them like a whirlwind, the stars gathered in a crowd playing blindman's buff, a whole throng of spirits billowing off to the side, a devil dancing by the light of the moon and tipping his cap when he saw the smith riding past, a broom flying back home, on which a witch had obviously just ridden to see about a thing or two. They came upon much more riffraff. On catching sight of the smith they would all stop for a moment in order to look at him, and then they would fly on about their own business . . .

With good taste Gogol avoids what is excessive, as in general a wise restraint in regard to details is characteristic of him: he never falls into the manner of many "folkloristic" writers, who pile up trifles in order to produce a "vivid" picture of life.

The Empress, her favorite Potemkin, and the famous author of comedies Fonvizin are drawn with a few brief characterizing strokes. As elsewhere in Gogol, it looks as if it were history, but in reality it is not.

The representation of devil-inspired gossip and rumors was a strong point of Gogol's from the very beginning. The conjectures in regard to Solokha's witchery in the village (again a strange pig plays a role in it) are crowned by the report of "some cowherd, Tymish Korostyavy" [the scaly-skinned], who is introduced, only to disappear again immediately. Strange persons always turn up in Gogol's works when rumors are involved.

> He did not miss the chance to tell how once in the summer, just before St. Peter's Day, as he lay down to sleep in the stall and was stuffing straw under his head, he saw with his own eyes that the witch, with her hair down, began to milk the cows only in her chemise, while he was unable to move, so enchanted had he been and smeared his lips with something so revolting that he kept spitting for the rest of the day.

The whole episode has not the slightest thing to do with the course of the real plot, and in the context is completely senseless; the cowherd himself plays not the slightest role in it—but Gogol tells the story in such detail that one involuntarily assumes something and is captivated by it. Note such precise indications as "just before St. Peter's Day" or "after he had stuffed straw under his head." The illusion of a concrete reality is produced by means of such precise details; the reader's imagination is constantly kept in suspense and he finally loses sight of all division between the real and the unreal—and that is exactly Gogol's intention.

Gogol is quite successful in the love scenes here because of one partner's mocking tone. This circumstance keeps him from slipping into operatic arias. As in many of his tales, here too Gogol speaks of the heroine's nudity. Psychoanalysts have made the most of this complex, and its striking character is not to be denied. At night in bed, Oksana thinks of the supposedly dead smith and cannot sleep. "Soon, in enchanting nakedness that the darkness of night concealed even from herself, having thrown off the covers, she scolded herself almost aloud." Such episodes occur frequently, sometimes quite suddenly, as, for example, in "The Story of Ivan Ivanovich and Ivan Nikiforovich," and they even aroused the derision of contemporary critics. But Gogol needs them for the composition. For him they are heightening effects intended to avert the danger of monotony; and he applies them so skillfully that he attains his goal completely.

Here Gogol succeeded in writing a splendid comedy in short-story form, and despite the fact that many strange things in it cause us to doubt the security of the world, this time the conclusion is encouraging.

To this positive mood and to the outwitted devil a diametrically opposed aspect is contrasted in the very next tale, "The Terrible Vengeance." Negation in every respect is the leitmotiv, and evil is more alarming and more powerful than ever before. Comedy is followed by tragedy—so gloomy and horrible that even in Gogol's dreadful fantasy world it occupies a special position. It is the one work of Gogol's that does not reveal even the slightest trace of humor. Gogol replaces his usual comic detail by repetitions of detail contingent on style and composition. In general the whole tale represents a collector's item of stylistic filigree.

Suspense is determined by structure. The legend told at the end by the traveling singer finally resolves all the questions and obscurities of the real plot.

Betrayal of a friend out of envy is the theme of the legend. The cossack Petro murders his companion Ivan and his little son because he begrudges him the glory of the victory over the Turkish Pasha. He pushes the bodies of the two over a precipice in the Carpathian Mountains, and leads a happy life afterwards. But before God's judgment, Ivan is permitted to select the punishment for his murderer, and he thinks up a terrible revenge. All of Petro's descendants shall be unhappy on earth, and the last member of the family shall be the greatest scoundrel the world has ever seen. And with each of his misdeeds, his ancestors shall rise up out of their graves in anguish, which they suffer because of him; but Petro is to grow so large beneath the earth that his bones will no longer be able to rise. And when the last scoundrel is to die, God shall raise Ivan from the abyss to push him off the same precipice, and all his forefathers shall climb out of their graves and plunge after him and gnaw the bones of their descendants. But Petro shall not be able to raise himself, and shall suffer terrible tortures beneath the earth, "for there is no greater torture for Man than to want to avenge and to be unable to avenge." God grants this request, but on account of his cruelty, Ivan is also not to be permitted to enter the kingdom of heaven, but is destined to always look into the abyss where the last of Petro's family is being torn to

Evenings on a Farm near Dikanka

pieces. And so it happened when the time was fulfilled; and if there are still earthquakes, they stem from the fact that Petro's corpse is trying to rise and is unable to do so.

So much for the legend; the end of the last scoundrel's life is now the content of the actual plot, which, without previous knowledge of the key, presents a succession of mysterious horrors.

The last of Petro's family is a sorcerer, fallen away from the faith of his fathers, in league with the devil, gifted with supernatural powers, which he uses, however, for the destruction of his fellow men. He burns with sinful love for his own daughter, the pure and beautiful Katerina, whom he abandoned as a child after murdering her mother, and whom he finds again, after his return from Turkey, the wife of an honest cossack and mother of a one-year-old son. But Katerina's soul is pure; the magic of the impure incantations is powerless against her purity. Once, her father succeeds in deluding her by means of a skillful disguise. She lets him escape from captivity so that he can save his soul. When he deceives her, she remains firm in the face of his new attempts and atones for her crime when her father murders her husband, her son, and finally also her. In ever-increasing tempo, in a crescendo of dread the misdeeds accumulate until the measure is finally full when the evil sorcerer murders the holy hermit who is unable to pray for him. And now God carries out Ivan's revenge.

All of this horror would hardly be bearable and would even have a comical effect, if Gogol had not struck the only narrative tone possible for such contents. He finds the language appropriate for this story in a brilliant, rhythmic prose, imitative of the style of folksongs, folk ballads, and *byliny*,[2] making use of a great deal of alliteration, assonance, repetition, pathetic lyricism, inversion, hyperbole, and metaphor, to name only the most important of the stylistic devices employed. The effect is carefully calculated down to the smallest detail. Every little episode, every descriptive stroke, every ever-so-tiny detail has a critical significance for the work as a whole. *Red* is the color of the silk embroidery on the little cloth with which Katerina

---

[2] Russian folk epics.

dries the face of her little son, *red* the fire in the father's pipe on the Dnieper trip, *red* the kaftan of the evil sorcerer, and *red*, finally, even the cossack captain's pipe which he hands to the child shortly before it is murdered. The same word in Ukrainian —*lyulka*—means both cradle and pipe. Fire in the pipe, blood of the murdered child in the cradle, red as color of evil—all this combines to produce a striking effect.

Gogol achieves a strange mood, in which all reality is dissolved, by building up the tale largely on the negation *ne* (not). Doom, death, the end are clarified purely stylistically by this device. This "not" accompanies above all the person of the father. The guests are most astonished by the fact that Katerina's "old father had *not* come with her. . . . He would have told a lot of wonderful stories. How could one who was in a foreign land for such a long time *not* tell stories. There everything is *not* like here, the people are *not* these, and there are *not* any of Christ's churches; but he had *not* come."

Through this technique the nature descriptions lose all concreteness:

> It is lovely to look at the high mountains, the broad meadows, the green forests from the middle of the Dnieper! Those mountains—are not mountains: They have no base: Above as well as below—a pointed peak, and beneath them and over them the lofty heavens. Those forests that stand on the hills are not forests: They are hairs growing on the bristly head of the forest demon. Down below his beard washes in the water, and beneath the beard and over the hair are the lofty heavens. Those meadows are not meadows: It is a green belt which girds up the round sky in the middle, and in the upper as well as in the lower half the crescent moon promenades.

Just as unreal as this picture is the famous description of the Dnieper at the beginning of Section X—a companion piece to the description of the summer day in "The Fair" cited above. Gogol views the picture from the perspective of a bird in flight and achieves it with such dazzling hyperboles that the splendor of the words he chooses smoothly glosses over the impossibility of what is said. But Gogol is also capable of presenting real scenes that are wonderfully poetic. "A quiet light is shining over the whole world. It is the moon, which had appeared from behind the mountains. With precious damask muslin as white as snow it covered the mountainous shore of the Dnieper and the shadow retreated further into the thicket of fir trees."

This genuine lyricism is contrasted with genuine horror, as when the corpses rise from their graves during the nocturnal trip along the Dnieper, in the last scenes of revenge, in the enigmatic, inserted Section XII, when the dead Ivan is fetched to his post and the end approaches, in the brilliant scene of Katerina's madness, and in the many extremely concise, sometimes only intimated murder scenes.

We find a blend of horror and lyricism in the scenes of sorcery, which interweave dream world and reality. Katerina does not know what her soul knows. Probably for the first time in Russian literature is the world of the subconscious portrayed with such economical means and in such a strikingly palpable manner. No wonder that Dostoyevsky took notice of this tale and made it the basis of his "Landlady." We find the same blend in Katerina's lament for her dead husband, which is built completely on folksong motifs, and finally in the speeches of Katerina and Danilo, which, despite their tense pathos based on songs and incantation formulae, acquire a pulsating vitality in this context. It need hardly be mentioned that this tale, which employs rhetorical devices of both folk and literary origin with such brilliant virtuosity, is practically untranslatable. Gogol here attains the high point of his tragic art, which he entirely abandons after "Viy."

The following tale, "Ivan Fedorovich Shponka and his Aunt," does not fall within the frame of the cycle, but is nevertheless quite significant, since it destroys the myth, popular in Gogol scholarship, of his "periods."

One cannot speak of a development in Gogol's artistic works. They are concentrated into one decade, and only the accent shifts somewhat from the obvious fantasy at the beginning to the detailed description of apparent reality at the end. But all the elements are present from the outset. Proof of this is to be found in the fragment in question, which probably dates from the end of 1831.

The designation "fragment" hardly gives the true picture, although the tale obviously lacks a conclusion. A later special preface by the beekeeper who is doing the editing explains this by the fact that his "old woman" took pages from the notebook, in which the story was written, to line the baking tin. But if we think of Laurence Sterne and his abrupt conclusions, then we can hardly doubt that Gogol was following a literary example here that corresponded very well to his wishes. The plot is of rather secondary interest; most important is the detail, which by means of skillful arrangement produces a unified whole. It possesses an artistically rounded form without the so-called content playing the important role that is usually ascribed to it. Gogol clothes the skeleton of an incomplete plot with such refined, such lively details that each of the characters involved in the action exists as psychologically complete and the continuation of the actual plot appears unimportant. Gogol imitated the spendid lesson of *Tristram Shandy* in his own manner; the fact that he did not have to bother about developing the plot proved very useful to him because he was entering an area for the first time where the old legends and their ready-made plots could not help him, and his creative imagination always left him in the lurch in this regard. Ivan Fedorovich Shponka, a small landowner, is the prototype of Akaky Akakiyevich of "The Overcoat," goodnatured and hopelessly narrow-minded. His aunt Vasilisa Kashparovna, a resolute virago, is filled with a touching but tyrannical love for her nephew. After an exemplary (in regard to conduct) period of schooling and after exemplary service with the army, in which he advanced to the rank of lieutenant in the "brief" period of eleven years, he returns again to his estate, at his aunt's request, in order to manage it himself. On his return she decides to have him married. A neighbor's sister appears to be suitable as a wife, but the first encounter produces no results, on account of the shyness of the wooer and the absolute stupidity of the girl. The hero, who according to his own words "was never married" and is therefore afraid of marriage, has a nightmare. This, together with the hopeful promise of the author to tell of a new plan of the aunt's, concludes the story.

Hardly a single stylistic device of the later Gogol is missing in this story. The mentality of the officers of the regiment to which Shponka belongs is in no way inferior to that of the officers in the later "Carriage." The manner in which Gogol proves the culture of the regiment—drinking ability, mania for gambling, ability to dance the mazurka, of which the colonel is especially proud,—is a study in miniature for the description of urban society in *Dead Souls*.

Shponka's reading material reminds us very much of that of Ivan Ivanovich *(Mirgorod)* and of the townspeople in *Dead Souls:*

> He did not like to read books in general; and if he sometimes would glance into the soothsaying book, it was only because he liked to come upon familiar things in it, things he had already read several times. In the same way the townsman goes to the club every day, not in order to hear something new there, but to meet there those friends with whom he had already been accustomed to gossip at the club since time immemorial.

His manner of expressing himself in incomplete sentences and particles reappears in the speech of Akaky Akakiyevich and Podkolesin *(The Marriage)*. As in "The Overcoat," Gogol remarks: "It is not superfluous for me to remark at this point that he was not at all generous with words. Perhaps this happened out of shyness, but perhaps also due to the desire to express himself more choicely!" None of the conjectures, naturally, are entirely correct: the smallness of his mind is responsible. A striking similarity exists between Ivan Fedorovich's yard and Korobochka's farm in *Dead Souls*. The description of the pack of dogs especially is executed with similar means in both cases.

Storchenko, the fat neighbor, is a blend of Nozdrev and Sobakevich from *Dead Souls*, and he is described with equal mastery. His appearance at the table wearing his napkin, according to Gogol, is reminiscent of barber signs, and it reminds us of a similar scene from "The Nose."

His mother, "a coffee pot in a bonnet," resembles Pulkheriya Ivanovna from "Old-World Landowners." The blonde sister could be an Agafya Tikhonovna *(The Marriage)*, and the scene between her and Shponka in which they do not get beyond the statement that there are many flies in summer has a striking parallel in the famous love scene in *The Marriage*. Even piquant insinuations, which Gogol likes to toss out in passing, are not lacking here. In the opinion of the aunt, the late owner of the neighboring estate has left certain landed properties to her nephew. Storchenko is supposed to have pilfered the deed of gift. The aunt tells of this in the following manner: "He, I must inform you, began to visit your mother even when you were not yet born; of course at a time when your father had not the habit to be at home . . ." As one example among others, one may compare the manner in which Ivan Ivanovich's family affairs (*Mirgorod*) are discussed, or also the "female relative" of Ivan Nikiforovich, who as a type is not far removed from the aunt.

In the style as well, Gogol is already employing many of his typical devices; for example, echoes of the characters' manner of expressing themselves in the author's speech, by which a comic effect is attained: Ivan Ivanovich would say of his turkey hens: "Believe me, my most honored sir, when they walk around my yard it is even a disgusting sight—they are so fat." And some paragraphs later we read: "Now Ivan Ivanovich was very offended; he kept silent and began to finish off the turkey hen, although it was not as fat as those whose sight is disgusting."

The dissertation on the aunt's carriage in scholarly style has several parallels in Gogol's later works: "I consider it my duty to inform the reader that this was the very carriage in which Adam had already traveled. And therefore if someone should pass off another carriage as Adam's carriage, this is a complete lie, and the carriage is without doubt an imitation. It is entirely unknown in what manner it survived the deluge. We will have to assume that in Noah's ark a special coach house was set up for it . . ." Obvious nonsense is treated with complete seriousness.

Inappropriate designations which do not fit the subject are already used here by Gogol to achieve comic effects; when he concludes the very one-sided dialogue between aunt and nephew with the sentence "With that, the conversation came to an end," that may still pass; but when, in connection with the statement concerning the quantity of flies, we likewise read: "At this point the conversation again came to an end," this is clearly irony—as it is again used in similar form after the conversation of the two peasants at the beginning of *Dead Souls*.

Even more decisive, however, is the fact that Gogol's conception of the world is also already present in this fragment in sharpest outline: the world of completely useless petty philistines, who only "get the sky sooty," while they think they are God knows how important—this world already stands here before us. Without any religious overtones, which one can perhaps find only in "The Overcoat" and then in the second part of *Dead Souls*, Gogol proves through the manner of his presentation how small and how unessential the things are around which the world turns. People go on living in complacent egotism, do not trouble themselves about their neighbor (like Storchenko, who immediately begins to speak of the cockroach which crept into his ear and brought on his deafness, when it is a question of hearing about the concerns of another), and sink down so deep into their narrow dullness and absolute futility that the absence of the conclusion can also be explained on this basis. It simply is not worth while to write any more about these complacent nonentities or to present variations on the same blasé pettiness. The first part of *Dead Souls* could also end at any point without the over-all impression being damaged by it; but it could also be continued *ad infinitum*, and one would still laugh about the way in which the unessential is presented, but never lose the bitter aftertaste from the knowledge that this represents the great majority of the human race, so full of dangerous stupidity. In this regard as well *Dead Souls* brings nothing essentially new. Gogol's talent had matured early and stood here already complete. Not the least cause of his creative sufferings was that he himself felt his incapacity for further development.

From the very beginning, the devil plays the dominant role in Gogol, whether as a half-romantic, half-real being or as the dangerous adversary of men, who causes them to sink into the swamp of everyday life. Hardly a word about God is found in his works. As much as he longed to proclaim God after his conversion he was never able to do so.

"The Enchanted Spot," which concludes the cycle and which originated in 1829–1830, draws its effects from the completely abrupt transitions between the supernatural and inexplicable to prosaic reality. A constant swing of the pendulum from one to the other is felt in these few pages. It is not without reason that Gogol placed this story, an end product, as it were, in the final position. The constant encroaching of evil and the irrational becomes more than clear, and the intimations of a natural explanation—drunkenness or here, a feeling of dizziness from dancing—are distributed so illogically and so inconsistently that everything remains fundamentally unclear—like the whole unclear world.

Gogol states here his basic theme very openly:

> Yes, you have expressed yourself to the effect that Man can master, so to speak, the Evil One. Sure enough, that is, when one thinks about it properly, all sorts of things happen in the world. . . . But don't say that now: If the diabolical power really wants to ensnare someone, it *will*! . . .

Not only the old grandfather, whom the devil fools by having him dig up his field for a treasure which turns out to be but rubbish, falls into Satan's snare; but the last paragraph of the *Evenings* also has a double basis: "Thus the Evil One fools a man! I know this ground well: Afterwards the neighboring cossacks rented Father's land for planting melons. A fine soil, and the harvest was always so magnificent; but there was never anything good at the enchanted spot. They sow, as is proper, but such things grow that you can't identify them. It's not a melon, not a pumpkin, not a cucumber . . . I don't know what the devil it is!"

The *Evenings* derive their strange, exotic form (Andrey Bely compares them to miniature Japanese lacquer paintings) from the interlacing of two kinds of style. While the pathetic impulse of one strives toward the heights, the minute and cunningly selected detailed painting of the other moves beneath the level of living realism. The two are equally distant from living reality. The blend of fullest lyricism with dead tissue to form a life that is more real than reality—herein lies Gogol's specific skill.

His literary models are numerous but they serve him only as material on which he places his own unmistakable stamp.

His prologues clearly reveal the influence of Sir Walter Scott (Jedediah Cleishbotham in the prologues of the Waverley

Novels, e.g., *The Heart of Midlothian*). It is here that Gogol could have borrowed the homely conversational tone of his beekeeper. The fact that he places the tale in the mouths of representatives of certain classes enables him to draw his literary effects from their particular manners of speaking. Laurence Sterne's compositional technique and use of dialogue is apparent, especially in "Shponka."

There is no doubt that E. T. A. Hoffmann, the great German Romantic writer, was the model for the combination of reality and fantasy; also many episodes might be derived from him (compare, for example "Ignaz Denner" and "The Terrible Vengeance"). In addition to Hoffmann, many passages suggest that Gogol was familiar with the works of Ludwig Tieck; parallels can be drawn between many situations in "The Terrible Vengeance" and Tieck's "Pietro von Abano," and between "St. John's Eve" and Tieck's "Liebeszauber." In general, Gogol appears to have been better acquainted with the works and the *Weltanschauung* of the German Romantics than has been generally assumed.

On the Ukrainian side, in addition to folk-literature, Ivan Kotlyarevsky (the author of a very successful travesty on the *Aeneid*) should be mentioned; from him Gogol borrowed several chapter epigraphs. Kotlyarevsky's picture of the patriotic Ukrainian (everything is funny except the fatherland) and his combination of sentimentality and comedy are also reflected in Gogol's works. Gogol may also have taken many details from Vasily Narezhny (1780–1825), the originator of the picaresque and adventure novel in Russia, even though his style as a whole is completely different from Gogol's. The search for the essence of the Ukrainian people in their myths, songs, and customs may have drawn Gogol to his compatriot and friend, the literary historian Professor Maksimovich. Maksimovich was also interested in F. W. Schelling's philosophy, so that many of the ideas of this important romantic philosopher and also many of J. G. Herder's could have become known to Gogol through this channel. The journalist Orest Somov, who was also familiar with Schelling's thought, had dealt with Ukrainian folk-beliefs in his stories shortly before Gogol; it is hard to stay to what extent a concrete influence is really present here.

2 · Fragments and *Arabesques*

AT THE TIME he was writing the *Evenings*, Gogol was apparently working on a longer story, which was not finished.

From the two chapters that were published in the *Literary Gazette* of 1831, it is hard to form any conclusions about the course the plot of "The Terrible Boar" would take (See p. 32 above). The first of these, "The Teacher," tells of the arrival of a private tutor, an incompetent, over-aged seminarian, at a Ukrainian country estate, of his doubtful intellectual qualities, and of the magnificent impression that he makes, both on the old mistress of the estate as well as on the inhabitants of the village, and mentions his blossoming friendship with the cook. The conclusion contains the suggestion that the female sex was completely alien to him. The second chapter, "The Results of the Errand," tells how the cook plays the role of matchmaker for the lovesick teacher with the beautiful Katerina, a cossack's daughter, even though he loves her himself. When he hears in the course of the conversation that Katerina returns his love, he puts his friend's wishes out of his mind. The two are caught kissing ardently by the gossipy, malicious proprietress of the village inn. The chapter concludes with a description of the cook's emotional conflict.

"The Teacher" is well written and contains *in nuce* almost all the technical stylistic devices that are characteristic of Gogol and that he later masters with absolute sovereignty.

The guesses of the village inhabitants about the teacher's role in the administration of the estate develop into the conjectures about Chichikov in *Dead Souls*. The ironic pretense of fear and respect in the description of the fair sex—who then get to hear extremely unpleasant things in an apparently respectful form—or the seemingly approving ridicule of the stupidity and vanity of men in general are handled with great virtuosity, even in these early works.

The juxtaposition of lofty ideas with low reality, as, for example, the mention of jousting, which is *not* practiced by the inhabitants of the village, the designation "Orestes and Pylades of the Modern World" for the friendship of teacher and cook, or the quotations from Seneca and Socrates—these sound just as funny here as they do later in the great novel.

Exaggerated descriptions with personal interpolations by the author, such as the glaring green eyes of the teacher, "with which, to my knowledge, no hero in the annals of the novel has ever been gifted . . ."; farfetched, precisely executed comparisons that carry the reader far from the starting point (from the women who quarrel with each other to the miser who reaches for his side pocket "when the street turns off into an empty part of town and only a lonely street light casts its dying light onto the straw-yellow walls of the sleeping city"); surprising turns of expression (such as: "sunburned faces armed with black and gray mustaches"); the baroque and incongruous personified descriptions of nature (e.g., the description of the thickly overgrown garden whose "gigantic inhabitants slumbered on, wrapped in dark green cloaks, crowned with wondrous dream scenes, or suddenly freeing themselves from their dreams, they cut through the agitated air with their branches, as if with the sails of a windmill, and then incomprehensible speeches passed through the leaves, and the temperate, majestic motions of their bodies reminded one of old actors who conjured up the great shades of the dead to the battleground of Melpomene . . .")—all of this is already genuine Gogol.

The second chapter, "The Results of the Errand," is weaker. Here too, of course, we encounter strange images: "The clamor of many canine voices cut through the cloud of deep thought that enveloped him, and his thoughts flew away in all directions like startled ducks"; a beautiful elliptical comparison (pot and soldier), and various other stylistic surprises, which make the texture of Gogol's speech into a kind of technical hocus-pocus, are always situated in the right place; but Gogol's great weakness—his complete inability to write highly emotional dialogue that is also convincing—produces a disturbing effect.

In the years from 1831 to 1834 Gogol wrote a number of small essays on aesthetics, art criticism, history, and geography, some of which he abandoned; others he published in journals, and still others he gathered into book form and published under the title *Arabesques*.

The article "Woman" reveals Gogol's familiarity with the philosophy of German Idealism and German Romanticism. In the twenties, translations of Tieck, Wackenroder, Schlegel, Novalis, *et al.* cropped up again and again in literary journals. Schelling's philosophy was in the air; academic and literary circles were discussing it, so that someone interested in literature simply could not overlook it.

The fruit of such philosophical readings is Gogol's short essay; the exact source has not yet been established.

Telekles, a handsome Athenian youth, curses the magnificent Alkinoe, who has deceived him. Indignantly he reproaches the sublime Plato for his doctrine of the divinity of women; but the master quietly replies: Yes, Woman is to be forgiven everything, for her beauty reflects the divine idea of the beautiful on earth. Through her, Man is inspired to great deeds; she impels the artist to create; she is the mitigating force, the conciliatory beam of light in this harsh world, which would go to ruin without this divine, spiritual beauty. Beauty kindles love, the divine love for the idea of the beautiful and good, which the soul once knew and which it still remembers—this alone is the true love, not the raging destructive impulse toward the individual, which represents a mistaken idea of love. Overwhelmed, the youth sinks to the ground, as the beautiful Alkinoe advances toward him, like a confirmation of the master's speech.

Plato's philosophy, seen through the eyes of German Romanticism and interspersed with Schillerian tones, provides the content; while in the style there is a solemn cascade of apostrophes, hyperboles, and rhetorical questions. One might call the description of Alkinoe a conventional series of metaphors, if the uninhibited flight of the words did not impart a peculiar quality to the whole. An antithesis of special importance in Gogol turns up here: beauty conceals dangers; evil lurks behind the godlike surface; if for a moment one takes his eyes off ideal beauty, the passions rage and pull everything around them to destruction.

Platonic-romantic trains of thought are also found in the unpublished article on Pushkin's tragedy *Boris Godunov*. An introduction, set in the bookstore, records the opinions of the "cold world"; then follows Pollior's fiery monologue concerning divine art, which is capable of satisfying Man's yearning and of resolving his restless seeking into blissful harmony.

"Sculpture, Painting, and Music" is the title of a third essay of Gogol's, composed in 1831 and incorporated into *Arabesques*, published in 1835. Here Schelling's influence, as transmitted by his Russian interpreters—the university professor and art historian Galich, the professor and journalist Nadezhdin, the poet Venevitinov, and members of philosophical circles—is tangibly present.

The romantic hierarchy of the arts, arranged according to the degree of their "spiritualization" lies before us. The poet raises golden goblets of sparkling wine to each of the arts and thus obtains the frame for his work.

The pagan art of sculpture is subordinated to the Christian arts, painting and, highest of all, music. They give us an intimation of the divine, they awaken our "mercantile souls," they drive away the "cold, dreadful egotism" that is about to seize our world. Again a basic motif of the author's: the petty mercantile souls of this narrow-minded egotistical world are gaining the upper hand; if aesthetic feeling leaves us, if music leaves our age, both decrepit *and* youthful—what will then become of our world?

Later Gogol merely put religion in the place of art. Here his dualistic world system is already solidly established.

The remaining essays do not contain anything noteworthy. Perhaps Gogol published them so that, in view of his professorship, he could also point to scholarly achievements; but the very tedious and much too verbose articles were completely overshadowed by the three stories which he incorporated into this variegated collection.

The three stories in *Arabesques* are set in the capital. The rustic fantasy and the popular mythology are transformed into urban fantasy. The devil is not confined to the countryside alone.

"The Portrait," on which Gogol worked in the years 1833–1834, is concerned with the problem of art. The painter Chertkov buys a portrait of an old man from a second-hand dealer with his last bit of money. He is fascinated by the weirdly lifelike eyes of the old man in the painting. The gleaming of these eyes so frightens him that he does not venture to take the picture along with him; later, however, in a mysterious manner he comes upon it in his house. During the night, the old man climbs out of the frame; he promises the painter success and riches if he will work, not for the sake of art, but for the sake of money. As if in confirmation of his power, a bundle of gold falls from the picture. Chertkov succumbs to the temptation. Success and riches flow to him—but his inspiration dries up; he becomes a workman at the craft of superficial portrait-painting, until the sight of a splendid picture by an artist of his own age, who had remained faithful to art, arouses first his despair over his own wasted talent and then his envy. In outbursts of madness, he buys up good pictures in order to destroy them, and finally dies in hate and anguish.

The second part of the tale brings a solution to the mystery of the portrait. At an auction it causes a sensation, and one of the buyers tells its history. In Kolomna, a district in St. Petersburg, there once lived an old usurer, originally from the Orient, who through his ruthlessness and strange good fortune had acquired very great riches. The father of the narrator, a pious and gifted painter, was called one day to the side of the dying usurer, and the old man demanded that he paint him immediately, before his death. The old man's eyes were terrifying; a dreadful evil power spoke from them, and the painter succeeded in capturing this very feature; frightened by the evil gaze, he refused to continue the work. Pleading for him to continue, the old man revealed his secret. He had sold his soul to the devil and the torments of hell awaited him, but half of his life-force would go over into his portrait, and as long as this remained on earth, he would not be sent to hell. Terrified, the painter continues to refuse, and the usurer dies; but when he comes home, he finds the picture on his studio wall. The ghost of the old man, who is pursuing him, makes the same proposals to him as he had to Chertkov; every time the pious man wants to unburden himself to the priest and ask him for advice, something horrible happens in his family life that keeps him from telling his story. In despair, he enters a monastery as a painter-monk in order to consecrate his art to the Almighty; there the following knowledge is revealed to him:

For a long time now, the Antichrist has wanted to come upon the earth, but he can be born only in a supernatural manner. The laws of nature are still firmly intact; and so his arrival is impossible. But the earth is getting older and older; the laws of nature are getting weaker, and the bounds which contain the supernatural can no longer completely hold. Evil is breaking through and now and then becoming incarnate in men who already at birth carry Cain's mark of evil. The devil himself was within the usurer; and horrible are his wiles! Since he cannot remain on earth any longer than the body which he chooses for himself as a dwelling, he is seeking to preserve himself in the picture. The picture that the painter painted is now wandering indestructibly somewhere on earth, bringing with it disaster and seducing pure souls (Chertkov's case serves as an illustration of this pernicious activity), and it would still be around, had not the pious life of the painter-monk touched the heart of the Mother of God. It will last only fifty years, and then its secret will be revealed to the world, and through divine intercession it will disappear. The time is now at hand. When the son has finished this story, and when the tensely listening crowd of buyers looks toward the picture, it has vanished—an insignificant landscape hangs in its place.

Gogol deals with a problem here that was to torment him all his life: evil is capable of infecting even artistic inspiration. Through this means it does the greatest harm, for they are indeed the best who engage in the arts or take pleasure in them. How great, therefore, is the responsibility of the artist, how he must control his actions! Nature, which has passed through an artistic consciousness and thus resulted in the work of art, is raised to a higher sphere of universal validity; but there is a limit beyond which art leaves its proper domain. The highest mastery of art gives the artist the means to go beyond this limit, to advance beyond art to the ultimate, to the first causes of Nature, into that reality which is the basis of all reality that is perceptible to the senses. The artist who reaches this stratosphere of art "steals something that cannot be produced by human action; he tears from life something living which animates the original." And this original reality, which is perceived by the artistic imagination, when strained to the utmost and propelled by a blow from without, it flies off its axis, is truly terrible. It is revealed to him "who thirsts for this reality, when in his desire to comprehend beautiful Man, he opens him up with his scalpel and catches sight of the repulsive Man within."

Thus, basically the same theme as in the Dikanka tales is present here: beneath the surface of the beautiful world the chaos of evil bubbles, and according to God's decree the world is to end after it has been tempted by Satan. The older the world, the stronger the power of the devil. "Wonder, my son, at the terrible power of Satan," says the old monk, "he will permeate everything: our works, our thoughts, yes, even the inspiration of the artist. Countless will be the victims of this hellish spirit who lives on earth invisible and shapeless." And is there any escape? "No" is the unspoken answer, for according to God's laws, so it is to be; the reprieve gained by the pious artist in years of renunciation is only a rare exception, attained through the intercession of the Mother of God. But the world is drifting helplessly toward its destruction—no sanctity is capable of saving it. But Gogol is less concerned here with the religious problem, for which reason he carelessly leaves the question open. It is the problem of the essence of art that excites him, and nowhere do we perceive so clearly his struggle to find a definition of that irrational effect produced on men by a great work of art as in this tale. The description of the good picture that causes the radical change in Chertkov is an example of these efforts. The "inexpressibly expressible" is the formula he comes upon. He is aware of the difficulty of the creative process; he knows how much work is involved in producing the apparently simple in art, for "everything unforced and light for the poet and painter is attained only forcibly and is the fruit of great exertions." Only one who dedicates himself to pure art will be able to achieve something great. The artist must serve art alone; if he lives only for his work, it can happen that in a mystical experience, knowledge of the coherence of the world within the divine order is revealed to him—but only if he does not strive for this knowledge, but rather serves art alone and dedicates himself to his work.

It is not hard to see that Gogol is here following the romantic conception of art. Pushkin had also accepted the *l'art pour l'art* principle of philosophical romanticism. His conception of art influenced Gogol; it is not without reason that the devil calls upon Chertkov to work for "profit." Pushkin had turned decisively against "profit" in art; against this "profit," for example, his verse tale "The Little House in Kolomna" was directed; it appeared at the same time, and the description of Kolomna that Gogol gives in "The Portrait" bears many a trait that reminds us of Pushkin. But these connections will be studied below in the discussion of "The Nose." It becomes clear that E. T. A. Hoffmann was also an influence when one thinks of "Die Elixiere des Teufels" (especially the chapter "Aus den Aufzeichnungen eine alten Malers" and the painting of the Blessed Virgin); in addition one can hardly overlook the common traits shared by the usurer and Hoffmann's evil spirits: Albano ("Magnetiseur"), Coppelius ("Sandmann"), Dappertutto ("Das verlorene Spiegelbild"). Usurer and Satan—this combination is also present in Hoffmann.

In regard to the particular effect of the horrible picture, especially the eyes of the old man, one finds a suspicious parallel at the beginning of C. R. Maturin's novel *Melmoth the Wanderer*, which Gogol certainly knew.

Gogol built up his material with great stylistic skill. The tale consists of two parts, which are not apparently connected with each other, but stand next to one another like two unrelated tales, yet in both of them, the mysterious picture is the center point; the first only becomes comprehensible after a reading of the second as an episode explaining the fatal effect of the picture. The author's tone is serious, and only at times are there flashes of satiric light (e.g., the policeman, the distinguished lady and her daughter) or traces of Gogol's humorous stylistic devices (e.g., "slight disagreements" used to designate absolute contradictions in the chatter of the lady, or the section on "the old women who pray, the old women who get drunk; the old women who both get drunk and also pray," etc., the account of "the sons of Mars, retired"). In the second part, which is narrated by the "buyer," any attempt to have the language sound like that which is really spoken is given up, so that the scattered apostrophes produce a jarring effect. Several uncertainties in expression, false pathos ("He threw himself on his knees and was completely transformed into prayer"), and superfluous sentimentalities, especially in the religious scenes, prove that Gogol was not entirely successful here with the serious, solemn style which he later worked so hard to perfect. The second version of "The Portrait" (1842) is discussed in Chapter 8.

In the second story, "Nevsky Prospect," [1] however, Gogol succeeded in achieving an absolutely flawless structuring of his material.

There are indications that as early as 1831 Gogol was thinking of a story in which St. Petersburg street scenes would play a prominent role. "Nevsky Prospect" was completed in October 1834 and immediately sent to Pushkin for his approval. He reacted most favorably. As he was always to do hereafter, Gogol feared the interference of the censors, who treated *this* story, however, relatively mildly.

The structure of the plot, in so far as one can speak here of a plot, and the idea are very similar to those of "The Portrait." In "Nevsky Prospect," likewise, two tales stand side by side, very loosely connected in plot (the hero of one knows the hero of the other), but antithetical in idea. Two attitudes toward the beautiful and toward love are described; through the crass, abrupt transition from one to the other they are made especially clear.

Gogol simultaneously combines two different literary genres: the gruesome naturalistic *roman-feuilleton* of late French

[1] The name of the main street in St. Petersburg.

romanticism with its strongly sentimental tendency and an anecdote recounted in the style of a farce. Thus the principle of mixture of styles, which he had already employed in *Evenings*, is taken up here in a new variation.

The plots of both tales are very simple. The idealistically oriented painter Piskarev follows in the street a beautiful woman whom he takes for a higher being. But she is really a prostitute from a brothel. When his attempt to save her ends in failure, he commits suicide.

Lieutenant Pirogov also follows a beautiful woman and finds out that she is the spouse of an upright German tinsmith. When the husband catches the two of them in an ambiguous situation, he soundly thrashes the lieutenant. The latter forgets all too soon his intention to wreak a dreadful vengeance.

A description of the main street in St. Petersburg, Nevsky Prospect, constitutes both the beginning and the end of the whole work. Both adventures begin on this street. In the introduction the changing appearance of this avenue according to the time of day is described in an apparently admiring, positive tone—but in reality, a fair of human vanity and stupidity is passing by. As soon as the sun sets, the action of both stories immediately begins; at the end of both stories we again find ourselves in the twilight on Nevsky Prospect, just as the street lamps are being lit. And now the author shows his cards:

> Everything is deceit, everything is a dream, nothing is what it seems! . . . It lies at all times, this Nevsky Prospect, but most of all when night presses against it like a condensed mass and outlines the white and straw-colored walls of the houses, when the whole city turns into thunder and glitter, myriads of carriages swarm the bridges, the outriders shout and hop up and down on their horses, and when the demon himself lights the lamps only to show everything differently from the way it really is.

We have again come to Gogol's theme: the devil is lying in wait for Man, and there is no escape from him. The painter who thinks he sees the ideal of womanhood when he takes the beautiful exterior for the mirror of the soul is in reality meeting a whore. His dream, which he seeks to prolong by means of opium and which is turning into real life for him, cannot save him in the long run. Our life involves a contradiction between the ideal and reality, but the imagination does not have the power to deliver Man—a conception which essentially distinguishes Gogol from his literary model at this time, E. T. A. Hoffmann. The stupid, unimaginative, crude, run-of-the-mill Lieutenant Pirogov lives more happily than anyone, as he forgets his righteous anger with some pastry and a mazurka, and on the next day is ready to go out on a new adventure of the same sort. The two dull-witted beauties who are the heroines of the two stories are also happy. (Gogol inserts a charming observation on the beauty of married people at this point.) But what terrible happiness it is! It is the happiness of the enslaved beast, for the devil already has power over such a man. Incapable of any higher impulse, his soul is paralyzed, and he will fittingly join the crowd on the streets which conceal its gaping inner emptiness beneath a brilliant appearance and vain splendor. It is again noteworthy that at this time Gogol does not speak a word about God or religiosity. His conception of the world is one-sidedly pessimistic: Evil rules. In art and in love a glimpse of salvation is granted Man; it is shining somewhere as something lofty and noble in which Man feels the need to believe. But Satan holds his deceiving prism in front of everything so that Man cannot see the truth. And what is truth? . . . Man stands in the world uncertain and alone—will he find in himself something to hold on to? Thus the Nevsky Prospect becomes a symbol of the world:

> Oh, do not trust it, this Nevsky Prospect! I always wrap myself tighter in my cloak when I walk along it, and I take pains not to look at the objects around me at all.
>
> Our world is oddly arranged! I was thinking as I strolled along the Nevsky Prospect recently and called to mind these two events. How curiously, how incomprehensibly our fate plays with us! Do we ever obtain what we desire? Do we attain what our powers are apparently predestined for? Everything goes awry.

As is always the case with "jolly" Gogol, the merry tale ends in complete hopelessness. And yet Gogol's great artistry lies precisely in the fact that he is able to relate these sad things while preserving a full range of humor.

The description of the Nevsky Prospect itself is a skyrocket of wit. Impossible generalizations:

> You will meet sideburns here: unique ones—pushed beneath the cravat with unusual and amazing skill, sideburns like velvet, like satin, black as sable or coal, but alas! only belonging to the Foreign Office. Providence has denied officials of other ministries black sideburns; to their great displeasure they must wear red ones;

syntactical illogicalities and ironic assertions: "a Russian peasant *speaks of a ten-kopek piece or of seven copper pennies,* the old men and women wave their arms about and speak *to themselves* . . . but no one listens to them . . . except, perhaps, for the boys in cotton smocks with empty bottles or finished boots in their hands, who dart along the Nevsky Prospect like streaks of lightning"; elevated designations for very prosaic things: "Beggars gather in front of the doors of the cafés, from which the sleepy Ganymede, who yesterday flew back and forth with the chocolate like a fly, creeps, with the broom in his hand and without a cravat, and tosses them stale cake and leftovers"; learned formulations for stylistically inappropriate subjects: "One can state with certainty that at this time, i.e., before 12 o'clock, the Nevsky Prospect represents an end in itself for no one, but only serves as a means . . ."; comical comparisons: "A thousand sorts of hats, gowns, kerchiefs, bright colored and light, which sometimes continue to please the ladies who own them for as long as two full days, will dazzle the eyes of everyone and anyone on Nevsky Prospect. It seems as if a whole sea of butterflies has suddenly risen from the flowerstalks and is now billowing like a brilliant cloud over the black beetles of the male sex"; impossible juxtapositions: "The fourth is wearing a pair of pretty eyes and an astonishing little hat"—these all follow one after the other without stopping.

The gloomy-sentimental Piskarev story is detached from the Pirogov anecdote, which presents excellently drawn types, first the hero himself, then the upright German craftsmen, and finally the tinsmith's pretty but stupid wife. The tinsmith is introduced, by the way, in a very witty manner. Pirogov follows the beauty into the house:

> He was surprised by a very curious sight: Before him sat Schiller—not that Schiller who wrote *William Tell* and *The History of the Thirty-Years War*, but the well-known Schiller, master-tinker on Meshchanskaya Street. Alongside Schiller stood Hoffmann,—not Hoffmann the writer, but a rather good shoemaker from Offitserskaya Street, a good friend of Schiller's . . .

Pirogov's manner of speaking is perfect in its stereotyped narrowness and anticipates Khlestakov's chatter; no less perfect is Schiller's Germanized Russian.

Here Gogol had found his style: it consisted in a heedless disregard of all literary schools; in the purposeful mixing of all elements of tone and expression, and in the apparently complete disdain for form which, however, reveals his sovereign mastery throughout. Sterne's influence on Gogol bore its fruit. In addition to Hoffmann (scholarship has repeatedly pointed out the parallels between Anselmus in "Der Goldene Topf" and Piskarev) the influence of the French contemporary writer, Jules Janin, whom we shall discuss below, begins to stand out more and more distinctly. The Russian scholar Victor Vinogradov demonstrates striking parallels with De Quincey's *Confessions of an English Opium Eater*, a book that was much read in Russia at that time. The fact that Piskarev turns to opium is in itself suggestive, but the contents of his dreams are also indicative of this source. Vinogradov is able to prove that Gogol used De Quincey's book as a thematic and stylistic guide in the transition from the village to the feverishly bright-colored milieu of the city.

How deeply Gogol was occupied with Hoffmann at this time is revealed in a fragment that belongs to the tale "The Terrible Hand," which in turn was supposed to appear in a book entitled *Moonlight in the Shattered Window of the Attic on Vasily Island, Line 16*. One night through a crack in the window of a house in a gloomy St. Petersburg suburb, a student from Dorpat catches sight of a wonderfully beautiful woman in a splendid white dress and beside her a gentleman in a black frock coat. The student immediately falls in love, and there is little doubt that the gentleman will eventually reveal himself as an evil magician. The style of the fragment and the situation possess all the characteristics of Hoffmann's tales.

"The Diary of a Madman" was written in the years 1833–1834 and was originally to be called "Diary of a Mad Musician." This fact already points to E. T. A. Hoffmann and his Kapellmeister Kreisler. Later Gogol gave up these plans and made his hero a minor government official, a forerunner of Akaky Akakiyevich in "The Overcoat." But one can detect reminiscences of *Kater Murr* and of "Nachricht von den neuesten Schicksalen des Hundes Berganza" in the correspondence of the dogs in Gogol's tale.

It has already been pointed out that Gogol was preoccupied with the problem of madness at this time. *The Order of Vladimir, 3rd Class*, an unfinished comedy which he later destroyed, treats the same theme.

Here again Gogol interweaves naturalism and the fantastic in an aesthetically convincing manner. The development of the mental disturbance into delusions of grandeur as a consequence of an inferiority complex resulting from an unhappy love affair is described with realistic detail and considerable empathy. However, the hero writes his memoirs himself, and, in addition, in the madhouse—a complete impossibility. The letters of the dogs are represented as really existing and their contents are so *normal* (in contrast with the memoirs themselves), that in spite of the precision and detail of the description, one constantly feels oneself in a fantastic and unreal atmosphere. The fact that the comedy of events and ideas has a bitter aftertaste is quite understandable in view of the subject chosen. The plot is only faintly intimated: Poprishchin, the elderly minor official, loves the daughter of his department chief. He himself knows how senseless any hope is, and slowly the unfulfilled yearning undermines his mental faculties. Obvious delusions of grandeur break out when he reads in a letter written by the young lady's dog to another dog that his idol is making fun of him, and that she is going to marry a dazzling young nobleman. Gogol contrasts the sober presentation by the dog, which makes its mistress out to be a superficial little goose, with Poprishchin's romantic dream fantasies. His inferior social rank is responsible for the fact that he is not able to compete; and some dreams that he is perhaps not at all what he seems to be finally lead him to the discovery that he is the King of Spain. This idea displaces his feelings of love and completely absorbs him; he ends up in the madhouse.

It would be wrong to try to see in this tale a social bias on Gogol's part. He is concerned with something higher; as the King of Spain is assuring the object of his affections of his favor, he suddenly breaks off to cry out: "Oh, she's a perfidious creature—Woman! I just now realized what Woman is. Up till now, no one had yet recognized with whom she is in love: I am the first to discover it: Woman is in love with the devil. Yes, no joking. The physicists write a lot of nonsense that she is this and that—she loves no one but the devil." Woman is the devil's tool—with Gogol, this old theme of Russian ascetic literature takes on a profound significance. Passion for earthly things is the snare of the devil, who thus changes the world into a dead-end of absurdity; and whoever succumbs to him can assert with doctrinaire gravity that the moon is usually manufactured in Hamburg and that noses inhabit it, that every cock bears a Spain under its tailfeathers and that China and Spain are one and the same country.

In Poprishchin's eyes the gruesome, extremely matter-of-fact treatment of the mentally ill in the madhouse acquires another aspect; he interprets it in his own way and ascribes a new meaning to reality. Is this not what we do in this devil-directed world? Where is the fixed point by which truth and illusion can be distinguished? Even when complete nonsense is related, the style of a factual report is brilliantly maintained. Only when the hero thinks of his beloved is it interspersed with stereotyped interjections which are intended to strengthen the artistic unity of the work as a whole. But in the last paragraph it is suddenly interrupted by a highly emotional lyric outburst, which, in its unreserved humanitarianism, produces a shattering effect:

> No, I have not the strength to bear this any longer. God! The things they are doing to me! They pour cold water upon my head! They do not listen to my pleas, they do not see me, they do not hear me at all. What did I do to them? Why are they

torturing me? What do they want of poor me? What can I give them? I have nothing. I have no strength, I cannot endure all their torments, my head is burning, and everything is spinning before my eyes. Save me! Take me away! Give me a troika with three steeds quick as the whirlwind! Climb up into your seat, my driver, ring out, my little bell, rear up, my steeds, and carry me out of this world! On and on and on so that nothing, nothing more is to be seen. There the sky is billowing before me; a little star twinkles in the distance; the forest flies by with its dark trees and the crescent moon; blue-gray mist spreads beneath my feet; a musical string twangs in the mist; on the one side the sea, on the other Italy; and there Russian huts are already glimmering. Is that my house looming blue in the distance? Is that my mother sitting by the window? Mother dear, save your poor son! Let a tear fall on his sick head! See how they torture him! Press the poor orphan to your breast! There is no place for him in the whole wide world! He is being pursued!—Mother dear, take pity on your poor sick child! . . . And do you know that the Dey of Algiers has a wart right under his nose?

The question about the wart under the nose of the Dey of Algiers introduces the last mad flourish which strikingly reveals the hopelessness of the situation. The comic stylistic devices, attributable here to the madman doing the writing, become, in a more subtle form, Gogol's own peculiar style, the true tone of the author's voice.

Nowhere does Gogol so clearly reveal the vanity of the world as in this story. All sense of reality is abolished; and absolute nothingness rises up in its stead. All of Man's ambitious striving, which, according to Poprishchin, is caused by a worm as tiny as a pinhead in a pimple under the tongue, is senseless and causes him to consider things important which are only illusions produced by the devil. But at this time Gogol saw only the negative side; at this time he was not consciously aware of the positive side, which allows the kingdom of God's grace to appear behind the dissolved world. The radical change which took place in him in 1840 enabled him to envisage the ideal of the highest eternal beauty and truth. Only after this, did he find a positive complement to balance his negative world-view and to round off his image of the world. His tragedy as an artist was that he lacked the words to represent the positive side.

3 · Mirgorod

THE CYCLE *Mirgorod* was published in the beginning of 1835. In this work, Gogol returns to the style of *Evenings*. When he published his collected works in 1842, he subjected *Mirgorod* to a close inspection, after which "Viy" and especially "Taras Bulba" underwent some changes. The latter tale was expanded (twelve instead of the original nine chapters); new situations and new details from the life of the times in which the story took place were added. As a result of this revision, the work, weak as such, became even weaker.

The cycle consists of two parts with two tales in each; but it is not at all necessary to read the tales in the order in which they appear. Three of them, the first, the third, and the fourth are masterworks in every respect.

As in *Evenings near Dikanka*, the basic tone here is also tragic. Three tales end with the death of the hero; and even though the two main figures in "The Story of How Ivan Ivanovich and Ivan Nikiforovich Quarreled" remain alive, its hopeless pessimism still exceeds anything that Gogol had written up to that point.

The first tale, "Old-World Landowners," was presumably begun at the end of 1832. It is an idyll written in the first person. The "I" views the persons and events from a friendly but superior vantage point with benevolent irony, and the unifying tone of the narrator gives the tale its splendid finish.

It describes the life of an elderly married couple who live a completely vegetable existence on the family farm. There is no plot in the proper sense of the word. Nature in the Ukraine provides superabundant resources for living, and the good, simple-minded people think of nothing but meals, the variations of which are almost inexhaustible. Filled with a deep love for one another, kindly toward the servants, touchingly hospitable toward all strangers, they lead an uneventful, unchanging life (the use of adverbs like "usually," "always," "often" and of iterative and imperfective verbs in the description of this existence excellently conveys in Russian the feeling of something lasting), far from the doings of the evil world, whose questions and cares they are not at all able to comprehend. Gogol describes the luxuriant, overflowing nature, which bears fruit independently, without measure or limit (a fine humorous twist: the inexplicable pregnancy of the maids), with unsurpassable color and assurance (compare the beginning of the story). No less genuine is the little house with its little, overheated rooms, with overstuffed furniture, and with doors that squeak in various ways (certainly a comical exploitation of a recollection from *Tristram Shandy*); and so true and valid, so humanly genuine are the inhabitants that one begins to live with them and to feel their griefs as one's own sorrow. Gogol's art has here succeeded in elevating the lowest level of human existence to the level of a Platonic Idea.

This life is made up of ridiculously trivial details, and a ridiculous detail ends it. The little gray cat which the old lady believes to be her death (we do not know why) destroys the idyll, and a tragedy, shattering in its simplicity, takes its inexorable course. Stupid people are not to be convinced, and death and grief gain their entrance through narrow-minded supersitition. Afanasy Ivanovich's grief over the death of his wife is, in Gogol's concise description, a masterpiece of narrative art. "What has more power over us, passions or habit?" This question, which Gogol asks at the sight of human affliction, the "corrosive grief in a heart already grown cold," introduces a new theme—the power of habit—which was to play a prominent role in Gogol's thought.

But death causes the old dread to return. In broad daylight, in the blazing sun, Afanasy Ivanovich hears a voice calling his name, and he knows now that he must die. In his childhood, says the narrator, he also heard this voice at times, and it filled him with dread, and he ran till he met a person whose appearance dispelled this "terrible wilderness of the heart." Again, evil breaking out in brilliant daylight!

In spite of the complete dullness of this patriarchal life, the narrator loves it and so does the reader. Invectives against innovators who want to overturn the old order are found side by side with spiteful remarks directed at dishonest servants. It is amazing that "socially" thinking people always try to represent Gogol as a defender of the "oppressed." He always describes the lower classes—especially servants and peasants—as contemptible and stupid creatures interested only in thievery. In his works there are no positive figures from the lower levels of society. Sterne's Trim and Scott's sturdy squires have left no trace in Gogol's writings.

Stimulated by his historical studies, Gogol tried again and again to write a historical novel in the style of Walter Scott. Just as Scott treated English history, so Gogol wanted to treat Ukrainian history, to try to give a picture of olden times through characteristic types, through the abundant use of folklore detail, and through the exploitation of old legends and songs. A suspenseful plot was supposed to make the history lesson acceptable to the reader. But Gogol here too wanted to use his exceedingly successful system of blending styles. In "The Terrible Vengeance" he had seen Ukrainian history through the prism of German Romanticism, with Hoffmann and Tieck in the forefront. In his new efforts, the French *école frénétique* and the Parisian *roman-feuilleton*, which represented a continuation of the English horror novel transposed to the big city, were introduced. Gogol read Charles Robert Maturin, the last representative of the English school, with enthusiasm; his French successors, Jules Janin, Eugène Sue, Frédéric Soulié, and also, in part, Balzac, were the most widely read authors in Russia in the 1830's. They were concerned mainly with the "underworld of the big city," with improbable criminals, intrigues, and mysteries, in which the naturalistic description of atrocities of every sort constituted the main attraction.

Since about 1831, Gogol tried to work this new literary trend (without which Dostoyevsky's great novels would also be inconceivable) into his historical tales. His weak talent for constructing a plot is probably responsible for the fact that most remained fragments. Among his sketches we find several chapters of a historical novel which was to bear the title *The Hetman* and whose hero is a historical personality, Stepan Ostranitsa, the colonel of Nezhin. A chapter from this novel was anonymously printed in the almanac *Northern Flowers* (1830) under the heading "Chapter from a Historical Novel." Another chapter, "The Bloody Bandura-Player," was intended for the journal *Library for Reading*, but was banned by the censors because the conclusion of the chapter was far too "gruesome." Gogol included the beginning of this chapter in the second part of *Arabesques* under the title of "The Captive"; the conclusion was not published until 1917. From the material at our disposal, it is not entirely clear how these sketches are connected with the printed chapters. Presumably, "The Captive" is a part of the *Vorgeschichte* of *The Hetman*, for the action takes place in 1543, while at the beginning of the unpublished sketches for *The Hetman*, April 1645 is mentioned. It is even possible that two different novels are involved here.

The sketches have as historical background the culmination of the Ukrainian War of Liberation against the Poles. Cruel but noble, courageous, and at times sentimental cossacks are contrasted with the ignoble Poles. With great fullness of details, particulars of their daily life are recounted, but they themselves remain lifeless stereotypes, and Gogol's desperate efforts to breathe some life into the story are all too clearly evident. They speak like stiff history books, and Ostranitsa's love scene sounds like an opera parody despite the fact that Gogol makes use of Ukrainian folk songs. In the midst of all this, we encounter quite unnecessary details from frénétique literature: "I have never seen my father," Ostranitsa recounts, "he fell in the war before I was born. Of my mother I have seen only her blue, swollen, cut-up body. They say she drowned. They fished her out and cut me from her womb, unfeeling, lifeless . . ." etc.

Gogol's use of this tone reaches orgiastic proportions in "The Bloody Bandura-Player." [1] "The Captive," in prison turns

---

[1] The Bandura is a Ukrainian string instrument.

out to be a woman whose naked body is put to the rack by some bestial Poles. Cruelty and eroticism are intermingled here, as was the custom in the French novels of that time. In Jules Janin, for example, we read: "Imagine the following operation: A young, healthy man lies on a broad black stone; and two skilled torturers pull off his steaming, bloody skin, like a rabbit's, without even ripping a single shred from the whole." This passage seems to have inspired Gogol. In "The Bloody Bandura-Player" we read:

> They were paralyzed with horror. Never could a more dreadful phantom have appeared to a man. It was . . . nothing could be more horrible or repulsive than this sight. It was . . . what man's fibers, indeed his whole being, would not tremble. It was . . . hideous! It was a man . . . but without skin. The skin had been pulled off him. He was all congealed blood. Only the veins glimmered blue and branched out throughout his body; . . . Blood dripped down from him! A bandura on a rusty leather band hung over his shoulder. In his bloody face, his eyes gleamed weirdly . . .

There is no need to feel sorry when Gogol departs from this course, which was completely unsuited for him. Of *fantastic* horror he was a master; but *realistic* horror merely turned into a jingle of words when he attempted it.

A further chapter, with the author's note, "From the novel entitled *The Hetman*," was printed in *Northern Flowers*, literary almanac for the year 1831. It tells of a Polish courier who is sent on a secret mission to the colonel of Mirgorod. When he loses his way, a peasant takes him into his house. When the exhausted Pole is least prepared for negotiations, the peasant reveals himself as the very colonel who is being sought.

The colonel is an idealized figure—clever, brave, decent through and through—like Scott's old warriors, but with a dash of Ukrainian cunning. The courier, a noble, inexperienced knight, with whom presumably a love intrigue (with Brigitta) was to be connected, is likewise in the style of Scott. Inserted in the piece is the horrible story of the hanged priest and of God's vengeance on the arrogant evil-doer. It is a wild, devilish piece that employs many motifs from *Evenings*.

In regard to style, we find vulgarisms (here especially in the direct discourse) and lofty speech on the part of the author intentionally combined with the personifications so loved by Gogol—as when there is talk of trees "which on all sides dipped their curious boughs into the yard as if low bucolic life could offer them, the majestic ones, an interesting spectacle." Gogol never succeeds with affectionate speech: here the father speaks a strange and stiff language with his children.

However, Gogol did produce a finished work that unites Walter Scott, Jules Janin, Ukrainian folksongs, German Romanticism, and, for good measure, Homer, whom Gogol esteemed very highly. This work is the second tale of *Mirgorod*, "Taras Bulba." There is no plot in the strict sense of the word. It is a description of cossack life and some cossack campaigns in which Gogol does not tie himself down chronologically (first he speaks of the fifteenth century, then of the sixteenth; at the same time, however, many details suggest that the action takes place in the first half of the seventeenth century) and also does not present any concrete events but merely generalizes and typifies the period of the Ukrainian War of Liberation against Poland (sixteenth to seventeenth centuries), its events and personalities. The whole work suffers from this use of types. Even the heroes, the cossack colonel Taras Bulba and his sons Ostap and Andriy, are abstractions which come alive only in a few episodes. On the one hand, Gogol would like to render a faithful picture "of that rough, cruel time" (for this, the above-mentioned French novels are very helpful); on the other hand, however, he wants to patriotically glorify (as is customary in the epic), and the results are idealized beasts whose deeds one reads of with a feeling of embarrassment because they lack inner truth. The drowning of the Jews (who are always represented as lower forms of humanity in Gogol's works, as are also servants and peasants), the "murdered babies, cut-off breasts of women, the skin pulled off the feet up to the knees of men who are then set free," the little children, which are speared by the cossacks on lances and thrown into the flames of burning houses —these are only a few examples of the deeds displayed for the glory of the fatherland. And this is how they act, one and all, casually and enthusiastically. Gogol's inclination toward hyperbole here becomes fatal. This bloody construction is completely lacking in any power to convince. Gogol revels in cruelties. The description of the conditions in the besieged and starving city, and Ostap's torture, for example, leave nothing more to be desired in regard to gruesome scenes, but they all somehow sound very literary. The battle descriptions are veritable orgies of horror: an *Iliad* faithfully transposed into modern times, but without its human breath. The idea of creating a Ukrainian epic caused Gogol to turn to Homer, but he makes use only of Homer's technique of describing battles—naming of the individual names of otherwise unknown heroes along with a short biography and an account of their character and physical appearance before the description of their death, precise statement of the horrible kinds of wounds, and very detailed comparisons expressed in tensely rhythmic speech. At times Homer and folksong are combined—in which case expressions like "sugar-white teeth" are added to the Homeric lexicon.

Taras Bulba's character has no unity. He does not reach even the level of the stereotype of the brave warrior with the golden heart and the rough exterior for which Gogol strove; this is made impossible by his deviousness and the inhumanities which can supposedly be excused by casual references to "that cruel time," but which are not at all appropriate for the picture of a hero who is intended to be altogether admirable. His son Ostap is also a cold abstraction of heroic blamelessness. The love story involves the youngest son, Andriy, with the beautiful Polish girl, of whom Gogol can say only that "her breast, neck, and shoulders were enclosed within those sublime limits which are appointed to fully developed beauty."

Their love dialogues, moreover, strike one as only embarrassing declamations. Andriy's betrayal is not motivated from within; and even less motivated is his passivity when about to be murdered by his father. Undoubtedly one can again see in this story Gogol's old theme of the destructive power of diabolical beauty which causes one to forget all other values. It seems unjustified to make of it the cardinal point of Gogol's aesthetic system, as has been done in philosophical Gogol scholarship. Andriy's adventure with the Polish girl has hundreds of literary parallels in every detail.

Serious pathos is not Gogol's forte. He immediately becomes rhetorical and hollow. It is interesting to observe how his normal style breaks through in many places (e.g., in the comparison of the captured Andriy with the misbehaving schoolboy, which is absolutely unsuitable under the circumstances, or in the enumeration of the many Pysarenkos among the cossacks). At once the tone tightens and becomes natural. Gogol also succeeds in nature descriptions which, however unreal, possess an astonishing glow. The times of day and the night on the steppes are very well portrayed; details such as the cossacks galloping in the tall grass or the swans in the evening sky illuminated by distant fire (even if this image may not be originally Gogol's) are fashioned by a great artist.

There is no doubt that the image of the burning orchard is Gogol's own:

> It seemed that one could hear the trees hissing, veiled in smoke, and when the fire sprang up, it suddenly illuminated with a phosphorescent, lilac-fiery light the ripe clusters of plums or transformed yellow-glimmering pears here and there into reddish gold, and right there under them, the body of a poor Jew or monk hanging on the wall of the building or on the branch of a tree stood out blackly and perished in the flames with the building. In the distance, high above the fire, birds flew back and forth, which looked like a cluster of tiny dark crosses against a fiery background.

Gogol's intention to represent the sentimental patriotism of his Ukrainian homeland fails because he obviously tried here to abandon his proper domain—irony. In the much shorter "The Terrible Vengeance," he succeeds in producing a unified piece of work, presumably on account of its very concentration. In "Taras Bulba" he uses literary stereotypes to patch together episodes that occasionally succeed in their pathos, and loses in this way the great vitality of language that could make such a delicate subject as the idealizing of the fatherland artistically bearable. Of course it need hardly be mentioned that "Taras Bulba" belongs among the most popular and most widely known of Gogol's works. Outside Russia especially, he is known as the author of "Taras Bulba," even though this very work is least characteristic of him.

While in "Taras Bulba" Gogol does not succeed in organically uniting the heterogenous stylistic elements, in the third tale of the cycle, "Viy," he is much more successful. Gogol began work on it in 1833. Abridgements which he planned for the 1842 edition of his works tightened the development of the plot, and especially the last scenes gained a great deal in conciseness. The plot is again very simple. A young theology student Khoma Brut kills a witch who, in the guise of an old woman, was tormenting him. In reality, however, the witch was the young and beautiful daughter of a rich and powerful cossack colonel. Before her death she requested of her father that Khoma read the prayers for the dead over her coffin for three nights. She wants to revenge herself, and she finally succeeds in doing this through the help of the earth spirit Viy.

Basically, Gogol continues here the style employed in *Evenings*, but the realistic element is strengthened and the fantastic intensified to the point of uncanniness until it approaches the limits of possibility.

The intrusion of supernatural evil produces a shocklike effect because the account begins completely innocently with a humorously vivid description of the seminary at Kiev, the so-called Bursa, with its three classes of rhetoricians, philosophers, and theologians, of the Kiev market-place, and of the school-boys going off on their holidays. The three students whom we accompany are as realistic as possible, and the replies of the "theologian" Khalyava, in their indolent meagerness, are a good mirror of his mind. The adventure of the "philosopher" Khoma Brut with the witch in the sheep-pen begins so abruptly and develops with the nocturnal ride, the transformation and murder of the witch, with such fantastic speed that the transition to the day in Kiev, which follows without pause, makes the whole affair appear like a feverish dream—an effect that was well calculated by Gogol. The consequences of the adventure are now related in a carefully planned crescendo. From now on, even the most realistic detail acquires sinister overtones. So vividly are the estate and the servants of the rich colonel described, that it is as if one finds oneself in another world on which a strange curse weighs. This impression is produced not only by the fact that the corpse of the beautiful daughter is lying in the house, but a weird, paralyzing atmosphere lies over the whole story, and Khoma's unsuccessful attempts to flee heighten the feeling of an oppressive sway.

The days that Khoma Brut spends in expectant anxiety, full of choked, forced gaiety, are masterpieces in reproducing a mood, and the three dreadful nights in the church with the corpse of the witch are masterpieces in describing cold horror. It is amazing how Gogol produces a sinister atmosphere with such scanty means; admirable also is his good taste, which preserves him from any overexaggerations.

The feverish atmosphere that was so successfully maintained in "The Portrait" is conveyed here with even greater tension. Gogol achieves his effect by eliminating intermediary stages from the descriptions of motion, showing only completed states (hence the effective use of perfective verbs) and suggesting, as it were, the intervening sinking into unconsciousness.

> One could hardly hear the soft crackling of some far-away candle or the faint, lightly popping sound of a drop of wax falling to the floor. What if she should get up now? . . . She raised her head. He looked wildly and rubbed his eyes. But she indeed is not lying down any more but sitting up in her coffin. He turned away his eyes and then again focused them with dread on the coffin. She got up . . . she is walking about the church with closed eyes, continually stretching out her arms as if she wanted to catch hold of someone.

Tremendous suspense prevails throughout the second night, which is compressed into a single paragraph and which is very impressive without repeating effects. Then the third night, culminating with the appearance of the earth spirit Viy, brings the usual solution: Evil triumphs.[2] The church and the Holy Scripture are not able to protect the harmless, cheerful, and goodhearted (although certainly not pure) Khoma. He is destroyed like Mikita, the overseer of the dog kennel, who burned to death because of impure love. From Gorobec's reply at the end (which was added later) we can conclude that the Divine

---

[2] A certain influence on Gogol in these church scenes can be ascribed to V. Zhukovsky's translation of Robert Southey's "The Old Woman of Berkeley. A Ballad, Showing How an Old Woman Rode Double and Who Rode Before She."

Might would indeed have the power to conquer if Man himself would help it by his attitude. But Man does not have the only correct attitude possible and therefore has helplessly succumbed to the evil power. Here it is symbolized by earthly, sensual beauty. Khoma's vision, as he storms away with the witch on his back, is significant:

> He felt a consuming, unpleasant and at the same time sweet feeling that swelled up into his heart. He lowered his head and saw that the grass that lay almost under his feet apparently grew deep and far and that above it stood clear water like that from mountain springs, and the grass appeared to be the bottom of some sea that was bright and clear even to the utmost depths. . . . He saw how, instead of the moon, some sun was shining there; he heard blue-bells bowing their little heads and ringing. He saw a water-nymph swim up out of the reeds; a back, a leg darted by, arched, elastic, made of nothing but luster and trembling. She turned to him—and there is her face with bright, sharp, flashing eyes, with a song that penetrates the soul and already approaches him, now on the surface, and quivering with glittering laughter speeds away, and now she lies on her back, and her breasts like little clouds, like unpolished porcelain, translucent in the sun at the edges of their white, gently elastic circumference. The water covered them with little bubbles, like beads. All of her trembles and she laughs in the water . . .

Khoma felt a diabolically sweet feeling; he felt a "piercing bliss full of longing and dread," and the "terrible, brilliant beauty" of the corpse clearly reveals how dreadfully close beauty and evil lie, and how easily beauty can become a tool of the devil.

It is a proof of Gogol's considerable artistic power that he was able to introduce flashes of humor against this gloomy background to intensify the horror and to make it more real and more genuine. The description of the drunken cossacks, the conversation of the servants, the mass snoring which transforms the farm into a factory, Khoma's implied love affair, his manner of speaking and thinking, the well-rendered conversations with the colonel, for example, are recounted with a knowing irony. The comparisons are comical and yet somehow sinister. When the old cossack tells a joke, the shepherd lets "such a heavy laugh resound as if two oxen had planted themselves opposite one another and begun to bellow together."

By means of short sentences, Gogol increases the weird effect of those scenes which are contrasted with comic scenes and which are so skillfully shaded: after Khoma's wild dance, the action moves to the church for the third night.

> On the way the philosopher continually looked in all directions and made feeble attempts to start a conversation with his companions. But Yavtukh kept silent, even Dorosh was not in a talkative mood. The night was hellish. In the distance, wolves in a pack howled. And even the barking of the dogs was somehow frightening. "Something else must be howling there: That's no wolf," said Dorosh. Yavtukh kept silent. The philosopher did not know what to say . . .

These few staccato lines contain a world of horror.

Noteworthy also are the small scenes in which something of universal validity is felt. After the second night, Khoma is able only to stammer—"Those who had gathered in a circle around him bowed their heads when they heard such words. Even a small boy to whom all the servants felt justified in assigning the job when it was necessary to clean out the stables or to draw water, even this poor boy gaped with astonishment." With classic brevity, a problem is suggested here which Dostoyevsky later verbosely elevated to his own domain.

In his note to "Viy," Gogol asserts that the whole story is a folk legend and that he was reproducing it exactly as he heard it. This is undoubtedly an attempt at mystification. Individual motifs are to be found in Ukrainian legends, but the whole is an original achievement of Gogol's; it represents the high point of the direction he began in *Evenings*.

The last tale, "The Story of How Ivan Ivanovich and Ivan Nikiforovich Quarreled," was printed for the first time in 1834 in the almanac *Novoselye* (Housewarming), which the publisher Smirdin issued on the occasion of his moving into a new house. We are certain that it was written before the other three pieces in *Mirgorod*. The censors had cut out several passages. For the *Mirgorod* edition, therefore, Gogol wrote a short preface in which he stated that everything recounted in this story belonged to the past and that today it has all turned out for the very best. The mockery was so obvious that the preface was forbidden at the last moment, and in order to avoid the costly rebinding of a book with the type already set, Gogol had to add two more pages to "Viy."

The story tells of two honorable citizens of the town of Mirgorod, friends of many years, who became deadly enemies because one had called the other a gander in the course of an argument. Attempts at reconciliation by other townspeople are spoiled at the last moment by the repetition of the fatal word. The courts drag out the mutual complaints of the two men; each is firmly convinced that he is right, and both find in the expectation of a favorable decision an absurd meaning for their lives. This is the entire plot.

It becomes more and more clear how unimportant the construction of a plot is for Gogol. A little anecdote is all that he needs to produce a work of art that touches all the depths of the human soul through the manner in which it is told. Again Gogol brings into play all his humorous technical devices and thus glosses over the disturbing gravity of the plot. The catastrophe occurs in the moment of greatest peace; in the midst of harmless comedy a radical change takes place which acts like a clap of thunder and which brings a sharp change in tone along with it. The vantage point from which the author was describing the action shifts with great suddenness. The tale begun in a cheerfully ironic conversational tone ends up in hopeless pessimism. "It's tedious in this world, my friends!" This now famous concluding sentence sounds like a last judgment, like the final product of a philosophical conception of the world, precisely because it stands at the end of such a lively, such a tremendously amusing story. And this liveliness, this amusing quality—they are but a senseless confusion of human desires and strivings that appear so important and so colorful when one participates in them oneself, but seen from the outside they turn into an irrelevant grayness.

The unity of the narrative tone is brilliantly maintained. The subtitle reads: "One of the unpublished true events related by the beekeeper Red-haired Panko." This enables the author to ramble on with apparent freedom, to act as if he presupposes extensive knowledge of the background on the part of the reader so that only an allusion, a name suffices to make him aware of what is going on. Since in reality this is not the case, this procedure increases suspense as well as comedy.

The first chapter is devoted to the description of the two heroes of the tale. Every paragraph begins with the declaration that they are fine men, but the proofs which follow are very strange: first an enthusiastic description of Ivan Ivanovich's coat, then of his beautiful house and splendid garden, then the information that he likes to eat melons, that the police inspector of Poltava knows him and visits him, and that some clergyman, Father Peter of Koliberda (who is not mentioned again), is of the opinion that he knows how to live. From all this it follows—and is repeated as a matter of course—that he is a fine man. Here Gogol uses on a greatly enlarged scale the device of intentional illogicality: a proof worked out stylistically which is logically no proof at all. Quite in passing and in subordinate clauses which remain entirely in the background, we also learn that Ivan Ivanovich actually does nothing else but rest (from what?), that he is a ridiculous pedant (registering of the melon seeds), that he has a swarm of illegitimate children (the amusing description of his maid Gapka and *her* children), that he is miserly (worrying about his keys), that his piety is limited to externals (his behavior in church), that he is frightfully nosy and devoid of compassion (dialogue with the beggar woman), and finally that he likes to receive gifts, without being generous himself. And somehow Ivan Ivanovich stands before us: a narrow-minded, average man who thinks he is important, while in reality he is a complete nothing —and this nonentity, that is also a man, becomes familiar and likable, strangely enough.

"Ivan Nikiforovich is also a very good person. His farm is situated next to the farm of Ivan Ivanovich," Gogol goes on to say. With a great deal of emphasis he asserts that Ivan Nikiforovich has never been married, in reply to alleged rumors which would claim the contrary. Rumor as profitable theme and showpiece of Gogol's turns up again. Here he suddenly declares that a rumor has been spread claiming that Ivan Nikiforovich was born with a tail in the rear: "But this fabrication is so absurd and at the same time so vile and indecent that I do not even find it necessary to refute it before enlightened readers who undoubtedly know that only witches, and even there only a few, possess a tail in the rear. Witches, however, belong to the female sex rather than to the male." In the style of a scientific treatise, with an appeal to the "enlightened readers," complete nonsense is spoken allegedly in order to refute an equally nonsensical assertion. This passage serves as transition to a comparison of the two heroes, from which comparison their human qualities will allegedly become especially clear. At first all goes well: one is like this, the other like that; one does this, the other that; but hardly has Gogol lulled the suspicions of the reader by means of the stylistic consistency of the comparison, when we suddenly read: "Ivan Ivanovich is of a somewhat timid nature. Ivan Nikiforovich, on the other hand, has wide breeches with such wide pleats that if they were inflated, one could comfortably store the whole farm with granaries and building in them."

The irrelevance of these people and their characteristics becomes strikingly clear by means of this stylistic illogicality. And yet after the pages of comparison, the two heroes—the lean, pretentious Ivan Ivanovich and the fat, crude Ivan Nikiforovich—stand before us as if alive. "However, in spite of a few dissimilarities, both Ivan Ivanovich as well as Ivan Nikiforovich are excellent men." Thus Gogol concludes the chapter in which, in a laudatory style, he has proven the exact opposite. In its composition, it reflects the absurdity of the world it describes.

The quarrel between the two described in the second chapter is simply the logical consequence of the conglomeration of human qualities governed by irrationality. Ivan Ivanovich wants to trade something of his for a rifle that he does not need, and Ivan Nikiforovich does not want to give it away even though he too has no use for it. When the negotiations reach their climax and the decisive word "gander" is spoken, it is completely incomprehensible why this particular word should be so offensive.

But the weightiest consequences result from this bit of nonsense. Agafya Fedoseyevna, a woman under whose power Ivan Nikiforovich has fallen in an obscure yet imaginable manner, interferes and stirs up mutual hate. The woman is indeed

Mirgorod

the devil's tool—she does it for no reason. The reversals of fortune springing from this hatred up to the point of Ivan Ivanovich's destruction of the goose pen are regretfully described by the allegedly thunderstruck author; the description of nocturnal nature in the conditional and the concise presentation of the deed help preserve the balance between serious suspense and parody on the stereotype of the usual romantic narrative. The subsequent description of the city of Mirgorod is a stylistic achievement on Gogol's part: in solemn, elevated language an absolutely trivial subject is described, and thereby its unimportance is revealed with striking clarity.

> A wonderful city is Mirgorod! What buildings one can find in it! Under straw roofs and under cane roofs and even under wooden roofs. To the right a street, to the left a street, everywhere an excellent wicker fence; hops twine around it, pots hang on it, behind it sunflowers stick out their sun-shaped heads, the poppy gleams red, big pumpkins are glimpsed— what splendor! The wicker fence is always decorated with objects that make it even more picturesque: Either with a petticoat stuck on it, or with a shirt, or with a pair of wide trousers. In Mirgorod there is neither thievery nor swindling, and therefore everyone hangs on the fence whatever comes to his mind. When you approach the main square, you will certainly stop for some time to enjoy the view; a puddle is situated there, an astonishing puddle! As unique as you have ever had an opportunity to see! It takes up almost the whole square. A splendid puddle! The houses and cottages, which from afar one could take for haystacks, surround it and marvel at its beauty. But I am of the opinion that there is no house more beautiful than the circuit court. I am not concerned with whether it is made of oak or birch wood, but gentlemen, it possesses eight windows! Eight windows in a row, facing directly on the square and out over the watery expanse of which I have already spoken and which the mayor calls a lake! . . .

In the same manner, the exterior and the interior of the building are described and also the people within, the judge and his staff. The "refined courtesy" of Ivan Ivanovich (who is presenting his complaint) is portrayed in an equally enthusiastic tone, as is, with ever-increasing improbability, the visit of Ivan Nikiforovich (who gets stuck in the door) for the same purpose.

The two complaints are clever parodies of chancery style. The increasing improbability reaches its climax in the theft of

Ivan Nikiforovich's petition by Ivan Ivanovich's pig. This is a parody on the retardation at all costs customary in literature and a demonstration of the freedom of the author, who is able to narrate a complete impossibility in such a way that it appears completely conceivable. The episode sounds even a bit sinister: the brown pig was offered by Ivan Ivanovich in exchange for the rifle and was indignantly refused by Ivan Nikiforovich for completely nonsensical reasons ("A pig is the devil [NB] knows what")—and this same pig now steals the petition. "When they informed Ivan Nikiforovich of this, he said nothing and merely asked whether it was by any chance the brown one?" From this passage we become aware of the fact that the surface of the world is again cracking up and that strange things are trying to come out. But this time Gogol bypasses the subject. Ivan Nikiforovich's new, second petition so far surpasses the parody in the first two that, in the chaos of quasi-official formulations, all sense is lost. (It is amusing to compare the ways in which some translators have tried to insert their own meanings into these *intentionally meaningless sentences*.) All attempts to reconcile the friends fail. The records are now filed away. "Many brides managed to get married, in Mirgorod a new street had been broken through, the judge had lost a front tooth and two molars, at the house of Ivan Ivanovich still more children were running around in the yard than before—where they came from, only God knows!"—thus Gogol characterizes the long period of time before the final reconciliation attempt at the mayor's reception.

This assemblage, as Gogol calls it, is described in enthusiastic tones interrupted by exclamations of delight, even though the things described are very commonplace, indeed even alarmingly commonplace.

After the comparison of the wheels in the mayor's court yard with the works of a clock, which is frightful nonsense even to contemplate, the delighted enumeration of the arriving guests begins, wherein names are mentioned which are completely strange to the reader and which never appear again. But precisely through the matter-of-fact manner in which people and events are assumed to be well-known to all, an intimacy of tone results, allowing the author the strangest disgressions about details.

> Oh, what a rout the mayor gave! Allow me, I shall enumerate all who were present there: Taras Tarasovich, Yevpl Akinfovich, Yevtikhy Yevtikhiyevich, Ivan Ivanovich, not *the* Ivan Ivanovich, but another, Savva Gavrilovich, our Ivan Ivanovich, Yelevfery Yelevferiyevich, Makar Nazarevich, Foma Grigoryevich . . .
> I can't go on! My powers fail! My hand is weary from writing! And how many ladies were there! With swarthy complexion and with pale, tall and very short, fat like Ivan Nikiforovich and so thin that it seemed as if one could stick each one in the mayor's scabbard. How many bonnets! How many gowns! Red, yellow, coffee-colored, green, blue, new, turned, remodeled, shawls, ribbons, evening bags. Farewell, poor eyes! You will be good for nothing more after this spectacle. And what a long table was opened up! And how everyone was talking at the same time, what an uproar arose! What is even a mill with all its millstones, wheels, mortars and flywheel compared to this! I cannot tell you exactly what was talked about, but we must assume that they were many pleasant and useful things, such as, for example: The weather, dogs, wheat, bonnets, stallions . . .

Gogol skillfully introduces Ivan Ivanovich's one-eyed namesake both to heighten the comedy and, by complicating the situation, to sharpen the attentiveness of the reader and thus increase his receptivity. This same namesake proposes to bring about the reconciliation.

> Everyone loved this one-eyed Ivan Ivanovich very much because he made jokes that were entirely in present-day taste. Even the big, lean man in the felt coat and with a plaster on his nose who had been sitting in the corner up till then and had not changed his expression even when a fly flew up his nose, even this gentleman got up from his seat and moved closer to the crowd that stood around the one-eyed Ivan Ivanovich.

Who and what is this man? He also crops up in *Dead Souls* when there is something afoot. Is he, as Andrey Bely thinks, the pithy demon of great mediocrity? Once more it seems as if something evil is trying to break out from beneath the surface. The man who is sent to fetch Ivan Nikiforovich has his parallels in the small boy in "Viy" and in Akaky Akakiyevich, the hero of "The Overcoat." He is a harmless, innocently suffering person, representative of that part of human society which is deprived of its rights, but seen not from a social point of view but rather from an ethical one. It is not in him to be a beast of prey, and he is therefore used by others as fool and plaything. He is deserving of sympathy and yet somehow repulsive. Gogol sees these figures with his characteristic objectivity; Dostoyevsky makes sublime heroes out of them.

The invitation scene draws its comic effects from the messenger's untrue sworn promises. The meal with the exotic-sounding Ukrainian dishes is described negatively; Gogol carefully enumerates what he purportedly does not want even to mention, and has an abundance of culinary products parade by.

The reconciliation scene itself, with the little detail that Ivan Ivanovich falls over a woman in a red dress, the devil's color, which is not a good omen, draws its effect from the smooth start that ends in catastrophe. "And this man," we read of Ivan Ivanovich, "a model of meekness, who would not let a beggar woman go by without questioning her, rushed out in a mad rage. Such powerful storms do the passions let loose." Again, pathos in connection with a ridiculous object. And somehow we are made to wonder if every object without exception is not ridiculous. Are there any passions at all in the world which would be worth such a storm? The connection of the gander with the solemnly pathetic "But, all is lost!" suddenly causes the whole world to appear absurd. Therein lies a radical change in tone.

The short final section is written in a concise style, pervaded by an infinitely sad melody. "The church was almost empty. Almost no one. One could see that even the most god-fearing were afraid of the mud. On this gloomy, or rather, sick day, the candles were somehow strangely unpleasant; the dark images of the saints were sad; the elongated windows with round pieces of glass were streaming with tears of rain." With resigned gravity, the author speaks of the changes in his heroes, of their being driven by absurdity. It's tedious in this world, my friends! In this world, apparently so colorful, so full of light.

4 · Two Masterpieces of the Short Form

IN 1833, Gogol began work on "The Nose," which is composed in the style of the three St. Petersburg tales. In 1836 it was published in the third volume of Pushkin's *Contemporary* after the *Moscow Observer* had rejected it as too "ordinary" and too "dirty." Pushkin provided the story with the following editorial note: "N. V. Gogol has objected to the printing of this jest for a long time; but we found in it so much that was unexpected, fantastic, merry, and original that we persuaded him to allow us to share with the public the enjoyment afforded us by his manuscript."

This judgment as well as Pushkin's interest in the tale in general should not be disregarded in its interpretation. There have been many attempts at interpreting "The Nose," but they all get lost in metaphysical or psychological constructs, and overlook the obvious.

Gogol's admiration for Pushkin is sufficiently well known. We know that he submitted everything he wrote to Pushkin for approval and that he accepted Pushkin's criticism without contradiction and was guided by it. Pushkin usually offered criticism based on a well-thought-out and rounded system of aesthetics. Its main thesis was the principle of art for art's sake, and it would absolutely not tolerate the concept of *profit* in the realm of art. Every non-artistic goal which the poet might pursue is necessarily injurious to his art. Ethics and morality have nothing to do with art; the poet is absolutely free in the choice and treatment of his themes. Pushkin never grew tired of affirming these theses against the usual conception that the writer should teach and edify. His famous poem "The Poet and the Mob" (1829) formulated very pointedly the autocracy of art. To mock those who always look for morals in literary works, Pushkin wrote his verse tale "The Little House in Kolomna," a smoothly flowing, somewhat frivolous ancedote told in irreproachable *ottava rima* from which, as the author affirms at the end, not the slightest moral can be squeezed.

There is little doubt that Pushkin expounded his favorite theory to Gogol. From Gogol's essays of this period we gather that he had to a considerable degree made it his own. The idea of writing a tale capable, merely by the form in which it is told, of making downright nonsense credible, suspenseful, and equal to all the demands that one places on a work of art could have been suggested to Gogol by Pushkin.

Gogol was predestined for such a work, because the ability to describe everyday details so vividly that the plot is completely forgotten was his strong point. "The Little House in Kolomna" was published in 1833, the same year in which Gogol began work on "The Nose." Gogol thought very highly of the little verse tale. In addition, one finds similarities between Pushkin's descriptions of the St. Petersburg suburb of Kolomna and those in Gogol's "The Portrait"; the action in the latter tale takes place in part in the same suburb. We should not overlook these facts when we attempt to interpret "The Nose."

Another element is also present. Gogol and Pushkin both thought very highly of Laurence Sterne. In *Tristram Shandy* they found the model of a novel that plays with form, that apparently neglects the plot completely, and that casually introduces the longest and most abundant of digressions. And in this novel as well, a nose plays an important and ambiguous role. In Book III, Chapters XXXI–XXXIII, Sterne repeats so emphatically the assertion that he actually means the nose and no other part of the body, scolds so indignantly the dirty minds of certain readers, and presents such well-chosen examples of his purity, that the double meaning can not be doubted. The gentle obscenity of this passage was quite likely to amuse both Pushkin and Gogol (both rather uninhibited in their letters). The dubious overtones that a tale from this sphere would have could only charm Gogol so much the more, since the ambiguity of the whole appeared to impart a meaning which, basically, was not there; for as soon as one tries to unite all the details that sound so convincing individually, the results are, properly speaking, downright nonsense. "The Nose" is to be understood as a game playing with the technical narrative devices and as a challenge to those who always look for a moral and for profit in art, who are too uncultured and narrow-minded to see that a real work of art can be created only for its own sake and that it is not at all a question of the *what* but of the *how* of the work. Similar to "The Little House in Kolomna," and presumably influenced by it, it derides the *mob*, which demands of the poet teaching and models of virtue. Both the psychoanalysts, who understandably go into ecstasies while interpreting this tale, and the metaphysicians, I believe, completely miss Gogol's true intent.

But precisely on account of the complete senselessness of the whole, all sorts of meanings can be read into the story, especially if one does not include all the details in the interpretation.

Naturally one can assert that Kovalev, the hopeless average man, is unable to bear to be conspicuous. The loss of his nose causes him to emerge from his inconspicuous mediocrity, and thus to lose his sense of security and come close to despair and madness.

If one considers "The Nose" in its second possible meaning, one can see in the tale the problem of sexual activity independent of the human being. A person like Kovalev who is completely absorbed in his sex life is depersonalized by the loss of his capacity for sexual activity; he becomes a nonentity, no longer has a "position" in life. There are still other possibilities of interpretation, but they remain mere possibilities.

Moreover, Viktor Vinogradov has shown that a veritable science of noses, presumably influenced by Sterne, had developed in contemporary Russian literature. Thus the theme as such was in the air. Gogol, however, made of it a total travesty. Again and again the nose is mentioned in passing in other works of Gogol's and in his letters in a very individualized manner or as a witty metaphor. It is clear that Gogol did not want a meaning in the tale, for he first thought of explaining the events as a dream of Kovalev's, but then gave up this intention. The dream would have meant the possibility of explanation; but this was precisely what Gogol wanted to avoid.

The story is made up of three sections. The first two have two different heroes and their plots develop independently; the connecting motif is the nose which someone cut off someone else (or was it not cut off?). The third section brings together both heroes in the shaving scene in which they both know of something that unites them, but do not mention it. The basis of the tale is completely fantastic, the story itself completely commonplace, completely realistic. Entirely as a matter of course, things are related which in reality are impossible; not the slightest attempt at an explanation is made: nonsense looks like reality, or reality proves to be nonsense.

On March 25, Ivan Yakovlevich, a St. Petersburg barber (whose family name "has been lost") finds a nose in the sliced loaf of bread which his malicious wife has just baked; with dread, he recognizes it as that of Major Kovalev, whom he usually shaves twice a week. Having wrapped it in a rag, he succeeds in throwing it into the Neva without being noticed, but as he tries to leave the bridge he is arrested by the police. "But here a complete fog covers this affair, and we have not the slightest knowledge of what happened after that."

The second section describes first the awakening of Major Kovalev, who in reality is no major at all, but merely occupies a position in the civil service equivalent to that of major and who in his vanity prefers the military rank. With stupefaction he observes that there is a smooth surface on that part of his face where his nose used to be. ". . . Kovalev jumped out of bed and shook himself: the nose is gone! . . . He immediately called for his clothes and flew to the chief of police." There is no consideration given to the possibility or impossibility of the incident. The characterization of Kovalev interpolated in the story shows him to be a vain, empty fop, a complacent egotist, completely faceless and lacking in personality, who is concerned with nothing but women and his career. His counterpart is Lieutenant Pirogov in "Nevsky Prospect." On the way he enters a café in order to ascertain in the mirror whether he had perhaps been mistaken.

> Fortunately, no one was in the café: The boys were sweeping the rooms and arranging the chairs; with sleepy eyes, some were carrying out warm pastry on trays; yesterday's newspapers, stained with coffee, were lying around on tables and chairs. "Thank God no one is here," he said, "now it's possible to take a look." He walked over to the mirror timidly and looked into it: "What the devil, confounded nonsense!" he said, spitting. "At least if there were something in place of the nose, but nothing . . . !"

A completely realistic, emphatically authentic picture of a café in the morning provides the background for the discovery that the nose is really missing. Kovalev's dread exceeds all measure when he sees that a state councillor who is getting into a carriage down the street is his nose. The nose rides to church—Kovalev follows. "He hurried to the cathedral, forced his way through a row of old beggar women with bundled-up faces and two openings for the eyes, at which he used to laugh so much, and entered the church." Again, a characterization and criticism of Kovalev is contained in this "at which he used to laugh so much": It is a procedure typical of Gogol's art to set up spotlights in subordinate clauses which are inserted without comment. The conversation with the praying nose (Gogol had to revise this passage by order of the censors and change the setting to a department store) is a splendid piece of humor. The nose rejects his claims and explains that it is "independent," and its high rank prevents Kovalev, who feels worshipful respect for ranks, from taking energetic steps. Distracted by a young woman, he does not notice the nose leaving the church. After the vain visit to the house of the chief of police, who is not at home (again a vivid conversation with the porter!), Kovalev comes upon the idea of advertising the loss of his nose in the newspaper; but the editors turn down his request. His visit with the superintendent of the police district, who insults him with the remark "that a decent man does not get his nose ripped off," is likewise of no avail. Kovalev is now convinced that it is Podtochina, the staff officer's widow, who, by magic means, robbed him of his nose because he courted her daughter, though not in a very pretty way, and then, instead of marrying her, dropped her to look for a richer bride. At this moment, the policeman who had arrested the barber on the bridge brings back the nose, which Kovalev delightedly holds in the palm of his hand. But it does not stick to his face. And the charmingly caricatured German doctor is unable to help. So Kovalev writes a threatening letter to the widow, to which he receives a rather puzzled answer that convinces him of her innocence. The widow's letter is a splendid example of the manner in which syntax and meaning go their own way in Gogol's writings, a device that he masters brilliantly: "In all honesty, I must confess to you, I never expected and still more in reference to the unjust reproaches on your part." So begins the answer of the staff officer's widow, and does it not reflect the psychic state of many, and is this not the style in which the world is managed by the grace of the devil? " 'In what way, by what fate could it happen? Only the devil will understand that!' Kovalev said finally and let his arms fall."

A number of rumors related to this event (minds were stimulated at that time by the discovery of the effects of magnetic forces on the psyche) are reported in an incredibly comical manner whereby one rumor is more nonsensical than the other, until . . . again the whole affair is shrouded in mist and what further happens remains a mystery.

"Complete nonsense goes on in the world. Sometimes all probability is lacking: Suddenly the same nose that traveled around with the rank of a state councillor and caused so much fuss in the city turned up again in its place as if nothing had happened—i.e., between Major Kovalev's two cheeks—This happened already on April 7." (The fact that on March 25, according to the Julian calendar, and on April 7, according to the Gregorian calendar, the Feast of the Annunciation is celebrated, has very much strengthened Professor Ermakov, the Russian psychoanalyst, in his assertion of the sexual significance of the nose.) Kovalev's jubilation is beyond all measure, and so is his narrowness. He has learned nothing from the espisode and soon he no longer gives it a thought.

So this is the story, that took place in the northern capital of our vast empire! Only now, after consideration of everything, do we see that it contains many improbable elements. Without mentioning that the supernatural separation of the nose and its appearance at various places in the form of a state councillor is strange—just how could Kovalev overlook the fact that it is not permitted to publish an announcement about a nose in the newspaper? I say this here not in the sense that I would consider it too expensive to pay for this announcement: That is nonsense, and I am by no means included among the number of greedy people. But it is indecent, impolite, and improper. [This is, no doubt, a swipe at the Moscow journal that refused to publish "The Nose"!] And then too—how did the nose get into the baked bread, and how could Ivan Yakovlevich himself . . . no, I do not understand that at all, I do not understand it in the slightest! But what is most strange, most incomprehensible, that is how authors can seek out such subjects. I confess, it is indeed completely inexplicable, it is really . . . no, no, I do not understand it at all. First of all, the fatherland does not gain the least bit of profit from it; secondly . . . but secondly there is no profit connected with it either. I simply do not know what it . . .

And yet, on considering all of this, although one can naturally grant this too and that and a third point, perhaps even . . . well, and where are there no absurdities?—And yet when one reflects, this all *does* contain something. Whatever one may say, but such things happen in the world; seldom, of course—but they do happen.

So ends this strange tale. The mention of the lack of profit confirms the interpretation presented above. Both the official on the editorial staff of the newspaper and the respectable lady want to see an interpretation of the occurrence published that will be profitable for young people, and the editor, moreover, wants it in *The Northern Bee*, Bulgarin's semi-official moralistic journal (an obvious jibe on Gogol's part).

It would be possible, within the literary tradition, to interpret "The Nose" as a parody of Gogol's on the romantic motif of split personality (e.g., Adalbert von Chamisso's Schlemihl, and Hoffmann's Erasmus Spikher). The tragic element in those motifs lies in the human significance of the person who is struck with misfortune; here Gogol develops the same subject on a lower level. Here it is the stupid average man who is the victim; this is why not the shadow nor the mirror image is made to vanish, but the nose. In this way comic overtones immediately appear. In the details, too, we find motifs from Hoffmann. The policeman who brings back the nose says: "and it is strange that at first I myself took it for a gentleman, but fortunately I had my spectacles with me and I saw at once that it was a nose. I am very shortsighted, you know, and if you stand in front of me, I only see that you have a face, but I notice neither the nose, nor the beard, nor anything else at all. My mother-in-law, i.e., my wife's mother, can't see anything either." The role of spectacles in the tales of Hoffmann is, of course, sufficiently well known. A special *"pointe"* is made by the mother-in-law, whose shortsightedness cannot, of course, explain anything.

Directly after writing this parody potentially loaded with metaphysical significance and full of nonsense, Gogol turned out a piece of virtuoso narrative craft. Gogol wrote the little tale "The Carriage" in 1835. It was published in 1836 in the first volume of Pushkin's *Contemporary*. It is quite likely that Gogol wrote it almost as an echo of Pushkin's *Tales of Belkin*, published shortly before. Every one of Pushkin's tales is based on an anecdote. Each of these anecdotes is related in a concise form emphasizing the essentials. Pushkin expands them into full-length tales by deepening the psychological motivation (this is conveyed by small details of the behavior of the characters or through brief exchanges), and by elaborating the descriptions in order to achieve a characteristic, illuminating, and concrete picture of the scene.

However, precise brevity remains the most characteristic element of this genre. At every word the author asks himself if it is really necessary for the construction of the whole, so that the finished work takes on the appearance of a pure distillate of crystalline transparency of structure.

The same is true of Gogol's little tale. The very beginning imitates Pushkin's manner, as with one stroke it begins *in medias res* and conveys a great deal in the smallest possible space: "The town of B. became much gayer when the ——— Cavalry Regiment took up quarters there. Before this, however, it had been dreadfully boring there." The anecdote itself is quickly related: The vain, simple-minded landowner Pifagor [1] Pifagorovich Chertokutsky, at a dinner given by the general, invites him and all the officers to a dinner on his estate scheduled for the next day, at which, in addition, a purportedly magnificent carriage, purchased for a great deal of money by the owner himself, is to be placed on display. He drinks too much, returns home late, and immediately falls asleep, completely intoxicated. When his wife awakens him at noon on the following day with the news that distinguished guests are approaching the house, all he can think of doing, since nothing has been prepared, is to have the servants announce that he is not at home. He hurriedly hides in the carriage which he had praised so highly the day before. The surprised general wants at least to see the carriage, and when the door is opened and the lap robe thrown back, the officers are presented with the sight of the master of the house, crouching in a peculiar manner, in his dressing gown.

At the beginning of the story, Gogol, in a few strokes, gives a vivid picture of the "dreadfully boring" provincial town. Every word reveals how intellectually barren, how gray, how stagnant everything is (the mayor is always sleeping). Then comes the change due to the appearance of the regiment—a surface brilliance that only emphasizes the essential hollowness. The officers all think that they are very important and take themselves very seriously, while in reality they are thoroughgoing nonentities, too intellectually limited even to be aware of their nothingness, and therefore very happy and content.

It is a characteristic device, frequently employed by Gogol, to introduce into the story unmotivated new elements; in this way his transitions become much more natural. When he wants to switch from description to narrative action he writes: "It is very regrettable that I cannot recall for what reason the brigadier general had to give a great dinner; the preparations for it were tremendous . . ." Instead of thinking up a reason and thus ponderously delaying the development of the events, Gogol usually achieves an effortless transition, with a brief reference to his forgetfulness, which makes it possible for him

[1] I.e., Pythagoras; an example of Gogol's peculiar use of names nonexistent in Russian usage.

to immediately continue with the story in the new mode; moreover, there is no doubt about the insufficiency of the "reason" given.

The description of the lunch and its participants is superb, as is usually the case in Gogol.

> The great quantity of bottles, long ones of Lafitte, short-necked ones of Madeira, the splendid summer day, the wide-open windows, the plates with ice on the table, the unbuttoned lower buttons on the officers, the crumpled dickies on the owners of spacious frock coats, the criss-crossing conversation, covered over by the general's voice and washed down with champagne—everything fitted together perfectly with everything else.

> The general, the colonel, and even the major had completely unbuttoned uniform coats, so that the fine silk suspenders showed a bit, but the officers, maintaining the due respect, remained buttoned down—with the exception of the three last buttons.

The kind of participants and their milieu is indicated in these few details: such things as the unbuttoned lower buttons, etc., of the officers make superfluous a flood of mood-painting words.

The implied mentality of Chertokutsky is illustrated by his talk. He praises his carriage: "How roomy it is! I mean, Your Excellency, I have never seen its like before. When I was still on duty, I could take along ten bottles of rum and twenty pounds of tobacco, besides I had with me about six uniform coats, underwear and two chibouques, Your Excellency, as long, with your permission, as a tapeworm, and in the pockets one could find room for a whole ox." Nothing more remains to be said about the mental level of the hero. His increasing intoxication and the drunken gathering are also perfectly portrayed in a few decisive strokes.

> In the other corner a rather heated argument about battalion drilling had developed, and Chertokutsky, who by this time had played a jack instead of a queen twice already, would at intervals suddenly break into someone else's conversation, and shout from his corner: "In what year?" or "From what regiment?," without noticing that the question did not at all fit into the context.

> The conversation at the table dragged on for an exceptionally long time, but even so it was conducted somewhat strangely. A landowner who had participated in the campaign of 1812 told about such a battle as had never taken place at all, and then he took (for what reasons, we do not know) the stopper from the carafe and stuck it in the layer cake.

This "for what reasons, we do not know" again belongs among Gogol's favorite devices—the innocent pretense of not knowing about something in situations that are only too clear.

Chertokutsky's return, the following summer morning, and the feelings of his wife (who, briefly sketched, stands clearly before us as a lovable, simple-minded, vain little goose)—these all lead to the catastrophe.

It is interesting how Gogol avoids the cliché and in a gentle parody presents a nature description: "The sun had come to midday and was scorching with all the power in its rays, but beneath the dark, thick rows of trees one could walk in the coolness, and the flowers, warmed by the sun, tripled their fragrance." Gogol does not say the customary "doubled," but "tripled."

The catastrophe itself is related very quickly and concisely, and the point comes through clearly faceted: "'Oh, you are here . . .' said the astounded general. After he had said this, the general immediately closed the door of the carriage, covered Chertokutsky with the lap robe again, and left together with *messieurs les officiers*." The general himself is an amusing figure, characterized only by the expanse of his belly, his bass voice, and the habit, when in conversation with young officers, of always asking "What?" the first time, and replying only when the sentence is repeated.

In this tale, Gogol is in no way inferior to Pushkin. Pushkin's irony, restrained by classical moderation, appears as funny, somewhat bitter mockery in Gogol's writing. His mastery of terse composition shows him at the height of his art. From here, the road to *Dead Souls* is not very long.

5 · Gogol's Theater Pieces

IN THE SUMMER of 1835 Gogol was engaged in the composition of a tragedy drawn from English history which remained a fragment; according to a later assertion of Gogol's, it was to be called *Alfred*. It deals with the famous English king (849–901) who fought against the Danish invaders and who was a noted ruler, lawgiver, scholar, and writer.

The first act and the beginning of the second have been preserved, presumably with certain gaps.

At the university Gogol lectured on the history of the English Middle Ages, among other things, and in addition carried on extensive research in this area, so that the choice of the theme is not at all hard to understand. His sources, as far as we have been able to ascertain, were, above all, Henry Hallam's book *View of the State of Europe during the Middle Ages* (in French translation, Paris, 1821), Paul de Rapin-Thoyras' *Histoire de l'Angleterre depuis l'établissement des Romains dans la Grande-Bretagne jusqu'à la mort de Charles I* (The Hague, 1721–1736), and Augustin Thierry's *Histoire de la conquête de l'Angleterre par les Normands* . . . (Paris, 1830).

This list is further proof that Gogol was well versed in the field and that he was well acquainted with the literature. The dramatization was undoubtedly worked out on the model of Shakespeare and of Pushkin's *Boris Godunov*.

On the basis of the fragment we can come to no conclusion about the further development of the tragedy. It probably was intended as a patriotic apotheosis of monarchy. Presumably

Gogol's Theater Pieces

Gogol was again unable to invent a tightly worked-out plot. The scenes were not printed during his lifetime, and the first edition appeared in 1856. The subject of the fragment is the Anglo-Saxons' struggle against the Danes. The first scenes characterize the Anglo-Saxon people, who are gathered on the coast excitedly awaiting the arrival of the new king. The following scenes portray the king himself in combat with the Danes, showing both his positive and negative sides. We perceive that the mainspring of the action was to be the inability of his rough, superstitious, egotistical vassals to understand his enlightened endeavors. The disunity and desire for revenge rife among the vassals are presumably the other motifs with which he intended to advance the action.

From the little that we possess of this work, we can hardly speak of its artistic qualities.

The whole work gives the impression of a dramatized history book, although in the scenes among the people there are a few faint flashes of Gogol's comic style ("I shall relate in succession how I saw him [the Pope]. When my aunt Markinda died, she left me only a half *hide* of land. Then I said to myself: Why should you, Brifrik, son of Hvihelm, cultivate the land, when you can win glory in combat? After I had told myself that, I traveled by ship to the French King . . .").

The earnest conversations of Alfred and the Danish leader with their respective followers are very similar to the bombastic and lifeless rhetoric of the cossack leaders in "Taras Bulba." ("Count, you are gray of hair, and you give such a piece of advice. No, noble thanes, every thing depends on us now, and on our determination. If we give up—we lose everything, increase the pride of the enemy. I swear we would give them the certainty of their invincibility as well, and who would then be able to do anything against them . . .").

Gogol never returned to the fragment; this is easily explained by his growing coolness toward the study of history.

However, at this time Gogol was constantly occupied with the theater. All his plays were sketched out during this period. Among them are two master works.

Gogol wrote *The Inspector General* in an astonishingly short period of time. On October 7, 1835, he asks Pushkin:

"Do me a favor and give me some subject, some purely Russian anecdote, comical or not comical. I am burning with the desire to write a comedy!" It is very likely that Pushkin complied with this request, for years later in "Confession of the Author," Gogol declares that he received the anecdote serving as the basis for *The Inspector General* from Pushkin. On December 4, the comedy is already finished, as is evident from a letter to Pogodin. Less than two months were needed for one of the greatest comedies of world literature.

The anecdote which Pushkin gave him and which is said to have happened to himself is simple. In a remote provincial town, a vain fop who happens to be passing through is mistaken for the incognito inspector general, whose imminent arrival has been announced. The authorities overwhelm him with servility and displays of respect, and he tolerates it with thoughtless audacity. After his departure, the mistake is revealed.

This plot corresponded to Gogol's wishes. He was extremely dissatisfied with the usual sterotyped techniques of comedy and rightly considered them outmoded. Always the same situations, always the same love intrigues—from this dead end the road could lead only to a complete renewal, which would have to be preceded by the elimination of the old stereotypes.

First of all, the deliberate omission of the love intrigue was decisive: in the four scenes of Act IV it is only parodied. Secondly, the utter lack of any didacticism; and thirdly, connected with this, an absolute refusal to divide the characters into good and bad.

Gogol's dismal view of the world—meaninglessness thought to be meaningful, against an ominous background—is also illustrated in this strange "comedy." The world is a curious confusion of misunderstandings; but the worst misunderstanding lies in the fact that the overwhelming majority of people believe that they are achieving something positive, something important, that they are something special, and also that they act in all good faith with the certain conviction that they are in the right —and thus only further the hopeless confusion. The forced attempts to stamp *The Inspector General* as a social satire, a social pamphlet, attempts which from its first performance to

Gogol's Theater Pieces

this day have not subsided, do not get at its true meaning. The work reflects the world—not a Russian provincial town at a certain time. Like the characters, the abuses exist only as symbols. The bribes taken by the mayor, the corruption of the officials, and the hint of an embezzlement are of course the only real crimes of which there is mention, but they have no structural function at all. Neither oppression of the innocent, nor interference with justice, nor any other shocking crime worthy of punishment play a role. There can be no question of social sympathy, for the "oppressed" (here the group of merchants and citizens not holding official positions) are either first-class swindlers themselves, like the merchants, or they are stupid and without dignity, like the noncommissioned officer's widow; and the only one who could possible arouse our sympathy, the locksmith's wife, considerably dampens the growing positive feelings toward her by her classic cannonade of insults.

In the very first scene it becomes perfectly clear that none of the characters is in his proper place. Yet the fates of other men depend on these men. None of them is really bad, but also none of them is really good. A dreadful, life-killing middle way, a cosmic mediocrity wafts toward the audience. Every individual is extremely satisfied with himself and with the whole: a stagnating confusion.

Into this atmosphere explodes Khlestakov, the false inspector general. While the upright, average men of the town are convinced of their importance, Khlestakov represents a second dismal possibility for a human type: he is convinced of nothing at all—and of everything, depending on the situation. He is a complete nonentity, a dummy without any center of gravity in himself whatsoever, for whom the border between reality and imagination is easily blurred; he is able to trip along over the waves of confusion which he himself has set in motion precisely because of his empty weightlessness. It was a brilliant move on Gogol's part to represent his hero as completely passive. He is by no means a conscious deceiver or a rogue—just a nothing, and this nothing prospers, this nothing attains glory. "I love good food. After all, one lives in order to pluck the flowers of pleasure." This sentence of Khlestakov's, both in form and content, characterizes him perfectly. What sort of world is it in which people of this kind live well and end well? The hero's instability is clarified by the structure. In the last scene, his simultaneous betrothal and departure are conclusively motivated psychologically in two independent parallel passages; the fact that the sum of these motivations, united in one person, results in a paradox both brands the character and proves anew the irrationality of existence. The mayor sees himself confronted with an incomprehensible discrepancy: he simultaneously experiences the greatest success and the greatest failure in his life (Khlestakov's betrothal and departure).

The whole comedy takes place in one day; the events develop with breathtaking speed, and only in this way is the delusion of the officials comprehensible and likely, for in their fear they leave themselves no time to reflect.

One man's senseless fear of another must necessarily lead to disaster—not the words of conscience are listened to, but the words of the authorities. Dobchinsky makes the following generalization: "When a high official speaks, one is frightened." And the whole play moves in this atmosphere of fear.

The plot is imbedded, as it were, between a flash of lightning and the thunderclap that one feels approaching inevitably and that is presented by Gogol in a technically very original manner. In deliberate contrast with Tartuffe, no punishment is imposed on stage. The gendarme merely reports the fact of the arrival of the real inspector general, and there follows only a sudden shift in the positions of the characters and then a minute-long silence.

The thunderbolt neither clarifies nor solves anything, and therefore its effect is all the more dreadful. Gogol later attempted to read into his comedy the idea of fatal retribution; the government, therefore, is supposed to be its tool—obviously a farfetched interpretation, for we see only a new increase of fear and nothing more. Why should the mayor not succeed in getting out of the situation this time too, as, according to his own statement, he has so often done before? The inspector general, as genuine as he now may be, comes, of course, from the same world; we have no cause to conclude that he is to be an ideal type. The lightning which strikes the morass does not have the triumph of justice as a consequence, as in Molière.

Gogol's Theater Pieces

Everything remains as uncertain and as threatening as in the beginning.

The wretched mediocrity of *all* the characters produces the oppressive effect of *The Inspector General*. Gogol does not describe individual wickedness and its evil action on good people, but a solid collective being with morals, habits, and customs in common that hold each one captive and from whose net there is no escape. He purposely leaves out the catharsis, and when he writes at a later date that the only honest and noble character in the play is laughter itself, it is at best a surface laughter, as in his previous works; not a liberating laughter of release, but a laughter over funny details that does not touch on the essentials.

At the very beginning, the mayor's ominous dream, which he associates with the inspector general, has a weirdly comic tinge: "Just as if I had had a presentiment: all night long last night I dreamed of two unusual rats. Really, I have never seen the like: black, of unnatural size! they came, sniffed about,—and went away again." Any farcical tone is neutralized by the fear in the background; the piece should never be allowed to pass over into burlesque. With sure good taste, Gogol softens the tone again and again and emphasizes in his stage directions that exaggeration would be the death of the whole performance—an author's wish rarely heeded by foreign stage directors. Strangely enough, they think that they can convey a "Russian milieu" by simply raising the volume, and not only do they fail to accomplish this but they also completely miss the point of this supranational comedy. Scenes like the mutual misunderstanding and fear between the mayor and Khlestakov, Bobchinsky's fall, the letter on the bill—all of this should be staged as if in passing, not for its own sake. Khlestakov's great scene with its brilliant, fireworklike crescendo of lies can only produce its full effect if it is spoken as if improvised. Khlestakov believes everything that happens to come into his mind during his torrent of words, becomes enthusiastic about his own lies, and finally goes into raptures, and the madder his hyperboles, the more overwhelmed is his stage audience with their naive authenticity. A conscious awareness in his speeches would destroy the effect. The requests for loans from the officials and the continual declarations of love to the mayor's daughter and wife likewise take place without any reflection; they simply develop from the situation. His clichés ("How I wish I were your kerchief, madam, that I might clasp your lily-white neck . . .") turn little by little into downright nonsense: a series of formulae without contents. To Anna Andreyevna's remark that she is married, "in a manner of speaking," he replies: "That doesn't make any difference! Love knows no distinctions; and Karamzin has said: 'The laws condemn.' We shall withdraw into the shade of fountains. Your hand, I beg of you, give me your hand!"

The ardor of this nonsense sweeps everyone along. Although Gogol has brilliantly individualized his characters, each one is seized with fear; each one has reason to be afraid. They stand before us as if they were alive, but Gogol avoids building any subplots on them. Zemlyanika's attempt to blacken the character of his colleagues comes to naught; the action is advanced by the least sharply delineated characters (Bobchinsky, Dobchinsky, the Postmaster). Gogol makes use of this procedure so that he can develop a second plot alongside the main action: the conflict between the officials and the exploited (although also dishonest) citizens, which maintains its tension thanks to Khlestakov's unpredictable behavior. This second line gave the comedy its social aspect, and because of its exaggeration by critics, *The Inspector General* has been labeled an exposé, a militant period piece. For Gogol, however, it was nothing more than an attempt at a mixture of styles (harmless comedy and satire); the customary tragic view of the petty world was to be the product of this combination.

The comedy that was finally printed in 1842 under the title *The Marriage—A Completely Improbable Occurrence* occupied Gogol for nine years, with prolonged interruptions. There are extant outlines of it dating from as early as 1833. The title was then *The Suitors*, and the plot was presumably to be developed in a manner completely different from that of the final version. The setting of the comedy was not St. Petersburg, but a Russian country estate; the girl and her suitors were either landowners or petty officials. There is no mention of Podkolesin and Kochkarev, the heroes of the later version. The development of the plot is not discernible from this fragment; in any case, the girl, in her eagerness to marry, does not want to lose any of the gentlemen brought to her by the matchmaker. Her reply, "I find them all very pleasing and I love them all," constitutes a climax, at which the fragment breaks off. The characterization is cruder in this sketch, the comedy in several passages cheap, although Gogol's fine sense of humor generally prevails. A comparison with the final version shows how Gogol eliminated all the flashy effects and sought to tone down the overly noisy passages. By the spring of 1835, the comedy had been fundamentally revised and probably was already very similar to the printed version. In 1835, Gogol read it aloud before a small gathering at Pogodin's house in Moscow. In a letter, dating from the fall of 1835, Gogol already reports that he is on the point of having his comedy staged—but this is certainly exaggerated. He had given it to Pushkin to read and he asked for its prompt return precisely on account of the staging. Pushkin probably sent the plot of *The Inspector General* along with the returned manuscript, and Gogol was so captivated by this plot that he went to work on the new comedy with fervor and abandoned *The Marriage* (as it was now called) for the time being. Afterward he was no longer interested in having it performed (presumably under the impression made on him by the performance of *The Inspector General* with all its real and imagined consequences), but when Shchepkin, who was looking for a rewarding role, urgently asked him for a play, Gogol returned again to *The Marriage*. But the work did not progress, and apart from occasional revisions, it was left lying till 1841. For the edition of his collected works in 1842, Gogol transcribed it once again and made minor corrections.

The first performance in St. Petersburg took place on December 9, 1842; the performance in Moscow, on February 5, 1843.

The St. Petersburg performance was a complete failure, and, in the opinion of Sergey Aksakov, the Moscow performance was also very weak.

The reviews, with the exception of Belinsky's, who expressed himself very approvingly (for doubtful reasons, however), were almost entirely negative and devoid of any understanding.

Neither the actors nor the critics—nor the majority of the public—were accustomed to this sort of comedy, and they simply did not know what to make of it. There was hardly any plot at all, the action developed very slowly, and the traditional pair of lovers was missing. The fine portrayal of the characters, the restrained tone of the whole, the gentle melancholy, which lies like a veil over the movements of the characters—the audience was simply not prepared to appreciate these things. But this time Gogol had expected no better reaction, for in general he regarded this comedy, unlike *The Inspector General*, with a certain amount of indifference. While he left very detailed stage directions for *The Inspector General*, he wrote to the Moscow actor Shchepkin: "You know yourself, I think, how *The Marriage* is to be performed, for you are no bachelor, thank God"; and then he speaks in precise detail of the new staging of *The Inspector General*. The reason for this is quite clear: Gogol now considered *The Inspector General* to be a didactic and moralistic play that could be given a religious interpretation, and this was of very special concern to him now, while *The Marriage*, with (as he states now) its "subject so harmless that not even the lowest police official could feel offended," in his opinion did not contain enough serviceable material. Little by little, not least, perhaps, through Belinsky's sympathetic reviews, the performances became better. Belinsky wrote quite frankly that the failure of *The Marriage* was a triumph for Gogol and an evidence of the intellectual poverty of his public, and that the time for a national theater in Russia had not yet arrived. But the official criticism with Bulgarin in the forefront was content to assert that this was a "creation, on a level lower than anything human talents have ever yet produced," "a labored Ukrainian satire against Great Russian officials," etc. Gogol was indifferent to all this: "The criticism of *The Marriage* and *The Gamblers* is entirely correct and the public has here demonstrated an instinct for what is right." To all the heated discussion Gogol reacted only with this disinterested observation.

Gogol's comedy signifies a decisive break with the usual traditions of this genre. Apart from a few unimportant attempts at original treatment, the comedy plot as such had become firmly established in world literature: in spite of certain complications, two lovers find their way into the harbor of marriage. "How weak this plot is even in the very best writers of comedy!" Gogol wrote, "how empty these theater lovers are with their cardboard love." Gogol considered such a plot to be stale and obsolete: "Everything in this world has long since changed. Nowadays, more dramatic tension is generated by attempts to attain an advantageous position, to distinguish oneself and to outshine another at any price, and to avenge oneself for neglect and for ridicule. Have not rank, capital, advantageous marriage now more electricity in them than love?" ("After the Performance.") Love is parodied in *The Marriage*. It is surrounded with such a swarm of banalities and clichés that it produces a simply ridiculous effect. In none of the persons involved is love the driving force of his actions; it is either greed for money or convention and convenience, or perhaps sensual attraction (Podkolesin, Zhevakin), in which there is no concern for the person of the girl.

The comedy is based on the completely unfounded but yet enthusiastic efforts of Kochkarev to get his friend Podkolesin married. Although Podkolesin wants to get married, at the critical moment he is seized with fear and he refuses "because marriage is somehow strange," since he has never been married. On the one hand he wants to give up his bachelor's existence, but on the other he is afraid of any change, has a dread of having to make decisions, believes that he can persist in his passivity without making decisions, and arouses Kochkarev to ever more decisive measures precisely through the ever threatening return to his original state. Podkolesin is afraid of life; his fear has something elemental about it; he reacts automatically to Kochkarev's pushing, which is intended to get him out of his rut. The stronger the push, the stronger the resistance: six times, with ever-increasing force, Kochkarev causes him to lose his balance, and six times Podkolesin springs back with equal force into his original position. Kochkarev's last and most powerful attack, which apparently brings complete victory, is followed by the catastrophe: a springing-back that literally hurls Podkolesin out the window. The sudden and abrupt appearance of fear at the height of apparent certainty is the compositional device which Gogol so ably employs in order to develop suspense. The stronger the reaction, the more surprising its appearance: the last time it occurs is in the midst of an enthusiastic soliloquy on the "bliss" of family life. Podkolesin's fear is contrasted with the unmitigated gall of Kochkarev, whose overflowing vitality passionately invades every field of activity. Why does he want to get Podkolesin married? He does not know himself; in his soliloquy (II, 17), which reaches its peak in the sentence, "Yes, just ask a man why he sometimes does this or that!" he logically concludes that he has no reason at all for trying to get Podkolesin married, and yet something is driving him to it. Obviously this is above all the instinctive reaction of the active man when confronted with the passive man, whom he cannot stand seeing idle; he fights for Podkolesin with touching pleas and rude insults in one breath, with an unparalleled display of energy, and with completely unconcerned impudence. The whirlwind that accompanies him is overwhelming and convincing.

His gall is equaled only by that of the matchmaker, a wonderfully conceived character, who speaks almost entirely in apt proverbs, which are always to the point, and who is unbelievably energetic within the limited scope of her profession. Her word duels with Kochkarev are extemely comical in the original Russian.

The parody on love and on writers of comedies is heightened by the fact that not one lover, but *four* appear upon the scene. The mixture of objectivity and of stereotyped expressions from the province of amorous sentiments, the mixture of business terms and words of love give the comedy its peculiar tone.

The rather exaggerated, bearlike Yaichnitsa, who is only concerned with the dowry, is the only uncomplicated character among the suitors. All the others, as so often in Gogol, have some little peculiarity which they cannot give up and which causes their narrow-minded mediocrity to stand out even more distinctly. Anuchkin, the retired infantry officer with a penchant for education (especially a knowledge of French), which he himself does not possess because his father was "a brute," but which he considers indispensable in a woman, already strikes

Gogol's Theater Pieces

dark tones. Petty fanaticism is just as reckless, egocentric, and dangerous as large-scale fanaticism. The naval lieutenant Zhevakin is almost a tragic figure. His memories of Sicily and the little Italian girls ("italyanochki") like rosebuds are symbols of his inhibited sensuality which remains always unsatisfied because he himself is not very attractive and is a man condemned by fate to be a flop. Although "a great amateur where feminine embonpoint is concerned," it is now the seventeenth time that he has been refused at the last moment, and his last soliloquy (II, 19) is one of the rare humanly touching passages in the play.

The heroine, Agafya Tikhonovna, is an ignorant little goose with no ideas of her own, ready to follow any advice, and Kochkarev has an easy time influencing her. She is firmly convinced only of the fact that she must get married; but it is a matter of indifference to her whom she marries, provided he is not a merchant. Since she herself comes from merchant circles, she considers such a match beneath her dignity. With her, there is no mention of love, either: only individual parts of the bodies of the suitors "please" her, and she would very much like to join these parts together in order to obtain the ideal man. Her narrow-mindedness combined with that of Podkolesin causes the first "lovers' chat," with its leaps from one subject to another, to be so completely unsuccessful. It is a distinguishing mark of all the characters (again a favorite device of Gogol's) that they are too intellectually limited to give comprehensible expression to their incipient ideas or their feelings. The fact that they constantly repeat the same arguments and get bogged down in details testifies to the limited range of their minds, which here attempt to come to an understanding in a very narrow area. The power of speech is given to Gogol's heroes only to demonstrate their complete lack of ideas.

Only a restrained performance, carefully avoiding all exaggeration, can do justice to the gentle sadness for this world intended as the keynote of this comedy.

In the edition of his collected works (1842), Gogol included the little comedy *The Gamblers*, four scenes from the unfinished comedy *The Order of Vladimir, Third Class*, and "After the Performance," a peculiar interpretation of *The In-*

spector General in dramatic form, under the general title *Dramatic Fragments and Individual Scenes*. All the pieces were written or sketched out much earlier (between 1832 and 1837, according to Gogol's own dating), and Gogol here only subjected them to revision.

The Gamblers was probably written in 1836, but Gogol thoroughly revised the text before publication. The comedy was performed for the first time in 1843 and had no success. Ikharev, the professional card sharp, falls into the hands of an even more clever band of swindlers, who cheat him out of the money he has recently won through cheating—this is the entire plot. There are no feminine roles and thus no indications of any love plot.

The original plan for the work was faulty: the humor was supposed to result from the deliberate cheating on the part of the gang that is acting out a comedy for the benefit of the swindler; such comedies are staged by Molière's swindlers in order to deceive the hero obsessed by a fixed idea. But it is not possible to construct a whole play on the basis of this device: too many improbabilities result, and in the end one feels dissatisfied with all the effort expended on a mere trifle.

The unpremeditated and the improvised work best in Gogol's plays. Here everything transpires for the purpose of deceiving the hero; the characters play prearranged roles, and the contents of these roles are perhaps humorous, but not the characters themselves, whom in two cases one does not get to know at all outside the roles they play within the swindlers' plot. Thus genuine characterization is impossible from the outset. Besides, the trick goes off much too smoothly. With a few *faux pas* on the part of the gang, Gogol would have been able to achieve some fine effects and would have increased the inner truth of the play. Once one is aware of the surprise at the end, one is amazed, on the second reading, at the clockwork development of the play, and one is astonished at how perfectly the members of the gang of swindlers are able to play Gogolian types.

Card-playing as the mindless occupation of empty men is often employed by Gogol to characterize his world; the upright

Gogol's Theater Pieces

officials and the stupid officers, for example, spend their time at it, and the more carefree ones do not take the honesty associated with it at all seriously. The fact that Gogol here takes card-playing as the theme of a separate comedy could perhaps be interpreted as a consequence of his new religious development: in the fragment that he had earlier abandoned, he could illustrate one of the most dangerous tricks of the petty devil. Some passages clearly reveal Gogol's new style, as for example Ikharev's maxim, "If a person loses himself for just a moment—then you can do anything with him," or Shvokhnev's observations on the narrowminded stubbornness of old people, who are firmly convinced that the bad luck that they had in some particular situation must befall everyone in the future in the same way. The "position" philosophy also crops up: the merchant thinks only of how he could get his daughter married to a general or how he could obtain a higher rank for his son, and this is what enables the swindlers to take advantage of him.

Gogol's revisions become still more evident in the four fragments from *The Order of Vladimir*.

The first, "The Morning of a Busy Man" (on orders of the censors, the title was changed to this instead of "The Morning of a Government Official"), had already been published in 1836 in Pushkin's *Contemporary*, and the changes here are very slight. Ivan Petrovich Barsukov, the busy man, who speaks of the medal several times, is the very official who is to go mad on account of this decoration. He and another very busy colleague talk of nothing but card-playing and are well disposed toward one another when face to face and ready for mutual assistance, but in secret they seek to hurt each other as much as possible.

The next fragment, "The Lawsuit," shows a friendly colleague in the process of setting a trap for Ivan Petrovich Barsukov, whose name has been changed here to Pavel Petrovich Burdyukov. His brother wants to start a most peculiar legal action accusing him of forging a legacy, and the colleague is ready to come to his assistance.

The third fragment, "The Servants' Room," was entirely rewritten, except for the last dialogue. As usual with Gogol, the lackeys are lazy, stupid, good-for-nothings, but the steward is a positive figure who sees the evil of the world—as does Gogol—in men's dissatisfaction with their positions:

> Proper behavior consists precisely in this: that every man must know his duties. If he is a servant—then he is a servant; if he is a nobleman—then he is a nobleman; a bishop—then a bishop. Otherwise, of course, everyone could begin to . . . I would immediately say: no, I am not a steward, but a governor or some other member of the infantry. But at that everyone would say to me: no, nonsense; you are a steward and not a general, that's what! It is your duty to see to the house, the conduct of the servants—that's what!

It is instructive to observe how Gogol's otherwise so convincing stylistic devices become awkward and ineffective in this didactic tone, how his lively figures threaten to turn into eighteenth-century comedy *raisonneurs*.

The last, untitled fragment was originally to be called "Scenes from the Great World," and also shows traces of dangerous comic stereotypes: a young man wants to marry a charming girl from a poor family, while his stupid and egotistical mother, proud of her nobility, seeks to keep him from getting married by slandering his beloved. Sobachkin, a character similar to the classic Nozdrev in *Dead Souls*—gossip, schemer, and cunning swindler—is entrusted by her with the task of obtaining material to be used against the girl. He intends to compose a false love letter which, through trickery, is to come into the hands of the enamored youth. Here the fragment breaks off. Only the weak-willed lover is so portrayed as to be an interesting character—the mother and Sobachkin are exaggerated and recall too vividly models from second-rate comedies.

"Leaving the Theatre After the Performance of a New Comedy" was first outlined in May, 1836. In 1842 Gogol completely revised this scene. The first version represented Gogol's argument with critical opinions after the first performance of *The Inspector General*; in the revised version he presents his new religious ideas and gives the dialogue a moralizing tendency.

The scene is set in the theater lobby. The author of the comedy just performed is listening, unrecognized, to the conversations of the public leaving the theater, for it is very im-

Gogol's Theater Pieces

portant to him to hear of his mistakes from representatives of every class. In rapid succession, favorable and unfavorable reactions reach his ear. Gogol reports the negative criticisms of his play and refutes them—all in the form of overheard conversations.

Only the observations on the necessity of a new comedy genre without a love plot are new; otherwise they are all discussions of the desired effect of a comedy on the audience. The fact that no good character appears for one to look to meets with almost unanimous disapproval, but Gogol has someone reply that a good character would attract all the attention and all the sympathy to himself, and everyone would forget only too easily the evil which now abounds so terrifyingly and which shall continue to abound. There is no doubt expressed concerning the didactic function of the theater: the episode with the "very simply dressed man," who wants to fill his position and who rejects for idealistic reasons the favorable change of position offered him—this episode, even in its style, clearly reveals the preacher in Gogol. After the multitude of mostly very superficial opinions expressed by the passing public, the author himself steps forward. He regrets that no one has noticed the only positive character in the comedy—laughter. The following theory of "laughter which liberates" that emerges from the bright side of human nature and acts upon evil, recklessly exposing it but also conciliatory, agrees exactly with Gogol's new attitude, for he believes that an improvement is possible in a scoundrel who has been instructed in what is good. The laughing good man is not able to feel anger, even though he clearly sees the evil. Instead he will want to help the evil person; but the evil person will be afraid of being laughed at and therefore give up his evildoing. The scene closes with the vindication of the author: his handiwork, which has been treated with such contempt by the crowd, is inspired by divine providence. Gogol's desire to make his art useful for mankind led him to write this commentary to his most successful literary creation and to point out its benefits for the soul. It presents in rapid succession the author's thoughts—but it has no artistic value.

6 · Dead Souls

GOGOL BEGAN work on *Dead Souls* in the fall of 1835. Probably as early as the spring of that same year he had obtained the idea for the work from Pushkin, for on his trip to the Ukraine, he made entries in his notebook that indicate he was at work on the subject. According to Gogol, Pushkin had advised him earlier to write a longer novel, and in order to further his work, gave him a subject that he himself had intended to use. "Pushkin was of the opinion," Gogol wrote much later (in "Confession of the Author"), "that the subject of *Dead Souls* suited me so well because it gives complete freedom to travel all through Russia with the hero and to introduce a multitude of the most varied characters."

On October 7, 1835, Gogol informed Pushkin that he had begun work on *Dead Souls* and that "a very long novel" would result from it. The project took six years and was carried on almost entirely abroad: in 1836 in Switzerland and Paris, and then in Rome. As was his custom, Gogol improved and polished the manuscript endlessly. It did not reach print before he had copied it five times. After the difficulties with the censors had been overcome, the book came out on May 21, 1842 under the title *Chichikov's Adventures, or Dead Souls. A Poèma.*[1] The censor had insisted on the first part of the title so as to soften the "offensiveness" of the second. Gogol did not decide on the designation *poèma* until 1836; previously he had simply called

---

[1] In Russian, *poèma* means a verse tale or a prose epic.

Dead Souls

his book a novel. Perhaps in so doing he wanted to shift the emphasis to the solemn lyrical passages which contain the ideological elements of the book; but it is more likely that Gogol intended a romantic mixture of literary genres as a deliberate approximation of and contrast to Pushkin's novel in verse *Evgeny Onegin*.

No doubt, in the process of work the scope of Gogol's book grew. The more he wrote, the greater the perspectives that opened up. The adventure novel which he began as an original recasting and combining of the narrative styles of Fielding, Sterne, and Lesage was to end up in the style of Dante. Chichikov, the hero, who was originally planned as a negative character, as an average man with predominantly negative qualities, was eventually to reach the stature of a purified hero. Even in the first part of the novel, toward the end, a twofold attitude on the part of the author towards his hero is evident. Gogol's situation here is similar to that of Cervantes with his Don Quixote, whose influence on Gogol, by the way, should not be disregarded.

All Gogol's peculiarities and merits are present in the first part of *Dead Souls*. He does not introduce anything essentially new, but all his stylistic and compositional devices are handled here with perfect assurance and his mastery of narrative art speaks from every line (with the exception, however, of the last chapter).

As always, Gogol draws from various literary sources. Fielding's blend of the bourgeois novel with the adventure novel certainly did not fail to influence him. Sterne's interruptions of the narrative with lyricism and with comedy had already been appropriated by Gogol. From Lesage (or his Russian imitators Narezhny or Bulgarin), Gogol could have taken the method of composition by accumulation of separate scenes. At that time in Russia there was no lack of socially critical, moralizing novels (this vein is present in Gogol's works too, although very faintly). Gogol certainly knew and made use of Alexander Izmaylov's *Evgeny, or the Fatal Consequences of Bad Education and Society* (1799); of the anonymous work of a certain S. von F., *A Journey of Criticism, or Letters of a Traveller, Who Describes to His Friends Various Vices of Which He Himself*

Was for the Most Part an Eyewitness (1818), and finally of V. Narezhny's *Aristion or Re-education* (1822).

In spite of all these influences, however, Gogol basically remains absolutely original. The plot that Pushkin gave him dealt with a swindle that seemed *theoretically* possible within the system of serfdom in Russia at that time. The landowners were obliged to report the number of their serfs to the authorities every five years for purposes of taxation. If the serfs had died within these five years, the tax on them had to be paid until the new report.

If a swindler could induce the landowners to sell cheaply the dead serfs who were still considered alive after the report and on whom the tax still had to be paid, and if he then mortgaged them at the normal price, it would be possible for him to make a tremendous profit in a very short time.

This is the very trick that Chichikov attempts. He travels from one landowner to another and persuades them to sell him dead serfs, officially referred to as "souls," with the intention of mortgaging them later. But these facts are made entirely clear only at the end of the novel, so that Chichikov's traveling around and his strange request are just as astonishing to the reader as to the landowners. Also, Chichikov's earlier life (the action begins *in medias res*), his mentality and character are not revealed until the last, the eleventh chapter, so that the reader is left in the dark concerning the origin and intentions of the hero throughout the whole first part. The second part, which caused Gogol so much anguish, dispenses with this element of suspense from the very beginning and was therefore much harder to write. Here it is a question of developing a definite character (which was not easy because of the unsuccessful presentation in the last chapter of the first part), whereas in the first part surprises are appropriate. The ideas of Chichikov as stated in the second part do not ring true because we know him and do not believe him; in the first part we might be taken in by them, and only later do they turn out to be a literary device, of the kind common in connection with the sly heroes of adventure novels in the manner of Lesage or the cardboard heroes of moralizing novels.

The first part consists of eleven chapters. The first tells of

Dead Souls

Chichikov's arrival in the provincial town of NN and reports of his visits with the high-ranking persons of the town. In passing he mentions his interest in the landowners of the surrounding countryside and in the condition of their estates. Chapters two to six describe Chichikov's visits with various landowners, partly on purpose and partly by accident. In the second chapter (on the estate of the landowner Manilov), the first mention of purchasing dead souls is made, which is then repeated with Korobochka (Chapter 3), Nozdrev (Chapter 4), Sobakevich (Chapter 5), and Plyushkin (Chapter 6). The reaction is different each time, depending on the character of each individual. The seventh chapter describes the final settlement of the purchase before the authorities; the eighth is the culmination of Chichikov's good fortune and at the same time the beginning of the catastrophe: at the governor's ball, Chichikov has an unpleasant encounter with Nozdrev, and Korobochka arrives in town. In the ninth chapter, a splendid piece of work on Gogol's part, there is an account of the rumors about Chichikov, which are circulated chiefly by the ladies. The tenth chapter contains the story of Captain Kopeykin and the death of the public prosecutor, which Gogol manages to present as a tragic highlight; in it Chichikov finally learns from Nozdrev of the rumors about himself. The eleventh chapter describes Chichikov's departure, and, as a rather inorganic interpolation, his childhood and growing up, and ends with the famous solemn apostrophe to Russia, which is compared to Chichikov's onrushing troika.

The events take place in a period of about three weeks. There is no plot, in the true sense of the word, for there is no intrigue. Chichikov's "falling in love" with the governor's daughter has compositional significance, inasmuch as Chichikov's bourgeois desire for progeny is a driving force in his actions, and the rumors are based on the supposed love intrigue. But it is so lacking in concrete foundations and is such a parody that it is only one episode among many. One easily forgets the real basis of the plot, the swindle with the dead souls, a proof of the fact that it is the episodes and the details that produce the organic unity, not the composition as a whole. Chichikov, the hero, stands complete before us, and nothing of the changes within him which are to be described in the following parts is evident in the first part. But again, the details are strung together so masterfully and recounted with such precision of language, they branch out so strangely and in such a bizarre manner and yet culminate in such surprisingly consistent phonetic and semantic effects that one stands amazed before this miraculous literary achievement, in which every little part reflects the whole and every nuance is guided by the law that determined the total work of art.

A multitude of characters appears, many only on the extreme periphery; but each one is characterized so extraordinarily, so uniquely with a few brief strokes, and there is so little resemblance to any stereotype that one never forgets them and proceeds from one surprise to the next, which—again something strange and inexplicable—never cease to surprise, even on repeated readings of the work. This is Gogol's secret, and the subtlest stylistic analyses have not yet been able to explain how he achieves this effect. Nowhere is it more evident than here that poetic invention can be more perfect, more valid than reality. All-decisive here is the manner of presentation.

Gogol tells his tale almost entirely in a humorously ironic manner. Absurdity and hyperbole are probably his most frequently used stylistic devices, and he employs them in a manner all his own. But not only that. He combines the most common words in such a way that they suddenly take on a new luster and sound more vivid than they usually do; he changes them in an unusual manner by means of little grammatical shifts. It is utterly impossible to give any idea of this in a translation. The Russian language with its sharp differentiation between perfective and imperfective verb forms, which are derived from one another by means of prefixes or changes in the suffix or infix; with its ability to alter adjectives by means of expressive suffixes (not to mention the many diminutives and forms expressing affection); with its manifold irregular case forms; and finally with its abundance of expressions that carry along a second meaning which can be comprehended only intuitively (hence the numerous faulty translations from the Russian)—all this offers an extremely fertile field for this kind of style.

In the midst of this furiously proliferating flow of words Gogol places the "lyric-pathetic" passages. These are partly

Dead Souls

personal recollections (of youth in the sixth chapter), partly reflections on human life in general, and on Russia and its destiny in particular. One should not overestimate the importance of the statements contained in these interpolations as Gogol scholars have often done in the past. They are employed primarily for the sake of their stylistic effect as a contrast to the narrator's own voice. It is evident that Gogol's main concern is not to use style to emphasize the important elements, since at times the most significant things are tossed off in passing as ironic asides, while on the other hand, magnificently constructed, gradually intensified sentences sometimes lead in the end to the statement of something meaningless. The combination of gravity of statement and pathos of style therefore means little in regard to the ideological weight of what is stated. Nor was Gogol striving to give a faithful description of Russian life. He himself once said that he had "never endeavored to be an echo of everything or to reflect reality just as it surrounds us." With Gogol, everything seems to resemble reality, but, on closer viewing an imperceptible intensification, skillfully concealed, transforms everything into unreality. "If someone should advise his students to learn writing from me, he would be acting imprudently; he would be forcing them to create caricatures," wrote Gogol himself, but people did not listen to him, and abroad, for example, it is believed that in *Dead Souls* there is to be found a faithful reflection of conditions in Russia. It is interesting to note that in 1854 in England an anonymous book was published under the title *Homelife in Russia by a Russian Noble*, which is an almost literal translation of *Dead Souls*. All realism was alien to Gogol. In ever-increasing measure, he concerned himself with something far more essential.

The background against which *Dead Souls* is set is the awareness that the world is somehow in a bad state, that it has taken the wrong path, that it is somehow cancerous and has irretrievably fallen prey to the devil. Chichikov is possessed with the desire for gain in order to secure for himself a commonplace existence of hopeless mediocrity. Completely captivated by earthly things, without even a thought of God or the Beyond (in the first part there is not a word about religion, even though at least in its external forms it must have played a role in a provincial town), he directs all his efforts toward a good income, a wife, and children in order to be able to vegetate in his well-being without a desire in the world. It would take too long for him to acquire this wealth by honest means. In his father (strangely enough, there is no mention of the mother), he had only an example of greedy dishonesty. "An example is stronger than rules," and from the very beginning the little boy thinks only of getting rich. His mind, as far as doing business is concerned, is brilliantly trained and of astonishing ingenuity, but otherwise he is in every respect an absolute mediocrity. Even the description of Chichikov's appearance is symbolic: "In the carriage sat a gentleman, not especially handsome, but not of ugly appearance either; not too fat and not too thin; you couldn't describe him as old, but he still wasn't what you might call very young either." Plump, friendly, insignificant, a rubber ball with a harmless inclination toward swindling—thus this hero of mediocrity stands before us. But the average is dangerous: it is the dynamic force that sets the world in motion if everything in the world is cut to the pattern of such hopeless mediocrity; and in this respect it appears as a confederate of the devil, as a retarding force that holds men back from what is real. The intellectual and spiritual limitations of human life are Gogol's theme.

They are so extreme that only one interesting side can reveal itself in each representative of the human species. There is no depth of soul. Representations of psychic experiences, psychological analyses are superfluous. It is not worth while to conduct diving experiments in a puddle. The incalculable in Man is charged to the account of his more or less great stupidity, but by no means to the labyrinthine mysteries of his soul, before which one must bow in reverence. The labyrinth consists of adjacent characters, each of which has his little peculiarity, his little quirk, which holds him fast in his mediocrity.

In this flat expanse it is extremely interesting to observe the numerous possibilities for variations on stupidity and on narrowness and their effects. But we should not promise ourselves any profound insights from such observations except just this one: the world is in a bad way.

Gogol sees no hope for improvement (where would it

come from?); he contents himself with the cold analysis of an ironical observer who sees no cause for either love or sympathy. Without being stated explicitly, it appears to be Gogol's opinion that there is no reason to be sorry for mankind; deep down, men really know what is good and yet do not do it. Only in the second part and in the *Selected Passages* is the task of the writer outlined: to point out to men what is good; the belief is expressed that after they have seen and have recognized the good, they will also act accordingly.

For the description of this flat expanse, Gogol has found the only possible tone corresponding to the irrelevance and monotony of the subject and one that permits the most carefree ramifications and describes the ridiculous twitchings of his puppets with cool irony.

The first chapter is devoted entirely to the representation of the mediocre. Everything is "as always," nothing is striking, like the hero himself.

The inn at which he stops is "like all inns"—but with all this ordinariness Gogol manages to include some features that make the universal also individual. For example, the spiced-tea salesman with his red face is said to resemble his samovar, so that from a distance one might think that two samovars were standing in the window if the one samovar did not have a pitch-black beard. The dining room is also "as always," however, a picture hangs on the wall "in which is portrayed a nymph with breasts so enormous that the reader has presumably never seen the like." This is followed by a satirical reflection on "Caprices of Nature" in pictures which are imported into Russia by art lovers. Gogol likes to introduce such little digs with a "by the way," which produces a still more comical and striking effect. He also does this in the account of the newspaper article on "The Municipal Garden," in which the townsmen's "hearts are overflowing with tears."

The town dignitaries visited by Chichikov are individual types in spite of their insignificant mediocrity: the soft-hearted governor who "even" embroiders on tulle, the public prosecutor with the blinking left eye, the well-read little postmaster, *et al.* Gogol's great skill lies in the fact that he knows how to set up lights in this sea of gray mediocrity, lights which make this gray sea even more evident and cause its infinitely monotonous wastes to stand out even more clearly. The action proceeds with assurance through a forest of digressions, which are not digressions at all. The mystery about Chichikov and about his interest in the circumstances of the townspeople and especially of the landowners comes up again and again; the "somewhat stiff" manner in which the hero speaks of himself is not explained by the author. One gets the impression of mediocre respectability to which, however, something strange and doubtful clings, although the hero can speak of virtue "even with tears in his eyes," just as he does, however, of the production of brandy, of playing billiards, etc. Gogol places virtue in the midst of this enumeration of absolutely unrelated and mutually incongruous things. From the abundance of little ironic side thrusts (presented in an objectively descriptive tone, they all are supposed to point out the failings of the world), the pseudoserious discussion proceeds to the successes of fat men in this world and to the protracted comparison of the gentlemen in frock coats at the ball with flies on a hot summer day. These lengthy comparisons cause the essentials to be almost completely forgotten due to the overly detailed description of the subject drawn on for comparison. They stand like islands, like interludes in Gogol's branched-out narrative, with all its diffusion of details. They turn up when least expected, and by means of their complete departure from the theme, they produce a skillful retardation in the flow of the narrative. Gogol's compositional technique is determined to a considerable extent by this use of comparisons in which he introduces into the action some remote object which is then discussed with the same precision. The conclusion of the chapter is formed by the comic enumeration of the favorable opinions about Chichikov and the delightfully abrupt little genre picture in Sobakevich's bedroom.

The suggestion that these favorable opinions would not remain that way for long again arouses interest and suspense in the reader.

The second chapter is devoted to the visit with Manilov. First of all, after an ironic apology, Selifan, the coachman, and Petrushka, Chichikov's lackey, are characterized. The author is allegedly distressed about having to take up the reader's time with people of a low class. He even has doubts because of the not very high official rank of his hero (probably an imitation of Pushkin). Both Selifan and Petrushka are stupid like all the servants in Gogol's works, nor does Petrushka's "peculiar odor" help to make him very likable. On their departure, "the passing priest tipped his hat," and "several street urchins in dirty shirts held out their hands with the words: 'Sir, give alms to a poor little orphan!'" As they passed through the villages, a few peasants were gaping "as usual," sitting in their sheepskin jackets on benches in front of the gates. From the upper windows of the peasant houses, women with fat faces were looking out, from the lower ones pigs were peeping out with their unseeing snouts. Gogol's coldness is expressed in such sentences: the poor, the children, and the peasants are sly or stupid cheats; there is no trace of social sympathy; the serfs are men existing on a lower level. Gray is the landscape that Chichikov passes through ("hummocks, fir groves, low, sparse undergrowth of young pines, charred trunks of old ones, wild heather, and similar nonsense"), gray and meaningless the weather: "The day was neither clear nor cloudy, but of some sort of light gray color, such as is only found on old uniforms of garrison soldiers, this, on the whole, peaceful army which on Sundays is not entirely sober." (A typical Gogol sentence!) This completely meaningless quality also colors Manilov. "It is much easier," writes Gogol, "to describe characters of powerful dimensions: Then one needs only to throw the colors onto the canvas with vigorous strokes: Black blazing eyes, overhanging eyebrows, the forehead cut through by a furrow, a black or fire-red cape tossed over the shoulders and the portrait is finished; but all these gentlemen, of whom there are so many in the world, who in appearance resemble each other very much, and yet at the same time, when you look more closely, you catch sight of many very elusive peculiarities—portraits of these gentlemen are so dreadfully hard to make." But Gogol is a past master of precisely this sort of portrait.

Manilov is a man who lacks even a slight quirk, such as almost everyone has. The "quirk" theory is here fully developed by Gogol. Manilov's environment (the chairs in his dining room, some splendidly upholstered, others still in a rough condition; his exquisite candlesticks, beside which stands one old zinc invalid) describes him.

Manilov is neither this nor that. Amid amiable, mawkish reveries, he leads a "sky-sooting," senseless existence (the neatly arranged little piles of tobacco ashes attest to this), of no use for anything, a parasite who is individualized by means of his mawkishly refined social forms. He and his wife, a woman quite suitable for him, are a pair of turtle doves who find everyone and everything very nice. Their two sons, Themistoklus (a "partially Greek name," as Gogol says) and Alkid, are described very believably, but again very coldly, as real children. Chichikov's conversation with Manilov exhausts itself in fulsome expressions of politeness (the "holiday of the heart" is perhaps the culmination of their mutual protestations of affection), until Chichikov finally turns the conversation to dead souls. Here Manilov's simplemindedness is revealed. He feels distinctly that something is out of order in his guest's proposal, but he simply cannot find the words to express his doubts: "But allow me to put this to you: Won't this undertaking, or to express the idea more broadly, so to speak, this negotiation,—well, would not this negotiation run counter to the civil regulations and the future prospects of Russia?" The inability to express oneself, as a symbol of intellectual poverty, frequently ends in a gesture in Gogol's writings: a movement of the head or of the hand that is supposed to express a meaning for which words are lacking. Chichikov, on the other hand, has a supply of clichés at his disposal which he makes use of according to the sort of person he is conversing with. (The comparison of his life to a bark in the midst of ferocious waves, and the following inimitable effusion are a good example of this.) The embarrassment in connection with the initial request for the purchase of the souls is well worked out. Manilov asks Chichikov why he needs the dead on his estate:

> The question, it seemed, caused his guest some difficulties; on his face appeared some sort of strained expression, from which he actually turned red—a straining to express something not easily amenable to putting into words. And as a matter of fact, he finally did get to hear such strange and extraordinary things as human ears had never heard before.

Manilov completely lost his composure. He felt that he had to do something, ask a question, but the devil knows *what* question. He finally ended up blowing the smoke out again, however no longer through his mouth, but through the nostrils of his nose [*sic*].

Manilov's reveries after his guest's departure provide in their irrationality the key, as it were, to Gogol's technique and to his manner of seeing life. Superficial nonsense is the essence of the average man. There are no depths, even though the author is capable of observing the finest psychological nuances. Chichikov promises little Alkid that he will bring him back a drum: "Then he kissed him on the head and turned to Manilov and his wife with the short laugh with which one usually turns to parents in order to indicate to them the innocence of their children's desires."

Chichikov leaves his friendly host with the intention of traveling to Sobakevich.

The third chapter begins with the monologue which the drunken Selifan delivers to his horses, while, content with the success of his visit—Manilov has turned the dead souls over to him for nothing—Chichikov engages in pleasant calculations. Selifan loses his way and finally tips his master out of the carriage into a trackless field in the pouring rain. Chichikov's indignation and Selifan's comical readiness to get thrashed, which disarms his master, is interrupted by the barking of dogs: "It seemed as if fate itself had decided to take pity on him." Chichikov reaches Korobochka's manor. The comparison of the barking of the dogs to a choir recital is again set up in such a way that the detailed description of the bass in the choir, with his unshaven chin, almost causes one to forget what is really being compared. The room that the guest enters leaves no doubt about the intellectual state of the mistress of the house: old striped wallpaper, "pictures with some sort of birds, between the windows small, ancient mirrors with dark frames in the form of curled-up leaves, and each mirror had either a letter, or a well thumbed pack of cards, or a stocking tucked away behind it; a wall clock with flowers painted on its face . . ." Korobochka's external appearance is now no longer described at all; it is only mentioned that she is one of those motherly creatures who always complain about losses and poor crops, but who hoard money in a stocking at the same time. These unused riches lie in the chest of drawers, although it appears as if there is nothing in it

> but linen and sleeping jackets and balls of thread and a cloak with seams ripped apart, which is to be transformed into a dress if the old one should somehow get scorched during the baking of cookies and all sorts of fritters, or if it should get worn spots by itself. But the dress will not burn and it will not get worn spots by itself; the good old woman is thrifty, and the cloak is fated to lie for a long time yet in its ripped state so as to be passed on, according to a will, along with all sorts of other rubbish to the niece of a female second cousin.

Inversions in the original Russian of this passage bring a note of pathos into the description of the most everyday things. Gogol's blend of two levels of style, through which he attains his effects, is especially evident here. The subsequent incident with the striking clock is a good example of Gogol's apparent gradations which end in inanities: the mysterious noise, the guest's terror, the room filled with snakes, and finally a sound as if someone were beating a cracked pot with a stick.

The famous conversation that Chichikov carries on with Korobochka next morning derives its effect from the simple-minded lady-landowner's answering all of Chichikov's arguments for the sale of the dead souls with the same objection—"but they are dead." When the purchase is accomplished after a great deal of effort, and when Korobochka is apparently convinced that she has not sold the unusual wares too cheaply, Gogol inserts another delightful eating scene in which the exhausted Chichikov develops an appetite that parodies Homer. Just as he is about to depart, Korobochka again becomes completely absorbed in an account of the details of her household; it seems as if Gogol wants to make us laugh at the triviality of her cares; but suddenly he breaks off:

> But why busy ourselves for such a long time with Korobochka? . . . in an instant the gay turns into the sad, and if you stand before it too long, heaven only knows what sort of thoughts will come into your mind.

> But why then amid unthinking, gay, carefree minutes, does another wondrous stream suddenly of its own accord break

upon us: The laughter has not yet entirely faded from your face, and already you have become a different person in the midst of the very same people, and your face now shines with a different light.

Whether in the highest spheres of society, or in the most extreme solitude, everywhere the same petty stupidity. A restrained tone of sentimentality lies over the last scene: the little girl who is showing the way and is happy to have sat up on the driver's box—we can see her clearly before our eyes, even though nothing about her was described except her mud-plastered feet.

The fourth chapter begins with a discourse on the Russian appetite and a description of the inn where Chichikov is stopping: again details that are simultaneously general and individualized—thus the fork with the two prongs, the knife with the yellowed handle, and the salt cellar which cannot possibly be set upright on the table. Nozdrev, who arrives by chance with his brother-in-law, is one of Gogol's favorite types: Khlestakov and Kochkarev, Pirogov and Kovalev reach their culmination here; a totally irresponsible parasite who lives exclusively on the inspiration of the moment and is utterly devoid of inhibitions or the slightest trace of an inner life. Everything, every notion, every chance thought, every momentary feeling is turned outward, let out in a torrent of words that flows on uncontrollably, without any logic. "Mizhuev, just look," he says to his brother-in-law. "Fate has brought us together: What is he to me or I to him? He has come from God knows where, I live around here too. . . . And how many carriages there were and all that *en gros*"—etc. The chapter consists almost entirely of Nozdrev's talk, senselessly splashing forward, extravagantly exaggerating everything, and possessing perhaps only one pole: winnings from card playing—but he only needs this money in order to be able to play again. He is the complete opposite of Chichikov, who wants to acquire and accumulate; thus the effects of Nozdrev's constant assertions that he knows Chichikov "as his own" are that much more comical. He imputes his own mentality to Chichikov as well as to everyone else with a certainty and a vigor that are irresistible. Gogol extracts the essence of Nozdrevianism: irresponsibility in speaking is also irresponsibility in acting. Led by a sudden intuition, with no sense or purpose, such a man is capable of doing the greatest harm, of slandering his neighbors, of deceiving, of lying. But his lack of purpose and his impulsiveness are too obvious: he practically radiates them. Thus a peculiar phenomenon results: people who just a short time before were tearing out his whiskers as punishment for his intriguing, associate with him again, and he with them, as if nothing had happened. Gogol illustrates the eminent vitality of this type by means of Nozdrev's whiskers, which through the astonishing "vegatative force" of his cheeks, always grow back again, even more beautiful than before. In brief, Nozdrev is the type of the stupid optimist who is always content in his ignorance: "He is everywhere among us and perhaps is only wearing a different coat now; but men are thoughtless and imperceptive, and a person in a different coat seems to them to be a different person."

Nozdrev persuades Chichikov to travel with him to his estate. The scene in which Nozdrev shows off his estate draws its humor from the host's exaggerations and lies, which are constantly branded as such by his brother-in-law, and from the abundance of technical expressions from horse and dog breeding which Nozdrev employs as a matter of course. Gogol individualizes the speech of every character with a mastery hardly to be excelled.

At lunch, Chichikov keeps emptying his glass into his plate, as Nozdrev, who drinks little himself, keeps refilling it with various kinds of bad wine. This is a somewhat hackneyed topos from the adventure novel, such as occasionally crop up in Gogol's writings, but of course so skillfully employed that they maintain their element of suspense, although basically they are out of place here: a good proof of the fact that in literature even a banal content can achieve an aesthetic effect through the right use of language.

The ensuing conversation about the sale of the dead souls is magnificent. Nozdrev's whole character is reflected in it; he is incapable of sticking to the point and offers the most impossible things to go along with the sale. Gogol's portrayal of the checker game the next morning is another choice item: both men's pretense of being inexperienced players, the sincere anger of the swindler Nozdrev over the fact that his attempted swindle has failed, and Chichikov's cowardly behavior. A hyperbolic comparison of Nozdrev to an impetuous lieutenant and Chichikov to a fortress is a good example of Gogol's concretization of metaphor:

> "Beat him up!" he yelled in the same sort of voice that some foolhardy lieutenant in a great assault bellows to his platoon, "Forward, lads!"—a lieutenant whose whimsical bravery has already become so well known that a special order is given to keep him in check during dangerous undertakings. But the lieutenant has already felt the tickle of martial fervor, everything is going around in his head; a vision of Suvorov hovers before his eyes; he strains forward toward a great deed. "Forward, lads!" he bellows, pushing forward, without thinking of the fact that he is hurting the carefully thought-out plan of the whole attack, that millions of rifle barrels are staring out of the embrasures of the fortress, the impregnable walls of which reach up into the clouds, that his powerless platoon will be blown up into the air like down, and that already the fatal bullet is whistling through the air which is about to silence his clamorous throat.

Effective as this description is, what coldness of feeling is expressed in it; or is it real indignation at the lieutenant's insubordination, which is about to ruin the wise plan of the general staff? One could easily project this onto a universal plane and relate it to the role of the self-confident person in it. The detail would then reflect the over-all conception of the work. The wisdom of the universal design in miniature is here symbolized by the decisive and proper behavior of the *deus ex machina* in the form of the police inspector who saves Chichikov from an extremely unpleasant situation.

The fifth chapter begins with the collision between Chichikov's carriage and that of the governor's daughter, as she is returning home from boarding school. This too is a cliché in the novel, similar to the disposal of the wine. Apparently Gogol is trying to introduce a love-intrigue, but the attempt never develops into anything; he is not able to construct a plot, and from the point of view of the entire work, the scene could be left out: it would suffice if Chichikov met the girl at the ball. But again the details are very funny—at the expense of the peasants, naturally, who are represented as a crowd of simple-minded dunces. Uncle Minyay and Uncle Mityay are downright caricatures. The assertion by social-minded literary scholars that

Gogol's criticism of the social order does not lie in the individual types, but in the fact that precisely in this faulty order such types were possible—these assertions are reduced to absurdity by Gogol's own exaggerations. A variety of stupidity common to the human species is ridiculed here; it is by no means an attack on serfdom. The description of the appearance of the governor's daughter would be a stereotype, were it not followed by the charming, prolonged comparison of her face with the fresh egg that the housekeeper holds against the sunlight.

In the course of the ups and downs of his narrative, right after the burlesque scene of the collision, Gogol introduces the melancholy generalization about the "same coach," that flies by everyone once in his life and lets him catch a glimpse of the beautiful, only to vanish forever.

As always, the surroundings of Sobakevich, whom Chichikov is now visiting, are in complete accordance with Sobakevich himself. Everything is like him—bearish or bearlike. He himself is roughly thrown together by Nature—by Nature, not created by God: here Nature is personified, something that would hardly be possible in the second part of the work.

The pictures on Sobakevich's walls represent Greek freedom-fighters, and the assumption is probably correct that they are hanging there primarily on account of their ringing names: Mavrokordato, Kolokotroni, Miauli, Konari, Bobelina. Among the Russian generals, it is Bagration whose sonorous name brings him to a position on Sobakevich's wall. In contrast to the garrulous reception at Manilov's house, silence prevails for minutes at a time at Sobakevich's, for his spouse, Feoduliya Ivanovna, who, on greeting Chichikov, makes a motion with her head "similar to actresses who are supposed to be representing queens" (Gogol likes to ridicule both real people and the theater in this way), has also appropriated the curt manner of her husband. While Manilov found everyone and everything enchanting, Sobakevich's opinions about the civic officials, in their apodictic, laconic unfriendliness, are quite disconcerting to Chichikov. During the subsequent, again Homeric, meal, which is commented upon by Sobakevich in detail and is sharply contrasted to the dishes served at the governor's house, there appears some sort of feminine creature of uncertain position and uncertain age, an example of Gogol's marginal characters, who are so well visualized and so well projected into universal validity. "There are persons that exist in the world, not as objects, but as foreign specks or spots on objects. They sit in the same place, always hold their head the same way, one is almost tempted to consider them pieces of furniture and to think that since birth not a word has come out of such a mouth, but sometimes one finds them in the maids' room or in the pantry, and then—oho!" In the course of the meal, Chichikov learns of the existence of the miser Plyushkin, on whose estate the people are said to be dying like flies, and who lives right in the vicinity; this, of course, makes him very excited.

After the meal, neither the host nor the guest is in a position to try the preserved fruits, which are very mysteriously described by Gogol as "neither pear, nor plum, nor any other sort of berry" (presumably on account of the beautiful sound effects of the intensifying *ni* and the alternation of bright and dark vowels in the Russian), and Chichikov resolutely begins to inform Sobakevich of the reason for his coming. This is followed by nine printed pages of bargaining about the price, as Sobakevich immediately shows that he is on top of the situation and evidently sees how things stand as soon as Chichikov opens his mouth. Outstanding is the devious manner with which Chichikov anxiously steers his way to his subject by the most roundabout route, while nothing is said of Sobakevich's behavior except always the stereotyped sentence: "Sobakevich kept on listening with his head cocked to one side." The enormous price that he demands while constantly acting as if it were a question of living beings and praising the capabilities of the corpses (a weird ambiguity) reveals him to be a rogue of the first order, who, behind the bearishness of his external appearance, conceals an unscrupulously clear mind. This clear mind is aimed only at the acquisition and maintenance of everything that surrounds it (in view of death, of which there is constant talk, a senseless undertaking); it is utterly earth-bound; Chichikov has here found a worthy match, and these hard stones rub against each other for a long time before the purchase is completed, and still Sobakevich succeeds in cheating the buyer out of some trifle.

Chichikov is burning with desire to visit Plyushkin, and quickly takes leave of the clever bear. On the way he asks a peasant how to get to Plyushkin's estate, and the peasant applies a very apt epithet to the miser that is not to be used in polite conversation. This provides a welcome opportunity for Gogol to contrast the long bargaining scene with a reflection on the Russian ability to invent apt nicknames. A patriotic hyperbolic interpolation in highly emotional, rhythmic prose contrasts the natural ingenuity of the Russian with the allegedly one-sided, nationally determined manner of the western peoples. For Gogol, patriotism is not seldom an artistic means of achieving a contrast. His real attitude in this respect disappointed the enthusiastic Slavophiles again and again.

The visit with Plyushkin in the sixth chapter is the culmination of Chichikov's purchasing visits. Gogol begins with a lyrical interlude. How happy he was in his youth when he passed through strange towns and villages, how he sought to fill out what he saw in his imagination, to guess the way of life of the strangers whom he saw from their behavior! Now everything is different. Age destroyed the happy emotions of youth without leaving a trace: "O my youth! O my fresh vigor!" is the final outcry. Old age is the theme of the chapter. At the end we are again urged to bring along all the good feelings from our youth, to lose none of them on the way:

> Take them with you when you leave your tender, youthful years to enter into stern, coarsening manhood, take them with you, the humane impulses, do not let them fall by the wayside, you will not retrieve them again! Ominous and dreadful is the old age that cometh upon you, and it gives nothing again and returns nothing once lost! The grave is more merciful than old age: On the grave will be inscribed: Here lies a man! But you will read nothing in the cold, unfeeling features of dehumanized old age!"

The picture of old age that Gogol paints in Plyushkin is a sinister one. Plyushkin's boundless greed is only an accompanying phenomenon of this corroding process of aging that has destroyed all good impulses as if they had never existed. Plyushkin's earlier normal life is described for us, his gradual sliding into the greedy piling up of senseless, worthless goods.

Dead Souls

What he is now is reflected in his surroundings, especially in his room, in the musty, dust-filled atmosphere of his existence filled with useless, rotting rubbish. As counterpart to this, Gogol introduces the luxuriant picture of the overgrown garden, the extravagant wastefulness of Nature in contrast with human stinginess. Extravagant also is the choice of words: complicated, unusual compounds (e.g., "trembling-leafed cupolas"), accumulations of sonorous names of trees, and a hyperbolic play with light and dark, with the glaring sunlight on the dark masses of leaves, all this conveys the impression of a tremendous abundance, of an unbounded productivity which stands in striking contrast with Plyushkin's sterile hoarding. Once again Gogol sums up the horror of the world in the image of the illuminated garden. In it no one

> is struck by something wild and threatening amid this forced illumination, when out of the thicket of trees a branch leaps out theatrically, lit up by the artificial light, robbed of its brilliant greenery; and high above, darker and more severe and thus twenty times more ominous, the night sky thereby appears, and far off shaking their leaves on high, fading deeper into the impenetrable darkness, the severe tops of the trees are indignant at this tawdry brilliance that lighted up their roots below.

The romantic conception of night here assumes a peculiar form. Because of Gogol the "realist," Gogol the romanticist is often all too easily forgotten.

These gloomy passages are scattered throughout the merry description of the miser, this "slit in humanity," and of his amusing negotiations with Chichikov. The latter is able to appear as a benefactor of the old man (who is completely possessed with the idea of accumulating more and more) and is thus able to make his best bargain. Undoubtedly, in the description of the miser there is a certain influence of Molière, but Gogol's miser is much more disturbing. The constant rumblings of Chaos in Man, which lies in wait to devour the human element in him, again and again becomes perceptible through all the comedy. Time and the process of aging kill any meaning of life on earth when Man clings to earthly things. How weird is the effect of the great comparison between the last ray of human feeling in Plyushkin's face and a drowning man!

Plyushkin's speech characterizes him both in the malicious way he speaks with people and about people—insistently repeating the same thing, constantly scattering terms of abuse because he suspects that everyone is a cheat—and in the tender way he speaks of *things*, the means to riches. This is an important nuance that is hardly discernible in translation.

Happy about the success of his undertaking, Chichikov returns to town.

The seventh chapter begins with a grandly constructed elegiac reflection on the fate of the writer whose characters are "everyday characters." At first, in ornate language, the fortunate author who takes for his subject the few rare exceptions is described. "All hasten after him applauding, and rush along after his festive triumphal chariot." But the "judgment of his contemporaries" (an anaphora solemnly repeated four times) does not recognize the author who describes little things, who tells "of the overwhelming slimy morass of minutiae that have ensnared our lives."

> Austere is his vocation, and bitterly will he feel his loneliness. And for a long time yet, I have been destined by a wondrous power to walk hand in hand with my strange heroes, to contemplate the whole of huge onrushing life, to contemplate it through my laughter perceptible to the world and through my tears invisible to it and unknown. And still far off is the time when the ominous storm of inspiration, like another wellspring, will rise up from the head veiled in horror and radiance and the majestic thunder of other words will be heard in the abashed trembling.

Here for the first time, Gogol clearly reveals his intention to write a purifying conclusion, to make from the merry tale a religious work with flashes of divine lightning.

The description, in a burlesque tone, of Chichikov's awakening (he leaps into the air wearing only a short undershirt, "Scottish fashion") is again followed by a lyrical interlude. As he reads the lists of names of the deceased that he received from the landowners, Chichikov engages in melancholy reflections on the Russian character in general, illustrated by the probable fates of the deceased. Only the fact that Chichikov's character is not yet clear to us enables such trains of thought to appear

Dead Souls

possible in him. The individual biographies of the deceased form a mosaic of genre pictures, which again draw their effect from the details, but which are very sentimental in tone.

As a contrast, a veritable orgy of sharp satire against the bureaucracy follows. The office in which Chichikov concludes his purchase is consistently called the temple of Themis; the officials are referred to as priests of the goddess who bring her sacrifices, some so zealously that their sleeves have burst through at the elbow. Again Gogol goes very far in concretizing the metaphor: he names parts of the body or articles of clothing instead of the person and executes this personification perfectly:

> Our heroes saw . . . bent heads, broad napes, frock coats, dress coats of a provincial cut, and even, simply some sort of light gray jacket which stood out quite sharply and, its head twisted to the side and lying almost right down on the paper, was nimbly and with full sweep writing down some sort of protocol . . .

(in most foreign editions one can be sure of finding the translation: "a gray jacket . . . whose owner" etc., by which the peculiarity of Gogol's style is completely lost—and it is like this in all analogous cases); that the noise of the quills was great "and sounded as if several wagons loaded with brushwood were driving through a forest piled with dry leaves a quarter of a meter deep" is an example of Gogol's use of hyperbole, which astonishes us again and again with its originality.

Chichikov is led to the president of the court (who is compared to Zeus and the sun, to the first because he is able to shorten and lengthen the work day at will) by an official, who thus becomes like Dante's Virgil. But the "new Virgil" feels so frightened on seeing the president that he immediately turns around, at which the threadbare back of his coat with a chicken feather clinging to it becomes visible. The conclusion of the purchase is described in this alternation of high and low; described just as comically and not interrupted by any digressions are the subsequent celebration with the chief of police, and the slightly alcoholic mood of the participants, at which Chichikov even recites a rhymed letter of Werther's to Charlotte. Slightly tipsy, Chichikov falls asleep back at his inn, and two unexpected flourishes conclude the chapter: Petrushka and Selifan's trip to a pub, which is related in a mysterious tone pretending ignorance; and, when everyone is asleep, there comes the story of the first lieutenant from Ryazan, who "obviously" is a great lover of boots "for he had already ordered four pairs and was just trying on the fifth. Several times he approached the bed with the intention of taking them off and lying down, but he did not accomplish it: the boots were really well sewn, and for a long time yet, he kept lifting his foot and looking at the deftly and wondrously turned heel." This first lieutenant does not turn up again, and yet how complete he stands before us; how successful generally is this lightly parodistic conclusion, which ridicules the romantic chapter endings with characters falling off to sleep!

Nowhere is the senselessness of this world portrayed with such apt artistic means as in the eighth chapter of *Dead Souls*. It begins with the conversations of townspeople about Chichikov's purchases. Most detailed discussions are carried on concerning a nonexistent object; detailed proposals are made for carrying out the resettlement of nonexistent peasants; the problem of how to act in case of a rebellion of these peasants is discussed. With objective clarity Gogol reports all the details, the whole verbal network, this busy blossoming of passions, all based on absolute nothing. Through his purchases Chichikov rises tremendously in the esteem of the town. Not that anyone would hope to draw some profit from his obvious wealth; no, the fact of wealth alone excites the respect of those around him —this is the way of the world. Stylistically, the description of the customs and people of the town which now follows is a masterpiece. The decisive factor is the revitalizing of hackneyed expressions; their triteness is emphasized by a preceding "as they say" or something similar: e.g., "In brief, he was, as they say, coddled"; "one would have to describe the qualities of their souls, as they say, in vivid colors"; "if anything like what people call 'this and that' should take place among them, it would take take place in secret!" In the contexts in which Gogol employs these customary expressions, they acquire a special significance, a life of their own—as if the stereotype of life itself were alive; a cosmic triteness is conjured up by the constant appearance of these clichés of everyday life.

Dead Souls

The society of the people of rank is also a sea of meaningless gray, even though the president of the court is able to recite the ballad "Ludmila" by Zhukovsky and the postmaster reads Young's "Night Thoughts" and Ekkartshausen, and in fact makes long extracts from them. By all this, the cultivation of the town is supposed to be proven. The gradation used here is rather curious: "The others were also more or less enlightened people: one read Karamzin, another *The Moscow News*, a third *even* read nothing at all." A rhetorical device is employed here in the reverse direction in order to illustrate nonsense. Gogol treats the world of women with malicious irony. Indeed, there is not even a hint of a positive trait to be found here. To his misfortune, the ladies are most interested in Chichikov. The letter which Chichikov receives from one of his female admirers is very funny, parodying as it does the whole romantic-sentimental epistolary style. As is always the case in Gogol's writings, the peak of good fortune and the catastrophe follow closely on one another. At the ball at the governor's house, there is again a whole fireworks display of ironic observations achieved by Gogol through the use of subtle stylistic devices. (In foreign editions, the latter are mostly obscured by the translators with great skill.) Here Chichikov meets the governor's daughter, the young girl who was in the carriage which collided with his.

> It cannot be said with certainty whether the feeling of love was really awakened in our hero; it is even doubtful whether gentlemen of this sort, i.e., those not exactly stout, but also not thin, are capable of love, but even taking all this into consideration, there was something so strange here, something of such a nature as even he could not explain to himself; it seemed to him, as he himself later confessed, that the whole ball with all its chatter and noise had for a few minutes moved far away; the violins and trumpets were shrilling somewhere on the other side of the mountains and everything was veiled in a mist, like a carelessly painted background in a picture. Out of this misty, roughly sketched-in background, only the features of the captivating blonde emerged clearly and distinctly . . .

Chichikov is intoxicated by the charm of her seductive youth and freshness. He attempts to entertain the girl and by this action draws upon both himself and her the anger of the ladies who are besieging him. But his conversational skill likewise fails. Gogol pretends not to understand why young lieutenants succeed so well in entertaining young ladies. Military men, presumably as representatives of the greatest human absurdity, always come off very badly in Gogol's works; the fact that they achieve success with the ladies, their worthy rivals in absurdity, is in itself only too understandable. While they say things that are not at all clever and yet succeed, all the attempts of a mature man come to naught. A knowing irony that is psychologically well founded pervades this section. Again typical of Gogol is the flourish that concludes these reflections: Chichikov has previously carried on similar conversations "in similar situations in various places, namely": and there now follows a long enumeration of the places and persons involved, in which one name is more bizarre than the next. These names, of course, have nothing to do with the development of the action and are only introduced for their carefully thought-out sound effects.

Next comes the encounter with Nozdrev, who loudly and clearly announces that Chichikov wanted to buy dead souls from him. Everyone listens, especially the irritated ladies. Very painfully, Chichikov plunges to earth from the peak of his good fortune. He leaves the ball deeply troubled and engages in highly unfavorable reflections on the sense of balls in general.

Again a flourish concludes the chapter. In a peculiarly mysterious tone, an event of great importance for the development of the plot is described—the arrival in town of Korobochka, who is still afraid that she might have sold the dead souls too cheaply. This event takes place at night; the squeaking of the ancient, ungreased carriage resounds throughout the whole town:

> The noise and squeaking of the iron clamps and rusted screws awakened the night watchman at the other end of town, who, with raised halberd, still half asleep, bellowed at the top of his voice "Who goes there?" but when he saw that no one was going there and that only a rattling noise was to be heard in the distance, he caught some sort of beastie on his collar, stepped over to a street light, and executed it on his nail, after which putting away his halberd he fell asleep again according to the regulations of his order of knighthood.

Here again is an example of a detailed episode employed by Gogol to attain comic effects. Very funny too is the personification of the gate to the archpriest's house which "with a great effort" swallows the watermelonlike carriage of Korobochka. The chapter ends with the promise to illustrate the consequences of this arrival in the next chapter by means of a conversation between two ladies.

The ninth chapter opens with this famous conversation. Its beginning already indicates the intellectual level of the participants in a most convincing manner: "One morning, even before the time assigned for calls in the town of N., out of the door of an orange-colored wooden house with a porch and blue columns, there fluttered a lady in an elegant checkered cloak . . . With unusual haste, the lady immediately fluttered up the let-down steps of a carriage standing near the entrance . . ." The twice-repeated "fluttered" and the blue columns excellently characterize both the light physical and the light intellectual weight of the lady. The mentality of the second lady is made no less clear in the description of the way her room is furnished that follows. Gogol's oft-repeated assertion that he was afraid to name names and indicate ranks because every chance possessor of a certain name or rank immediately felt offended here too causes him to describe the second lady only as the "lady agreeable in every respect" (as she is almost always referred to in the town of NN.), and the first one as the "simply agreeable lady": again a revitalizing of hackneyed clichés. The conversation itself shows how well Gogol has mastered the art of writing dialogue. In spite of all the irony, which is gently exaggerated in some passages, the tone of an average, excited woman's conversation is convincingly achieved. After the little digression on the subject of fashions that almost provokes a serious quarrel over a dress pattern, the "simply agreeable lady" begins her account of the news that she has brought. Chichikov's visit with Korobochka and his offer to buy are described as a veritable attack of brigands (he is even compared to the famous Rinaldo Rinaldini), in a headlong torrent of words, often interspersed with French expressions. Gogol seldom misses an opportunity to make fun of the efforts of the "cultured class" to "ennoble" the Russian language with fragments of French. Chichikov is said to have demanded at gunpoint that he be given the dead souls. The conclusion that the lady agreeable in every respect draws from this is more than astonishing: Chichikov, it turns out, wanted to abduct the governor's daughter and everything else is camouflage. Indeed, at first this logical *salto mortale* causes the merely agreeable lady to stop short, but in the next moment she is already convinced and has always thought so herself. The hatred of the older women toward the young girl because of her success with men is now expressed as both ladies attack the poor child with mutually contradictory accusations ("She is a statue, pale as death." "She is chalk, chalk, purest chalk." "She puts on rouge in a godless manner." "Rouge as thick as your finger and it even breaks off in pieces."). Their anger is then directed at Chichikov, and harmony is again almost disrupted when the assertion is made that "there are still some ladies to be found who were not at all indifferent toward him." But in spite of this, the news to be spread together is just too wonderful. The fact that the two ladies are so convinced of a mere conjecture should not appear strange to us, says Gogol. Even in the scholarly world it is customary to begin with a cautious hypothesis, which, in the course of its elaboration, grows into a positive assertion. A certain resentment against scholarship in connection with his professorship is evident in this somewhat abrupt insertion of Gogol's.

The two ladies manage to set the whole town in an uproar within half an hour. An extended comparison with the sleeping schoolboy into whose nostrils his comrades shoved a little bag of snuff is meant to illustrate the condition of the excited and perplexed townspeople.

> What sort of a tale is this, really; what sort of a tale are these dead souls? There is no logic at all in dead souls; how is one to buy dead souls anyway? Where is such a blockhead to be found? And how much money would he throw out for them? And to what purpose, for what business could one utilize these dead souls? And why has the governor's daughter gotten mixed up in this? If he really wanted to carry her off, why then buy up dead souls for that? But if he really wanted to buy dead souls, then why carry off the governor's daughter? Did he, perhaps, want to give them to her as a present? And really, what sort of nonsense have they spread around town? What kind of direction are things taking, that before you can even turn around, a tale is spread, and if only there were some

sense in it. . . . However, they did spread it, therefore there was some reason for it? What sort of reason is there in dead souls anyway? There isn't even a reason . . .

This is Gogol's masterpiece in describing the spreading of rumors and the distortion of facts. "The town, which had apparently been slumbering up till then, swirled up like a whirlwind." Weird and unknown figures appear: "Some Sysoy Pafnutyevich or other and a Macdonald Karlovich, both of whom no one had ever heard of before, turned up on the scene; suddenly, always sitting in the drawing rooms was some lanky, lanky person, one of whose arms had been shot through, of a stature so tall that no one had ever even seen anything like it."

A male faction and a female faction are formed; in the first, disorganization and uncertainty prevail, in the second, order and clarity, which are, of course, nonsensical. The mysterious and ominous aspect of these rumors spreads fear among the men. It turns out that each one has something to fear, each one has some sort of impropriety, if not something worse, on his conscience. Two horrible stories of manslaughter and murder, which had not been handled properly at all by the town officials, are related in an indefinite tone wavering between gravity and comedy. The officials are afraid that Chichikov is a government spy who is supposed to bring abuses to light (again the *Inspector General* motif). Two documents that the governor receives demanding that he watch out for a forger and a robber who might turn up in his province and the report that a new governor-general is going to put in an appearance to look over the situation, completely disconcert the town officials. Who is Chichikov? ". . . a person of the sort that must be arrested and imprisoned as unreliable, or, on the contrary, is he a person of the sort that can imprison and arrest all of *them* as unreliable?" Inquiries with the landowners who had had something to do with him and with the servants come to naught—only the character of each one is illuminated once again.

The tenth chapter begins with a conference of the town officials on the situation. They engage in conjectures as to Chichikov's identity and the postmaster tells the story of Captain Kopeykin, an armless and legless veteran of the Napoleonic

Wars, who energetically demanded his pension in St. Petersburg, was always put off by government officials, and finally became a robber. This story can be considered a virtuoso performance of personalized narrative speech (in Russian, *skaz*). Its value as social satire tends to be exaggerated. The whole is a baroque flourish which, as could be expected, leads once again to nothing and which has not the slightest value for the action as such. For, when at the conclusion of his tale, the postmaster is about to proclaim that Kopeykin and Chichikov are the same person, it is immediately objected that the captain was armless and legless—whereupon the postmaster only strikes his forehead and calls himself a veal chop. But other conjectures are no less absurd. Chichikov is even said to be Napoleon, and finally, the Antichrist. In the end they decide to ask Nozdrev, who is known to be a liar.

> Go ahead and try to figure man out! He does not believe in God, but he believes that when the bridge of his nose itches, he is sure to die; he does not notice the work of a poet that stands there as clear as day, permeated with the harmony and lofty wisdom of simplicity, but he throws himself straight into a work in which some audacious fellow has confused, twisted, distorted, and turned Nature inside out, and this will please him and make him shout: Here it is, here is the genuine knowledge of the mysteries of the heart . . .

More and more frequently such passages, reminiscent of the *Bildungsroman*, break through, always delivered in a solemn tone, interspersed with exclamations. Next comes a concretization of the proverb that a drowning man grasps at even a straw, achieved by use of significant detail. The drowning man, for example, does not think of the fact "that he weighs around 160 pounds, if not a full 200."

The bragging Nozdrev says such crazy things that even the frightened officials are not able to believe them, but the whole affair produces such an impression on the public prosecutor that he suddenly dies. The death of the little man is just as terrible as that of a great man: "He, who but a short time before was walking around, moving, playing whist, signing various papers and who was so often to be seen among the officials with his thick eyebrows and his blinking eye, now lay dead on the table,

Dead Souls

the left eye no longer blinked at all, but one eyebrow was still raised with a somehow quizzical expression. What the dead man was asking about, why he had died, and why he lived,— that only God knows."

Placed amid the crazy, comical whirl of rumors, this sad event serves as a transition to a great, highly emotional passage, from which it is clear that Gogol had decided to give his *poèma* a new, higher significance. Proceeding from a fictional objection from a reader that it is not possible to delude officials like that, there follows an apotheosis of error as the driving force in history, as the decisive factor in human life:

> What twisted, obscure, narrow, impassable paths, leading far from the main road, has humanity chosen in their endeavors to attain eternal truth, while right before them the straight road lay open, like the road that leads to the splendid mansion which is destined to be the emperor's palace. Broader and more splendid than all other roads it is, lit up by the sun and all night long illuminated by lights; but in the gloomy darkness, people hurried by it. And how many times already when understanding from heaven was about to guide them to it, here too they managed to recoil and go astray, managed in broad daylight to get into an impassable wilderness again, managed again to blow a blinding mist into each other's eyes, and dragging themselves after will-o'-the-wisps, they finally contrived to reach the abyss, only to ask one another in horror: Where the way out, where the path? The present generation sees this all very clearly; it is amazed at the misconceptions, it laughs at the lack of understanding of its forefathers, without perceiving that this chronicle is writ in heavenly fire, that every letter in it screams, that from every direction a piercing finger is pointed at it, at the present generation itself, but the present generation laughs and proudly and confidently begins a series of new errors, at which its descendants will also laugh afterwards.

What is this broad road, where is this splendid chamber? Gogol had seen them in a vision and introduces them into the description of the ridiculous, twisting paths and miserable huts as a magnificent contrast.

Chichikov, who is slightly ill, knows nothing of the rumors about himself. When after a few days he is recovered and sets out to visit his friends, he is either not received or his friends are so embarrassed and speak such stuff and nonsense that both finally feel ashamed. Disconcerted, he is sitting in his room at the inn when suddenly Nozdrev appears and informs him in a completely natural and approving manner that he is a forger, that he wanted to carry off the governor's daughter, that the public prosecutor has died of fright at this, and that a new governor-general is coming. Comically enough, the only thing he fails to mention is the matter of the dead souls. The deeply shaken Chichikov decides to leave the next day.

On leaving the town (Chapter 11), Chichikov meets the funeral procession of the public prosecutor. His reflections on the death of this man culminate in the assertion that despite all the usual encomiums addressed to the dead man, on closer inspection, his individuality consisted only in his thick eyebrows. The minor chord thus introduced is maintained throughout the last chapter. One elevated passage follows another. First comes the apostrophe to Russia with its desolate expanse (and as antithesis to this comes the immoderately exaggerated description of the southern lands), which nevertheless possesses a mysterious attraction and calls for a hero who is capable of mastering these great wastes; then, after a sudden interruption, the meeting with the courier, comes the lyrical elegiac passage on the benefits of traveling, with its glittering, spirited scenes of Nature, which recall the showpieces from *Evenings near Dikanka*. "And how many wonderful plans you have given birth to, and how many poetic dreams," says Gogol in addressing the journey, "how many splendid impressions were experienced while you lasted." The fact that Chichikov has fallen asleep gives the author an opportunity to tell the story of his life. He is not a "good man," whom the novelists have degraded into a "workhorse for their purposes." Gogol does not want a stereotype here either. Of course in the future a man of "godlike" qualities shall appear, or a "splendid Russian maiden, such as is found nowhere else in the world." At the moment, however, one should be content with an ordinary hero. The story of Chichikov's life which follows reveals as his most conspicuous quality, to which all other impulses are subordinated, the eagerness for gain. He wants to possess enough to be able to lead the carefree existence of a middle-class philistine. For him, any common, even low means of attaining this goal is acceptable. Then the ups and

Dead Souls

downs of his career are related. Through flattery and servility he manages to gain the favor of his teachers and superiors. His aspirations, however, are directed only toward making money, and his character, not at all bad by nature, is completely taken over by this obsession, this fixed idea. (A very passionate passage, which clearly shows that Gogol's pathos is largely determined by sound and structure, describes the joy and grief of a teacher at the help given him by his former students, in which, however, Chichikov does not want to take part: "The poor teacher covered his face with his hands when he heard of this action on the part of his former students: tears like those of a feeble infant gushed like rain from his expiring eyes.") With astonishing tenacity and energy, Chichikov pursues his goal. Setbacks only spur him on to new efforts, and in this vitality Gogol undoubtedly sees the possibility of regeneration; presumably Chichikov's ever-striving endeavors are to save him—a Faust on a lower level! After a debacle (an elaborately arranged smuggling venture of Chichikov's is discovered), he comes by chance upon the idea of the swindle with the dead souls, and not until this passage in the novel is his previous course of action explained.

> The reader has already seen how the first purchases were effected; how the matter will progress, what successes and failures the hero will encounter, how he will clear away and overcome more difficult obstacles; how colossal figures will appear; how the hidden levers of a novel planned on the grand scale will be operated; how its horizon will open up wide, and how it will assume a majestic, lyrical course—that we shall see later.

Again and again toward the end, there is reference to a continuation in a positive tone.

Gogol never tires of emphasizing the pernicious aspects of Chichikov's endeavors.

> Everything in Man transforms itself quickly; you can hardly turn around and already within in you a horrible worm has grown up that has imperiously drawn all your life juices to itself. And it has happened more than once that in a man born for the greatest heroic deed there developed not only a grand passion, but a petty little passion for something insignificant, forcing him to forget great and holy obligations

and to see something great and holy in insignificant baubles. As countless as the sands of the sea are the passions of Man, and no one of them is like another, and all of them, the base and the splendid, all are in the beginning subject to Man and only later do they turn into his terrible masters. Blessed is he who has chosen for himself the most splendid passion of all; his immeasurable bliss grows and increases tenfold with every hour and minute, and he enters deeper and deeper into the infinite paradise of his soul. But there are passions that are not chosen by Man. They were already born with him at the moment of his coming into the world, and he has not been given the strength to swerve away from them. They are guided by the highest designs from above and there is something in them, something eternally calling, something not stilled all through life. They are destined to complete the great earthly course: Regardless whether in a somber guise or flashing by as a radiant apparition causing the world to rejoice —they are equally called forth for a good that is unknown to Man. And perhaps in this very Chichikov, the passion that is drawing him on is not of his own choosing, and in his cold existence something is enclosed that will cast Man into the dust and onto his knees before the wisdom of heaven. And it is still a mystery why this figure has stepped before us in this *poèma* that is now seeing the light of day.

Here the stage is set for the purification of the hero. But it is still not stated what the "splendid passion" is. Noteworthy is the theory of predestination to a passion that is to lead to the good, which is never developed any further by Gogol.

The author rejects the possible reproach that he describes only "human poverty" by indicating that it is the writer's obligation to peer into the depths of the soul and point out what is wrong with it. The teaching role of the poet is emphasized more and more clearly.

Gogol answers the possible reproach of patriots that he disparages Russia with the parable of Kifa Mokyevich and his son Moky Kifovich (two very unusual and funny sounding names in Russian), which is intended to illustrate two types of Russians; the father, who is entangled in vain, abstract reflections and empty philosophizing, and the son, who wastes his tremendous energy in absurd crudities stand as symbols of the two generations that Gogol had witnessed. The philosophizing period of the 1820's and 1830's did not succeed in showing the

Dead Souls

newly powerful country the way to salvation. Senseless squandering of energy is the result. Must not the poet then warn and teach?

Everyone is a Chichikov in some corner of his soul; but no one has enough *Christian humility* to recognize this and to examine himself. Here, at the very end the decisive words are spoken.

The first part of the *poèma* concludes with the solemn comparison of Russia with an onward-rushing troika; but Gogol had by now decided to continue *Dead Souls* and to add to it two more long parts.

7 · "The Overcoat"

THE STORY "The Overcoat," which was printed for the first time in the third volume of the collected works (1842), combines all of Gogol's literary skills in the highest degree. In this case too, the work appears to have been planned long before it was finally written. Annenkov relates that in the early 1830's Gogol heard an anecdote among a group of friends about a minor government official who was a passionate hunter and who through great privations endured over a long period of time managed to save the money needed to buy a fine rifle. On this first duck-hunting trip, he placed the new rifle in the boat so awkwardly that without his noticing it was knocked into the water by the heavy reeds. This loss had such a shattering effect on him that he became severely ill and hovered on the verge of death. The unfortunate man did not recover until his office colleagues learned of his misfortune and took up a collection to buy a new rifle.

It is very likely that Gogol saw in this anecdote a promising subject for a story; and since in 1830 he himself wrote his mother that he did not have any money to buy himself a winter coat and that he went through the whole winter in his summer coat, it would be quite understandable that he should substitute his own overcoat for the rifle of the anecdote.

Evidently Gogol worked on the tale in the years 1839–1840, but did not complete it until 1841.

The simple little government clerk Akaky Akakiyevich

finds that he needs to buy himself a new winter coat, since his old one can no longer be repaired. By doing without things and by carefully saving his money, he succeeds in getting together the necessary amount; he is completely engrossed in his thoughts about the new overcoat, to which he looks forward like a child. Finally the coat is finished, and Akaky Akakiyevich's office colleagues invite him to a party to celebrate the occasion. On the way home that night he is fallen upon by thieves, and his new overcoat is stolen. In desperation he turns, on the advice of a colleague, to an "important official" with the request that he urge the police on to more intensive investigations. The "important official," only recently promoted to this position and fully aware of his power, throws him out because he imagines an intolerable familiarity in the utterly harmless manner in which the case is presented. The frightened Akaky Akakiyevich catches cold on the way home and dies a few days later. A strange epilogue follows: there are more and more cases of mysteriously stolen overcoats, allegedly the work of Akaky Akakiyevich's ghost. Even the "important official" has his overcoat pulled off, and this time, indeed without a doubt, by the dead Akaky Akakiyevich. This produces a profound impression upon the "important official," and even brings about his moral betterment. After this, peace returns and there are no more cases of stolen overcoats.

Gogol's "The Overcoat" is usually taken to be the beginning of the literature of "social sympathy" in Russia. "We all come from Gogol's 'Overcoat,' " became the motto of nineteenth-century Russian writers. Belinsky took "The Overcoat" as a source for the text for his social sermons about the part of humanity deprived of its rights; people saw in "The Overcoat" all the pathos of the injustice of class differences, and Gogol was represented as the champion of the "humiliated and insulted." It is understandable that present-day communist criticism enthusiastically proclaims this position, but it is less understandable that Western criticism mechanically repeats it.

Not only Gogol the humanitarian, but also Gogol the realist was supposedly at the height of his powers here. Realism in Russian literature—in fact, even its naturalism—allegedly has its beginning here. If one reads Gogol's tale with no preconceptions, one is amazed that such an opinion could have ever developed.

"Social sympathy?" But, after all, Gogol covers the poor Akaky Akakiyevich with scorn, according to the philosopher and the literary critic Vasily Rozanov, who was one of the first to attempt to revise the traditional view of Gogol. The hero's precarious situation is not in the least attributable to the "capitalistic structure of society," but to his own narrow intellectual horizon. Gogol explicitly remarks that a promotion had been planned, but Akaky Akakiyevich was capable only of copying, and when given a job that required a minimum of intellectual activity, he immediately broke down. In his narrow world, however, Akaky Akakiyevich is completely happy. His own beautiful calligraphy satisfied him entirely; it was his life. He would even take home official papers in order to fill up the rest of the afternoon with the same copying, and when there was no more official work to be done, he would simply copy out a paper for his own amusement. One can hardly say that Gogol was very skillful in choosing a hero if he wanted to champion the poor members of society who had been deprived of their rights. But nothing was further from his mind.

Since the 1830's social problems were in the air in all the literatures of the Western world. (Note George Sand and Victor Hugo in France.) The trend conquered the world and was even read into works where it was certainly not to be found. Social mobility and social developments in Russia furthered this attitude toward literature; in Soviet Russia it is officially proclaimed, even when they know better. In Gogol's tale, some highly emotional, humane passages seemed to call for this interpretation—it simply was not realized that they could have a function different from that of a sermon, even though closer examination leaves no doubt about it.

The same applies to Gogol's realism. There is constant reference to little details, as for example the hard toenail of Petrovich the tailor which resembles a turtle shell. But the fact is overlooked that this is almost the only bit of "concrete" description of this man that we have. Gogol is obviously making fun of the realistic school when he declares that one certainly should not speak any more of this tailor, "but since the custom has already been introduced that in a story the character of every person must be outlined with complete clarity, there is no helping it—we've got to have Petrovich too!" What follows then as "character" is only the statement that Petrovich got drunk every holiday and that he demanded lower prices when drunk than when sober—this, together with the above mentioned toenail, is just about the whole extent of the realistic description. The narrator is now obliged to describe the wife—he had inadvertently revealed the fact of her existence by a slip of the tongue. We are told that she did exist, that she wore bonnets, that she apparently could not boast of her beauty, and that she had trouble bringing the low prices of her husband up to a normal level—a strange sort of realism! It is always the same in Gogol: he knows how to arrange details in such a way that they awaken the *impression* of realism—he is not at all concerned with the exact reproduction of reality at which the realists aimed.

Gogol narrates "The Overcoat" in the chatty tone of a talkative eccentric. Now in objective, now in elevated, now in ironic, now in naive, now in jolly, now in mournful, now in cold-hearted, now in sentimental and emotional language, interrupted by anecdotes and digressions and studded with all the technical devices of his narrative art, he places before us a very strange mixture of styles. This mixture portrays the subject of his narrative with such palpable authenticity and such perfect certainty of effect that one might mistake it for our own familiar world, the world in which we live, except that we are learning to see the things in it for the first time and that those things which we have seen daily but have not comprehended are now raised, as it were, to a higher level of consciousness and gain a new and sharper reality. It is the secret of Gogol's art that he achieves this effect by such slight means.

It is the narrative style, therefore, that holds together these heterogenous elements. According to Annenkov, Gogol once said that for any novel or story to be successful it is quite sufficient if the author describes a room or street with which he is familiar. His skill in describing things in the tone of an individual whose personality is brought to life by his very manner of speaking, also giving unity to the story, is the inimitable aspect of Gogol's style.

Gogol's brilliant manner of reading aloud emphasized this absolutely personal element in his narative style. Prince Obolensky, who often had the opportunity to hear Gogol read, writes:

> Gogol read in a masterly manner: not only that every word stood out clearly, but by frequently changing the intonation of his speech, he caused it to sparkle in various colors and enabled the listeners to grasp the slightest nuances in meaning. I remember how he began in a gloomy, sepulchral voice: "Why always describe poverty and nothing but poverty. . . . And again we have come to the back woods, to an out-of-the-way spot." After these words, Gogol raised his head, shook his hair, and then continued in a loud and solemn voice: "But then, what sort of back woods, and what sort of an out-of-the-way spot!" With this he began a wonderful description of Tentetnikov's manor, which in Gogol's reading, sounded as if it were written in a certain rhythm . . . I was utterly astonished by the unusual harmony of the language. Here I saw how wonderfully Gogol made use of those local names of grasses and flowers which he collected so carefully. At times he obviously added some sonorous word—solely to attain a harmonious effect.

Gogol did not read like an actor. He characterized his figures when he imitated their voices, but always from the standpoint of the narrator: they did not live their own lives, but only in connection with him. Gogol did exactly the same with words: they would take on the new life that was breathed into them by the poet. He knew how to fill words with new meaning, new intonation so that within the context into which the author fitted them they sounded peculiarly effective. Gogol linked them together not so much according to the laws of logic as according to sound laws, sometimes barely perceptible assonances that produced in their context a garment of sound which was artistically convincing beyond any objective or logical significance. This skill of Gogol's is nowhere so evident as in "The Overcoat." Gogol plays with words: he lets them intertwine in the most diverse variations—from familiar puns to gentle reminiscences, from a torrent of lofty language to the chopped-up, unfinished sentences of a simpleton. Behind all this wonderful spectacle of sparkling verbal fireworks stands a brilliant comedian gifted with a knowing, superior irony, who smiles down from his high watchtower at the frailties of man— a warning smile, which recognizes at the same time the senselessness of warning.

"The Overcoat" is written in a tone of verbose familiarity. The characters hardly speak, but the chattering author is completely unconstrained. He tells his tale as if he did not know all the details—he apologizes, digresses, laughs, only to become tragic again immediately afterwards. A peculiar tension, a highly charged atmosphere is attained by these leaps.

The objective beginning: "In the bureau of . . ." is suddenly interrupted in an angry and irritated tone. The interruption is directed at people who immediately consider a whole class insulted when one representative of that class is attacked (since *The Inspector General* an ever-recurring invective of Gogol's), and before the story has even begun, the anecdote of the provincial police chief is woven in. The following description of the hero, Akaky Akakiyevich, is an untranslatable example of Gogol's play with assonances (changing the adjective suffixes so as to convey roughly the meaning of the English "somewhat"), which depict the subject merely through the sound sequence. The details concerning the family name of the hero, Bashmachkin, show Gogol's "art of the illogical": the name comes from "bashmak," slipper, although it is well known that the father, grandfather, and *even* the brother-in-law of Akaky Akakiyevich wore boots, "and they only had the soles changed about three times a year." This last addition gives the impression that it is not at all the connection between the name and its bearer that is being discussed, but the frequency of resolings. And yet in sound it fuses so perfectly with the beginning of the sentence that the lack of logic is not overly striking. A veritable orgy of strange sounds follows as supposed proof that it was not possible to give Akaky Akakiyevich any other name. The most curious, the most outlandish names from the Byzantine menology ring out, the most useless details are introduced: "His mother was still lying in bed facing the door, and at her right hand stood the godfather, a most excellent man, Ivan Ivanovich Yeroshkin, who served as a division chief in the senate, and the godmother, the wife of a police official from that district,

Arina Semenovna Belobryushkova, a woman of rare virtues." All this sounds as if it were important for the presentation of the proof, but naturally it is not that at all. These "trifles" are abruptly followed by the melodrama, the famous "humane" passage. The defenseless Akaky Akakiyevich is teased and tortured by his office colleagues:

> But to this Akaky Akakiyevich replied not a word, as if no one at all were standing before him. . . . Only when the joke became all too unbearable, when they jostled his arm and hindered him from doing his work did he utter: "Leave me alone; why do you pick on me." And there was something strange in his words and in the voice in which they were uttered.

A young man was so deeply moved by this that "some sort of supernatural power" pushed him away from his colleagues.

> And for a long time afterward, in the midst of the merriest moments, the little official with the bald spot on his head would appear to him with his piercing words: "Leave me alone; why do you pick on me," and other words rang within these piercing words: "I am your brother." And the poor young man shielded himself with his hand and he would often tremble later in his life when he saw how much inhumanity there is in Man, how much fierce coarseness in refined, cultivated worldliness and, O God, even in the man that the world considers noble and honest.

In the midst of this unrestrained flow of words, this solemnity stands as a stylistic source of tension that prepares the way for the fantastic conclusion. Here, as in similar constellations in *Dead Souls*, such elevated passages build up the energy-laden mechanism of the whole. The eminent literary critic Boris Eikhenbaum is correct when he says that the assertion about the soul of the author speaking here without a necessary direct connection with the artistic whole only shows the inability on the part of aesthetic scholarship to cope with the problem. No sentence in a work of art may be *only* a reflection of the author's personal feelings: everything is structure, a game played according to definite rules. The soul of the author must remain outside the bounds of his creation. To confuse a compositionally determined utterance with the contents of the poet's soul is inadmissible from the standpoint of aesthetics, and it shifts the value judgment to a level alien to aesthetics.

The crazier, the more preposterous the puns and fioriture of the chatter, the more solemn and stylized must sound the sentimental melodrama which interrupts this game. A simple, serious tone would not provide a contrast—the grotesque effect that Gogol is undoubtedly aiming at would be lost.

Right after the solemnity, the chatter begins anew; again Akaky Akakiyevich is made ridiculous (compare his manner of eating); a new attempt at solemn pathos follows

> Even at those hours when the gray sky of St. Petersburg becomes entirely extinguished and the whole tribe of civil servants is filled up and has finished dining, each as best he could, according to the salary he receives and his own whim, when everyone has already rested up after the scratching of pens at the office, the running around, their own unavoidable cares and those of others, and everything that a restless person voluntarily takes upon himself, even more than would be necessary . . .

which, however, after a suspenseful crescendo that takes up almost a full page, breaks off abruptly and ends up in trivia (". . . in short, even when everyone would be striving to amuse himself, Akaky Akakiyevich would not give himself up to any sort of diversion"). Here Gogol parodies, as it were, his earlier humanitarianism. There is no longer any doubt that Gogol intends a grotesque: in the artificial isolation of a limited world, figures and events lose their customary relations. Within the little world of Akaky Akakiyevich, the author can deal with reality any way he wants, can disguise it or shift it around according to his wishes. Gogol is not concerned with preaching sympathy for our humble brother, but with reversing the dimensions in a world separated from reality, with uniting what cannot be united. "There appeared to him in this copying some sort of *special*, varied, and pleasant world. Apparently nothing existed for him outside his copying." And in this closed-off world, a new overcoat is really a grand event: "He provided himself with spiritual sustenance by carrying around in his thoughts the eternal idea of the overcoat he was to acquire." Gogol even surrounds the overcoat with an erotic atmosphere: "As if he were not alone, but as if an agreeable life companion had declared herself ready to walk the path of life with him, and this life companion was none other than the very same overcoat, padded with thick cotton and with strong lining that would not wear out."

Dostoyevsky correctly discerned that there was no humanity or love to be found here, but only a grotesque play with words and values; in reply he wrote his *Poor Folk*, a work trembling with emotion, in which he substituted a real woman for the overcoat. But in art, both approaches have equal value, provided the motifs are woven together to form a valid whole.

The visits with the tailor, the waiting period, the first venture outside in the new overcoat, the visit with the office colleagues, the theft of the overcoat, the despair of Akaky Akakiyevich, his efforts with the police—all are splendidly recounted; Gogol places his accents with such certainty, presents the little genre pictures with such perfection, and such a clear and unbroken melody of language runs through and unites the work that one could quote any sentence as proof of Gogol's mastery. One has but to think of St. Petersburg in the evening, the erotic musings of Akaky Akakiyevich, his screams in the broad expanse of the square, the scene where his landlady is awakened in the night by his knocking. Gogol speaks of "the important official" with bitter sarcasm, but again, not for social reasons. The contrast between little Akaky Akakiyevich and the big, self-confident official has to stand out as sharply as possible in order to motivate the death of the poor hero. It is clear that Gogol is not out to stir people and that he is not writing tendentious literature, since "the important official" suffers pangs of conscience and asks for Akaky Akakiyevich, and after his death and reappearance even undergoes a moral awakening. His basically good heart is mentioned several times. After 1840 Gogol, now loyal to the government, always endeavors to praise government officials; and if he wants to criticize something, it is only the misuse of "position" or the ambitious striving to go beyond it.

The death of Akaky Akakiyevich is presented as a mixture of tragedy and comedy; as always in Gogol, the description of his feverish dreams is brilliant, as the unconscious becomes con-

"The Overcoat"

scious (compare his scolding of "his excellency"), and then the shift to the inheritance, which is carefully enumerated, though "the person narrating this story" is not interested in the people who are to receive the inheritance.

> And St. Petersburg was left without Akaky Akakiyevich, as if he had never existed there at all. There disappeared and vanished a being protected by no one, dear to no one, of interest to no one, a being, in fact, that had not even attracted the attention of a naturalist who would not fail to stick a common fly on a pin and examine it under a microscope: a being that had submissively endured the teasing of the whole office and that had gone to its grave without any special fuss; but before which, however, even though only right before the end of its life, a radiant guest had appeared, in the form of the overcoat, which animated for a moment his wretched life, and upon which being then misfortune crashed down bringing just as much torment as it does to emperors and rulers of the world . . .

This solemn sentence is followed by the coldly objective account of the manner in which the people at the ministry learned of his death, and then the unexpected "apotheosis of the grotesque," the fantastic conclusion—a sudden sliding into romanticism, which, however, is basically not at all more fantastic than what has gone before. There Gogol played with reality while placing it in the isolated area of the grotesque; here he plays with the fantastic while speaking of the most commonplace ideas and facts as if of fantastic things:

> The ghost suddenly looked around, and having stopped, asked: "What is it you're after?" And showed such a fist as one does not even find among the living. The policeman said: "Nothing!" and turned around on the spot. However, the ghost was of much greater stature and wore a tremendously large mustache and, turning its steps apparently toward the Obukhov Bridge, it disappeared completely in the darkness of the night.

If one wants to interpret "The Overcoat" from a religious point of view (and especially in this case it is possible from the standpoint of Gogol's own intentions and in view of the radical change in his religious attitudes), one could see in this tale the best illustration of Gogol's theory of the power of the devil, who makes use of "little passions" to divert men from their striving toward God, from the only necessary thing. God is the *centrum securitatis;* he alone should be in Man's mind. Worldly things, which settle down like immovable ideas in the aspirations of Man, lead him to destruction and damnation; whoever loses himself in the world and its enticements is lost. Akaky Akakiyevich's great passion for the little, insignificant thing—the overcoat—brings with it a gaping spiritual and ideational discrepancy, a precipitous falling from the heights into the depths, which Gogol manages to make clear both stylistically and compositionally. In his excellent essay on "The Overcoat," Dmitry Chizhevsky has investigated these connections. The extraordinarily frequent use of the word "even" (Russian *dazhe*) symbolizes the gap that exists between Akaky Akakiyevich's conception of the world and that of the reader. In the little world of Akaky Akakiyevich, the little is great, and through the constant repetition of this intensifying conjunction, which is not, however, always followed by the expected intensification and which in fact is apparently used at times without any logical reason (in the tailor's kitchen there is so much smoke that one cannot see "even" the cockroaches—one must mentally add: let alone Akaky Akakiyevich), the difference in size is also made completely clear by stylistic means. Chizhevsky interprets the smallest details without doing violence to them: Petrovich the tailor, the maker of the coat, as a symbol of the devil surrounded by the attributes of evil; his snuffbox, for example, with the picture of the general whose face is pushed-in and pasted-over with a little piece of paper, is, according to Chizhevsky, connected with the faceless devil of the folk legend —new evidence of the manner in which every detail in Gogol's work serves the general conception of the whole.

"The Overcoat" is the most mature, the most perfect among Gogol's shorter narrative works; nowhere else is his language so colorful, his composition so sure. The many and varied interpretations in the course of time have shown how rich the possibilities are of developing his store of ideas.

8. Gogol's Art after the Crisis

AFTER "THE OVERCOAT" (finished in 1841), Gogol's efforts in the smaller genre were less successful.

The fragment "Rome" was published in 1842 in the journal *The Muscovite*. It is a beginning of the novel of Italian life which Gogol started to write in 1839 and which was to bear the title *Annunciata*. The version of the beginning as we have it today is an 1841 revision of what had been written earlier; Gogol gave in unwillingly here to the urgings of his editor Pogodin.

On September 1, 1843 Gogol wrote to Shevyrev:

The idea of the novel was not so bad and consisted in showing the significance for living nations of a nation which has already died and died in beauty. Although naturally nothing can be deduced from the beginning it is evident that it is concerned with showing what sort of impression is produced by the developing whirlwind of new society.

It must be confessed that this is not so evident.

The exaggeratedly empty description of an improbably beautiful Italian girl Annunciata is followed by the inception of a love intrigue: "But who is he whose gaze even more irresistibly follows her footsteps? Who watches her words, movements, and the movements of thoughts in her face? A twenty-five-year-old youth, a Roman prince, offspring of a family that was once the glory, pride, and shame of the Middle Ages," etc. A digression follows which recounts the spiritual development of the prince and takes up almost the whole fragment. Although in the same letter to Shevyrev, Gogol asserts that the views of the prince are not his own (he does this under the influence of an absurd criticism of Belinsky's reproaching him with a lack of a sense of "reality"), one would certainly be correct in refusing to believe him. The stagnation of enslaved Italy, whose youth rebels against the Austrian oppressors in words alone, is contrasted with the pulsating life of Paris. A display of verbal fireworks paints the French capital, about which the young prince is just as enthusiastic as Gogol was when he first stayed there. But the first good impression fades on closer inspection. A yawning emptiness is concealed beneath the brilliant surface: "One strove, cost what it may, to outdo the other, be it even only for a minute." In other words—no one is content with the position which he has been assigned; everyone is obsessed with brilliance, with surface glitter. The French writers, "whose strange creations . . . shocked his young and fiery soul, those writers in whom everyone thought he heard still untouched strings and felt previously unseen turns of human passion," lost their charm for the prince: "The stories and novels endeavored to captivate the reader by means of strange, unheard-of passions and the ugliness of the exceptions in human nature." Gogol, who in the beginning was enthusiastic about the French *romans feuilletons*, went through the same development.

On his return to Italy, the prince sees it through Gogol's eyes. Rome, its ancient grandeur, its buildings, its easy-going people enrapture him. In the Italian churches, where one can really pray, he finds again the genuine belief which has been lost in those clever countries of Europe that he visited. The stone symphonies of architecture "harmonically subject to the well-considered idea," the "mighty works of the brush" develop his taste, cause him to hate the superficial fashion which seems to him to be the cause of that "indifferent coldness which surrounds our present age . . ." the early dullness of feelings "which have not yet had time to develop, indeed, to be born." It is the new Gogol who exclaims: "They have removed the images of the saints from the temple—and the temple is a temple no more: Bats and evil spirits dwell in it." Like Gogol, the prince recognizes in the history of nations the Great Finger "before which Man, becoming silent, casts himself in the dust,

Gogol's Art after the Crisis

—the Great Finger that ordains from above the events of the world." It becomes difficult to believe in the concrete existence of the Italian prince when we read that the splendid south exists for the purpose of tearing the inhabitant of the north, as if in a dream, away from his cold life and of making him, if only once in his life, into an excellent man, by means of its splendor. It is equally difficult to believe that this thought could actually be a source of consolation for an Italian prince. Here, as in his invectives against the Germans, he shares only too clearly Gogol's sentiments.

In this fragment Gogol did not stand above his work—it contains a great deal of his autobiography, his own thinking, and it belongs among his weak performances.

The only parts that are successful are a few descriptions of the Roman landscape, such as, for example, the color symphony of the fields:

> Then they appeared to be a boundless sea that radiated and swelled up through the dark balustrade of the terraces; the slopes and lines vanished in the light that embraced them. At first they still looked greenish, and here and there one caught sight of scattered tombs and arches; then they turned into patches of bright yellow in the iridescent shades of light, hardly revealing the old ruins, and finally they grew more and more purple as they also swallowed up the boundless dome itself and merged into a solid raspberry color, and only the golden strip of the sea sparkling in the distance separated them from the horizon, which was just as purple as they.

While the description of the Italian carnival does not have much of an Italian flavor about it, and rather recalls the amusements of the Ukrainian peasant boys from Dikanka, the fine picture of the inquisitive Italian women in the narrow Roman alley, which concludes the fragment, has a very authentic ring. Here Gogol is in his element again, and a merry genre picture is painted with a sure and steady brush. Peppe, the factotum with the incredibly big nose that hangs on his face like a hatchet and with the passion for playing the lottery, could perhaps have become a good Italian Gogolian type. The anecdotal digressions about him clearly reveal how Gogol's familiar style tries to break through again and again. But Gogol holds it back by force—he wants to become a serious writer who has ideas of his own to impart. In style and in ideas the fragment prepares the way for the second part of *Dead Souls*.

On the road away from the real Gogol, there also lies the complete revision to which Gogol subjected "The Portrait." The new version was published in 1842 in *The Contemporary*, and in the accompanying letter that he sent with the story to Pletnev, the new editor, Gogol writes: "I am sending you my story, 'The Portrait.' It was already printed in *Arabesques*, but that should not frighten you. Read it: you will see that only the embroidery frame of the original tale remains, that everything is newly embroidered on it. In Rome I completely revised it, or rather completely rewrote it—because of the remarks that were made about it in St. Petersburg." He is probably referring again to the remarks of Belinsky, who, for ideological reasons, was not capable of judging Gogol's tale as a work of art and who even denied that Gogol possessed a talent for describing the fantastic. Gogol, therefore, greatly toned down the fantastic element—to the detriment of the whole and without gaining the approval of Belinsky, who was still not satisfied with it and demanded the removal from the tale of the uncanny portrait itself.

Gogol narrowed the intellectual scope of his work considerably. Instead of the problem of the penetration of demonic forces into art, instead of the great apocalyptic vision of the world and its destruction, there only remained now the thesis that an artist who only works for the sake of money ruins his talent and produces a run-of-the-mill product instead of a genuine work of art. In connection with this, Gogol greatly reinforced the didactic element; his sarcasm in regard to "the great world" clearly bears the stamp of a sermon, which stands apart from the structure of the whole; again there is a galloping succession of hyperboles, but they only cover up an emptiness. The figure of the father which was so unified and successful in the first version is here an empty stereotype, and his teachings only repeat what Gogol himself intended to preach: the artist must have a pure soul in order to be able to create. Even the most ugly and trivial thing that passes through the purgatory of his soul thereby gains in his representation a splendor that stamps it as a real work of art. The artist must avoid all passions.

> Whoever conceals a talent in himself, his soul must be purer than that of all others. A man who stepped out of his house in bright festive raiment needs only to be splashed with some mud from a carriage wheel, and already the people stand around him and point to him with their fingers and speak of his uncleanliness, while the same people do not notice the multitude of stains on the other passers-by who wear everyday clothes. For one does not notice stains on everyday clothes.

In the first version, Gogol used religion only to clarify the sublime mission of art; he pointed constantly to the self-sufficiency of art, to its sovereign power in good and in evil. Now art is justified only in religion; it occupies a position subservient to religion. Only art filtered through a religious spirit is real and genuine. In the first part of the second version, Gogol demands only inner sympathy toward his subject on the part of the artist (these meditations of Chertkov's before the delirium are unrevised remnants from the first version); in the second part the prayer, too, is demanded. Gogol had finally switched from the art for art's sake theory to the art for religion's sake theory. The problem of Christian art was raised, which occupied him in the last decade of his life and which he finally despaired of solving.

The second version is far inferior to the first. The obeisance to the Church (it is a "clerical personage" who notices the presence of the devil in the picture of the father), to the monarchy (compare the repulsive flattery of Catherine II with the strange statement that poets flourish only in monarchies and not "during a period of ugly political phenomena and republican terrorisms, which up to now have unfortunately not given the world a single poet"), the patriotic eulogies of the one and only Russia—all these, together with the prevailing religious moralism, indicate a turning away from art. Only in one scene is the second version superior. This is Chertkov's brilliantly narrated delirium, in the course of which he twice thinks that he has been awakened, while in reality he is still dreaming. The atmosphere between dreaming and waking in the studio flooded with bright moonlight could not have been conjured up any better.

9 · Selected Passages from Correspondence with Friends

TO AN ever-increasing degree, Gogol felt that the second part of *Dead Souls* would hardly succeed in the manner he wished. He wanted to give shape to his insights into the meaning of life, but his artistic feeling told him that such a structure would lack inner truth. The search for a valid form for his ideas took too long; he wished to announce them to the world as quickly as possible; hence he turned to direct reporting, without any artistic garb. He chose the epistolary form, and by directly addressing the recipients, he imparted a lively tone to the presentation. Some of the letters really *had* been addressed to persons from among Gogol's circle of friends and were merely revised for publication, while some are fictitious letters, written solely for the book. Gogol had probably decided on the plan of proclaiming his ideas in this form as early as the beginning of 1845, but he only began work a year later, and continued it with great intensity. From July to September, 1846, he sent the individual letters to Pletnev, who was to supervise the printing, which was begun early in October. The censors forbade five letters (Nos. 19, 20, 21, 26, 28) and also struck out some passages from those that were approved. Gogol was beside himself:

> Only a third of my book was printed, in a mutilated and confused form, some sort of strange stump . . . and not a book. The most important letters which were to make up the most substantial part of the book were left out—letters that were intended to make people better acquainted with the evils

which occur within Russia through our own faults, and concerning the means to correct a great deal, letters by means of which I hoped to do the emperor and all my fellow countrymen an honorable service. [January 30, 1847 to A. Smirnova.]

His protests—he begs Pletnev to go to the Czar and ask him to intervene—were of no avail. Not until 1867 did the book appear in its complete and uncut form, in the edition of his collected works. It contains thirty-two letters and a preface.

In the preface Gogol says that he had been gravely ill and thought he was going to die. In his last testament he had asked his friends to publish some of his letters which in the opinion of their recipients "contain more that is necessary for Man than my works do." After his unexpected recovery, he writes, he himself picked out whatever "pertains to questions that occupy the public today" and added a few literary essays and the testament.

> My heart tells me that my book is necessary and that it can be useful. I believe this not because I have a high idea of myself or because I have confidence in my ability to be useful, but because up to now I have never felt within me such a strong desire to be useful. It is sufficient for our part to hold out one's hand with a desire to help; but it is not *we* who help, *God* helps, bestowing power on the powerless word.

There are above all two problems dealt with in the *Correspondence*: the Christian social structure and Christian art. They are closely related, for in the divinely ruled social structure demanded by Gogol, art can play only a very definite role—it submits to the hierarchy of a divine state as a servant of God, who inspires it; the artist is a priest who creates his works of art for the glory of God and preaches God's law in them. The testament, which opens the book, states: "I am a writer, and the duty of the writer is not only to provide a pleasant occupation for mind and taste; he will be held responsible if no benefit to the soul is disseminated by his works and if he leaves nothing for the edification of men."

The poet is called by God; he feels his calling within him, and it does not permit him to follow other, perhaps more lucrative professions. But this selection by God also involves obligations: "The poet must be just as blameless in the field of the word as everyone else in his own field" (IV). Gogol asserts that Pushkin also meant this when he said the words of the poet are his works, although it is quite evident that with this statement Pushkin had in mind aesthetic purity, certainly not ethical purity. After his spiritual transformation, Gogol generally showed a tendency toward reinterpretation of his idol in a religious direction, which at times assumes strange forms, as when he asserts that the addressee of Pushkin's poem "To N." was Emperor Nicholas I and invents an unlikely ancedote as proof, or when he quotes incorrectly Pushkin's famous imitation of Horace's "Exegi monumentum" (X).

Poetry is a power. He who knows how to handle it must be able to use it correctly, for it affects the heart, it is able to transform life. Gogol devotes a long letter (VII) to *The Odyssey* (in Zhukovsky's translation). The human grandeur of its characters, their magnificent and naive simplicity, and the healthy patriarchal customs that it reflects will not fail to make their impression on Russia. "Through the fragrant lips of poetry, something is wafted onto souls that no laws and no government could implant in them." The poet, who like the prophet is able to guess the fruit already in the seed, is chosen to interpret the present age. For the dramatic poet, the theater is a rostrum from which he has the power to speak a great deal of good; it is within his power to cause a thousandfold crowd of dissimilar individuals "to weep the same tears, to laugh the same laugh." His power is great, but it is not easy for him to bear this high gift: "The artist can only describe what he himself has felt," says Gogol in the letter on the painter Alexander Ivanov; he can only portray something about which he already had in his mind a perfect, finished, rounded-off idea.

Thus an artist cannot depict suffering unless he himself has suffered: the experience of suffering is an indispensable step towards artistic greatness. Like an echo, the artist must find in his soul a living response for everything that the world contains. Gogol names Pushkin as the poet par excellence: he possessed the rare gift of being able to transport himself mentally into another situation, even to foreign nations, and to feel in the same manner as they did. Everything that was human found an echo in him, in whatever garb it might appear. Long before Dostoyevsky, who based his famous Pushkin speech on this thesis, Gogol had pointed out Pushkin's universality.

It is, above all, suffering that forms Man; only through suffering does one become a true human being. How much, therefore, must the chosen man, the artist, suffer in order to be able to portray this most important factor in being Man.

But also the second requirement, that of a finished idea of what is to be depicted, demands much of the artist. Like a monk he must retire from the world before he sets about his work; even during his labors, he only lives for the work; nothing hurried (again and again, with a sidelong glance at himself and the urgings of his friends, Gogol attacks hastiness), nothing half-thought-out or half-felt may appear in his work. Only if God reveals to him the idea of that which he wants to represent will the representation bear the unique stamp of real art. How unjust people are who want to urge the artist on to faster work— they accuse him of laziness and do not see that he cannot create before God has granted him the power to see his work in its uniquely ideal form. Gogol defends the painter Ivanov against such attacks, but at the same time speaks for himself and defends himself against the friends who had demanded of him the second part of his *poèma*. The artist whose work, by God's decree, has become the mission of his soul can do nothing more: "His thoughts will be directed toward nothing else, however he may force and compel them. Thus a faithful wife who truly loves her husband will love no one else, will sell her caresses to no one for money, even if she could save herself and her husband from poverty by this means." This is Gogol's answer to suggestions that he write little stories for periodicals or have individual chapters of *Dead Souls* published for the sake of money. "I was not at all born to be epoch-making in the realm of literature. My task is simpler and lies closer at hand: my task is that of which every man, not I alone, must think. My task is the soul and the lasting and immutable *task* of life," writes Gogol in the letters concerning *Dead Souls*. The largest part of the surviving fragments of the second volume deals with the manner in which this life is to be set in order "lastingly and securely." The ordering of the soul, the "management of the soul," both of the individual and of society is prescribed by Gogol.

In the forefront stands the thesis that virtue can be taught. Man sins because he does not see his sins. "No, Man is not unfeeling, Man will become purified only if he is shown things as they are." Half of his sins he commits not out of depravity, but out of ignorance. He will embrace as his rescuer the person who will cause him to turn his gaze upon himself. The heart of the evil in the world is that everyone is dissatisfied with the position in which he is situated. "Position" here is to be understood both in a very general sense, as the place that a man fills as a personality, and also, in the narrow and concrete sense referring to the situation in Russia, as an official position within the hierarchy of government officials. It is a question of making it clear to Man that he was placed by God in the position in which he finds himself, that all positions are of equal value in God's eyes, whether they are high or low when measured by earthly standards. "Wonderful is the grace of God which has destined the same reward for everyone who honestly fulfills his obligations, whether he be the emperor or the very last beggar. There they will all become equal, for all will enter into the joy of their master and will continue as equals in God." The earthly problem of positions is solved in God—therefore, is there any sense in appearing discontented on earth? "It seems to everyone now that he could do a great deal of good in the position and post of another and that only in his own post is he unable to bring about this good. This is the cause of all evils. We must all consider now how we can do good in our own position."

The Russian state as such is in complete accordance with its destination; all posts therein are necessary and useful, for every problem is seen differently from every position. The occupants of these positions are responsible for the failure of the apparatus of the ideal state, which Gogol believes to be realized in Russia:

> It was not very long ago that I spoke with you about all the posts in our government. Considering each individual post within its lawful limits, we found that they are precisely what they should be, all of them as if created for us by heaven in

order to conform to all the demands of the customs of our state, and all became what they should not have become because everyone was trying to destroy the limits of his post or even to step completely beyond its limits as quickly as possible.

Allegedly following Pushkin, Gogol compares the state to an orchestra: every position is occupied by a definite instrument, and as long as every instrument endeavors to play its part as well as it can, the harmony is perfect; if an instrument tries to distinguish itself at the expense of the others, the balance is destroyed and dissonances result. Just as the conductor stands at the head of the orchestra, the monarch stands at the head of the state. Just as the conductor softens or increases the sound and indicates the rhythm and the tempo merely by a sign or a glance, so too does the emperor with the orchestra of the state. Without him, the law would be nothing but wood; only the ruler can breathe a human soul into it. Just as God assigns any other position, so too God assigns the monarch his position. He is the image of God on earth, the incarnation of God's love, which is to guide the state just as God's love guides the world. "The people will be made completely well only where the monarch comprehends his highest destiny—to be on earth the image of Him Who is Love itself." Gogol sees this requirement fulfilled in the Russian monarch. While in Europe it has not yet occurred to anyone to define the lofty significance of the monarch, in Russia the poets—not the legal scholars—have done this. Here is a task for the poets, and how brilliantly the poets of the eighteenth century solved it! Gavrila Derzhavin's significance, according to Gogol, lies particularly in the fact that he was able to sing the praises of three crowned monarchs. Love and good sense caused Russia's poets, who could see the divine calling of the czars in their own country, to sing their praise. Gogol cites the election of the house of Romanov to the throne of the czars as proof of their divine calling.

"In brief—everything is fulfilled and everywhere one feels the legislative wisdom both in the organization of the authorities themselves and in their relations with one another." But in this positive utopia of the existing order—as one could call Gogol's conception—the "devil of disorder" builds his nest, and causes men to lose sight of what is good. The devil begins with the human intellect. "Intellectual pride" is the vice from which evil originates, and never has this pride grown so tall as in the nineteenth century. "The devil has now entered the world without a mask. The spirit of pride has now ceased to appear in various forms and to frighten superstitious people: he has appeared in his own proper form." Man doubts everything, but he does not doubt his intellect, which is something sacred to him and in which he believes. Led astray by the intellect, mankind in this century has fallen in love with its own purity and beauty. But pride that is fed by the intellect is the beginning of ruin for the individual and for the nation—it is an unchristian vice, that which draws man farthest away from the imitation of Christ. "The intellect is not the highest faculty within us." It is subject to the passions, subservient to them; deluded by them, it often acts absurdly and stupidly. Gogol makes a distinction between the intellect and reason, which is above the passions. He probably means by this the "intelligence of the heart" which is attained through the cultivation of the inner man and of his moral capabilities. Nor is reason the highest level: it is wisdom, which is a gift of Christ's grace. It alone allows men to recognize that only humility can bring him to perfection. Only the Christian is always striding forward. He feels he is a pupil, always sees a wide scope for self-improvement, for new achievements lying before him. He knows that suffering is sent to him so that he might recognize his errors with humility and change his life. Suffering has a deep and sacred significance. All misfortune in the world purifies Man. Life was given to Man so that he might struggle with misfortune; in the example of Odysseus we have the symbol of our life before us.

> You need some sort of misfortune or shock. Pray to God that this shock will be granted to you, that some sort of unbearable annoyance in your employment will befall you, that some person will be found to insult you terribly and to cover you with shame before everyone so that you do not know where to hide yourself with shame, and that with one stroke he will tear apart all the most sensitive strings of your self-love. He will be your true brother and redeemer. Oh, how we have need of a public box on the ear, given in full view of everyone!

In the intellectual arrogance of his time Gogol sees its most important characteristic. A lack of love is the first consequence, then come separation between people, coldness, and abstraction. Everyone is ready to embrace humanity—but no one wants to embrace his brother. It is amazing how clearly Gogol has already formulated a central problem in Dostoyevsky: the alleged love for Man in the abstract which covers up the concrete love for one's neighbor. This alone is the truly Christian love, the other is an abstraction of the devil.

In their pride, men pass judgment on one another. But guilt has been distributed upon all so that it is impossible to distinguish the guilty from the innocent. Raging pride only causes men to sit in judgment on other men. There are innocent-guilty persons and guilty-innocent persons. Gogol arrives at the idea of a chain of guilt which is only to be broken by loving forgiveness. One needs only to show the criminal how he is guilty—not toward others—no, toward himself, for everyone bears within himself a good core, and when deeply shaken and enlightened he will give up his evil ways.

The second consequence of intellectual arrogance is boredom. Without faith, led only by cold intellect and evil passions, Man does not know what to do with himself and his life. Without anything to hold on to, driven by fear, he feels that he needs some sort of "longed-for center" which he lost along with his belief in God. Hard-heartedness, lust for power, egotism which looks on one's neighbor merely as a source of amusement, as a means for satisfying one's own desires—these are the consequences in the background of the "giant figure of boredom," which with every passing day attains an even "more immense growth." "Everything gloomy, everywhere a grave. God, it is growing empty and terrible in your world!"

Dostoyevsky's demonic characters and even modern existentialism reveal a close relationship with these trains of thought.

In Gogol's hierarchical ideal state, the church has the task of transmitting the word of Christ without participating in the life of the state. In Gogol's view, the Russian church has preserved the purity of Christian teachings more than any other church; her servants are to work on themselves in seclusion from the world and to attain true humility in order then to preach this genuine humility to men. They are to let "every stratum of society, every profession, every official position proceed to its lawful bounds and limits without changing anything in the state." Gogol sees the "ruin" of Roman Catholicism in the fact that Catholic priests take too great a part in the life of the world. One gains experience of life in secluded work on oneself and in the analysis of one's soul: "first find the key to your own soul; when you have found it, then with the same key you will unlock the souls of all." Godless people have not caused so much harm in the world as poorly prepared preachers of God. The Orthodox church has sat like Mary at the feet of the Savior, while the Roman church, like Martha, "hospitably busied herself about men, brought them the words of the Lord, which were not yet comprehended by the whole power of reason . . ." The Greek Catholic Church is not dead, as the Roman church claims. Through its conservatism, its apparent immobility, it has preserved the living word of Christ in its original purity, and precisely now, when society is faced with a crisis, when "everywhere the morbid grumbling of discontent, the voice of human dissatisfaction with everything that there is in the world" is becoming audible, when "diseases of the intellect with which the present generation is infected" become widespread—now the conservative church will reveal its treasure and announce to mankind the unadulterated truth of the teachings of Christ. The worldly Roman church has long since lost it; the perplexed world will find no center here to which it could hold fast, from which everything would acquire the proper norm. In the Russian church, soul, heart, and reason have equal potentialities for development; the Russian church illuminates Man's whole being.

Briefly summarized, then, Gogol's system is the following: the ideal state has theoretically been realized in the Russian state. The point is to convince men of the fact that everyone has to be satisfied with the position in which God has placed him, since he can do his best in this divinely ordained position. Men *can* be convinced of this; they do not want evil and only do evil because they do not see the good. Religion and art are the chief administrators of this teaching role; but everyone is authorized to teach, and the higher his rank, the more so. Whoever does not teach becomes guilty. The present age is a turning point: mankind has lost its belief in God because it overestimated its own intellect; anxiety and boredom are the consequences in a world that is now without meaning. But this condition will not last if all well-meaning people unite to instruct the deluded; paradise on earth, a true "city of God," is the final goal. Obviously, this conception, which in regard to particulars contains many apt formulations and many pertinent ideas, proceeds from assumptions which have to be believed. Gogol's mystical experience in Vienna, the "unusual spiritual event" of which he also speaks in the *Correspondence*, fills him with the firm conviction that he has seen the unique truth. The confident, didactic tone of the letters reflects this indubitable knowledge. Gogol's tendency towards exaggeration is especially harmful to him here, and one can partly understand the irritation felt by many contemporaries at his apodictic opinions. They produce an especially unpleasant effect when Gogol goes into detail as, for example, when he instructs the housewife how she should arrange her money for household expenses in seven "little piles" for her various needs or when he demands of the ideal landowner that he burn money in front of the peasants in order to prove to them that he is not concerned about his possessions but about his soul.

For Gogol's contemporaries, the thing that was terribly wrong with his theories was the fact that he did not oppose serfdom, but on the contrary even doubted whether literacy and education would be beneficial for the people. Because of this, Belinsky, foaming at the mouth in anger, heaped abuse upon him. Gogol's assertions that this was not at all what he was chiefly concerned with were not heard, so that he himself, although only for a short time, began to waver. However, it is completely clear that on the basis of his system of positions, serfdom had to be considered a divinely ordained institution, and education too could only mislead the peasant into stepping outside of his proper station. Proceeding from his premises, Gogol remained completely consistent. Some things he did not yet think necessary to consider, such as, for example, the fact that once the divine state had been attained, certain posts, for example that of the police, would become superfluous. For the present, his chief concern was to teach Man that humility and modesty and a cheerful contentment in trusting to God afford protection against the chief weapons of the devil: cold reason and—one might say, existential—boredom.

The assertion that the ideal state exists theoretically in Russia leads Gogol to a patriotism that at times is painfully embarrassing and that greatly annoyed the liberal Westernizing circles, so much the more since Gogol missed no opportunity to direct sarcastic remarks at "rotten" Europe. For this reason, the Slavophiles considered him one of their own. But he was only partly so: their militant nature was alien to him, very much in contrast to Dostoyevsky. Still, he believed in Russia's Christian mission to bring salvation to other nations, and at times strikes really messianic tones. Praise of the Russian people and Russian nature, the assertion that this and that positive feature is possible *only* in Russia are only all too frequent. It is no wonder that from many sides Gogol was reproached for base flattery for the sake of purely practical goals (e.g., the granting of a pension by the emperor). Even the censors considered unsuitable some things intended as praise, because in view of the real situation they sounded like mockery; on the other hand, they naturally crossed out the passages where Gogol dealt with the deviations in practice from the ideal theory.

There is no doubt that Gogol was sincere in his demands and articles of faith and did not mean to flatter anyone. He believed that it was important to show Man his positive side so that he might see that he was doing greater wrong to himself than to others when he did not develop his good tendencies; and he acted according to this rule. The accusation of "fierce pride beneath the mask of humility" that Sergey Aksakov directed at him certainly does not apply. Gogol's belief in the rightness of his ideas was so deep that he preached humility with the greatest, at times intolerant, emphasis, but his humility as such was genuine—the last years of his life and his death prove it.

It is really amazing that Gogol, who reveals such a deep knowledge of men in his artistic works, believed so firmly that only ignorance keeps men back from the path of virtue. He believed that the person "who would pay 100 rubles for a seat in the theater in order to enjoy the singing of Rubini would sell his last possession if he ever became a witness in reality of only one of those horrible spectacles of hunger compared to which all the horror and dread which are represented in melodrama are nothing at all"; he believed that after appropriate instruction one would not be able to keep back the flood of those who would apply for subordinate but indispensable positions; he believed that a superior can instruct his subordinates in the duties of Man in such a way that it will seem to both that two angels are speaking together in the presence of God, etc.

Many of these unrealistic statements are, of course, rhetorically determined. Gogol wrote his *Correspondence* in a definite style, which he surely and consistently maintained and which is entirely appropriate for the positive, idyllic utopia that results. It is the combination of the unctuous calmness of the sermon with the simple tone of an idyll, of plain colloquial speech between man and man with cleverly calculated, elevated climaxes. It is not the language of one searching, nor the speech of a fanatic who wants to force his opinion on others—fanaticism and humility generally are not easily united, and Gogol consistently calls the fanatic a cancerous sore on society—but the wise tone, one that is beyond all doubt, of a person firmly convinced, who does not need to take great pains to make clear what is evident. Antitheses, exclamations, and imaginary dialogues are far more rare than repetitions, intentional assonances, polysyndeta, and archaisms; a rich vocabulary, slightly archaic in sentence structure, is handled with great skill.

Again and again Gogol emphasizes the pre-eminence of the Russian language, which he calls the richest and most complete of all the European languages. It contains all shades of sound within itself and "the boldest transitions from the elevated to the simple in the same speech." Again and again Gogol points to these same bold transitions, the combination of "high and low words" such as exists only in Russian. He particularly stresses Derzhavin's courage in combining opposites, and since this is also Gogol's chief stylistic device, it is not without interest to point out that Gogol was aware of this peculiarity. Gogol's literary observations in the *Correspondence* generally show him to be very much concerned with form. He is surprised that the critics of his *Dead Souls* completely overlooked the formal side, and explains it by the "lack of practice in considering the structure of a work," hence the extremely small number of objections that pertain "to the art or science of creation." In Gogol's work particularly "the science of creation" plays an important role; and precisely this aspect in his works was hardly noticed by his contemporaries. Gogol had such great difficulties with the second part of his chief work for the very reason that he *was* so clearly aware of formal requirements.

The stylistic individuality and unity of Gogol's *Correspondence* give it too a literary rank.

In regard to ideas, Gogol draws from many sources, although the over-all conception, especially the "position" philosophy, bears his personal stamp. In addition to the Bible and the church fathers, there are above all Thomas a Kempis' *Imitation of Christ* (particularly concerning the important role of prayer during the purification of Man), perhaps Silvio Pellico's *My Prisons*, and Bossuet's sermons and tracts, which he uses as models. Dmitry Chizhevsky has pointed out parallels with Justus Möser's *Patriotic Fantasies*.

In reply to the critics of *Selected Passages*, Gogol wrote in 1847 the "Confession of the Author," which was not published during his lifetime. The work is intended as an *apologia*. In a dignified, offended tone, Gogol rejects all charges raised against his personal motives in writing the *Correspondence*; he defends himself against the malicious generalizations drawn from many of his theses, and in the main part of the work brings together the reasons which prompted him to turn away from his genre as "writer of comic entertainments." Basically, however, this is not the main point, but rather the reasons he gave up the art for art's sake theory of the whole period of creativity in which he was influenced by Pushkin and turned into an ethical-religious writer. No new ideas are to be found in this work, but Gogol's account of himself is very informative. The central thesis is that the writer can describe only what he himself has felt, what he bears within himself. Since it is the task of the writer to portray the good, *he* must be good—*only* then will he have the ability to tell something about the highest feelings

Selected Passages from Correspondence with Friends 245

and impulses of Man. The writer must be acquainted with all of life in all its ramifications in order to be able to write about it. "I pursued life in its reality and not in reveries of the imagination and came to Him Who is the source of life." Here Gogol adopts to a certain degree the false view of his contemporaries that he is a realist. This coming to Christ occurred in the midst of his work on *Dead Souls*; it was the illumination in Vienna which determined the radical change in Gogol. "I nursed in quiet the hope that the reading of *Dead Souls* would give some people the idea of writing their own memoirs, and that many would even feel a certain turning to themselves because also in the author himself at the time when *Dead Souls* was being written, a certain turning to himself was taking place." This "turning to oneself" in every individual is considered necessary by Gogol because the time was a period of transition: everyone felt the pressure toward a new order, searched for a cosmos of which he could become a part. In many souls revolutions are taking place ("inner spiritual revolutions," says Gogol, thinking of himself), enabling them to see in God this order. It is the duty of a writer who has experienced this illumination to pass it on to other men and to teach them; this applies especially to the writer who not only *describes* life, but who is able to *create* it. But this ability to create (naturally Gogol means by this artistic representation, which can be more true than reality) is a tremendous responsibility; life created by the poet influences men, transforms them—how, therefore, shall the poet venture to create when he does not yet feel himself purified? For this reason, Gogol considers it proper to lay down the pen of the pure artist, to resist the temptation to create, and first of all to work on himself until his creation becomes useful to Man on his way to God. Everyone should recognize, just as Gogol recognized, that our whole life is service, service before God, in whom we all have our place. Everyone's earthly position is at the same time his position before God; one should fill this position with a happy heart and to the best of one's ability. To recognize properly his position, Gogol had need of a mirror —this mirror is the attacked book, which reveals him with all his faults: "And thus my book, which originated out of the sincere desire to be useful to others, was useful, above all, to myself." Such a work cannot harm others, as some critics assert. Instead of abusing the author, they should help him, this author who is searching. "I know of no greater heroic deed than to extend one's hand to him whose soul has grown weak."

There is really no reason to doubt Gogol's sincerity. The elegant paradox of a literary critic, stating that Gogol speaks with disarming sincerity about his insincerities, does not do justice to Gogol's honest search.

Besides his work on the second part of *Dead Souls* and on the *Correspondence*, Gogol, until his death, was putting the finishing touches on a work that he had decided to write in 1845 and had completed in the course of the years: *Meditations on the Divine Liturgy*. It is a stylistically very impressive description and explanation of the actions, words, and chants of the mass according to the Greek Catholic rite and an interpretation of the symbolic meaning of these actions. In an admirable manner, Gogol maintains the solemn, archaic tone, making abundant use of Church Slavonic. Stylistically, these *Meditations* are Gogol's most homogeneous work. They show what impressive powers of word-formation lay at his disposal. The contents—the description of the ideal mass, which is celebrated by priest and congregation in a perfect spiritual state, the elevated mood in its ultimate ideal purity—are expressed in stylistically appropriate form, which may explain the powerful impression that this work produces.

10 · The Second Part of *Dead Souls*

ON FEBRUARY 11, 1852, Gogol burned the finished second part of *Dead Souls*. We possess only fragments of it which come from an early draft and were preserved by chance. The idea of expanding his book occurred to Gogol as early as 1836, as we learn from his letters. He probably began actual work on the second part in 1840, thus at a time when the first part was not yet finished. "I am healthy," he wrote to Pogodin in December 1840, "even feel fresh. I am engaged in corrections, stylistic changes, and even with the continuation of *Dead Souls*. I see that the subject is growing more and more profound. I even want to have the first volume printed in the coming year." In a letter dating from 1843 to Zhukovsky we read: "I am continuing with my work, i.e., I am continuing to throw chaos down on paper, from which the creation of *Dead Souls* is to emerge." But he was not satisfied with this "chaos," and attempted to organize it in the following two years. In 1845 he burned practically all of it. He wrote *Selected Passages from Correspondence with Friends*, and only after its publication did he again turn energetically to *Dead Souls*. The years 1848 and 1849 were spent in work on it. In July 1849, he read several chapters aloud to Madame Smirnova. In the fall of 1849 and the beginning of 1850 Sergey Aksakov also heard the initial chapters read. The judgments of both were very favorable Until the final catastrophe in February 1852, the work proceeded, interrupted by periods of depression. It is practically certain that the book was finished when it was burned.

Naturally the question arises: To which version do the first four chapters that have been preserved and the concluding chapter of the work belong? Scholarly opinions on the subject vary greatly. To me, the most likely conclusion is that they are to be dated between 1843 and 1845. The initial four chapters have been taken from a fair copy (with his painstaking manner of working, Gogol was accustomed to having several "fair copies"); the concluding chapter from a rough draft. Both manuscripts are filled with many corrections by Gogol dating from various periods, so that here too several versions can be made out. The number of variants is very great.

On the basis of the fragments that have been preserved, it is not possible to judge the artistic merits of the second part. The development of the positive characters that Gogol promised was probably to be put off until the third part, for in the second part there are only beginnings in this direction (e.g., Konstanzhoglo, Murazov, the governor-general). Gogol wanted to portray only the "more important" characters; "it was the purpose of the author here to penetrate deeper into the lofty meaning of life, which we have made so spiritually shallow, and not to show the Russian man merely from any *one side alone*" (letter to Markov, November 1847). Otherwise, however, the plan of the whole resembles the first part. The second part begins: "Why describe poverty and more poverty and the imperfection of our life, digging up people from the back woods, from distant corners of the empire? What is one to do if the author is of such a nature and, infected by his own imperfection, can describe nothing else but poverty and more poverty and the imperfection of our life, digging up people from the back woods and distant corners of the empire. And now we have landed again in the back woods, again chanced upon an out-of-the-way spot. But then, what a back woods and what an out-of-the-way spot!" This solemn introduction again uses Gogol's device of repetition. It is followed by an enthusiastic description of nature in this "out-of-the-way spot," the vast landscape of Russia. We find ourselves at the estate of Andrey Tentetnikov, a young landowner who leads a useless, "sky-sooting" existence here. We are told of the course of his spiritual development: he is the victim of false education, of a

The Second Part of Dead Souls

narrow-minded milieu. The idealistically disposed youth leaves boarding school with an abundance of sterile knowledge. With youthful enthusiasm he wishes to work for the welfare of mankind, he even belongs to a "philanthropic society" (an allusion to the many Moscow and St. Petersburg circles—predominantly student groups—which, from German idealistic philosophy, proceeded to French utopian socialism, and were looked on with suspicion by the government), thinks of a career as a statesman, but must learn from his highly placed uncle that good handwriting is the first prerequisite for such a career. Annoyed, the idealist returns to his estate in order to manage it in exemplary fashion and to compose a great work on Russia —but he gets no further than the intention. Laziness soon overpowers him. He is the predecessor of Goncharov's Oblomov, who is unable to accomplish anything because he is lacking in the inner strength needed to make decisions and because his social position makes it possible for him to live an inactive life. Even his budding love for Ulinka, the daughter of General Betrishchev, a neighboring landowner, is not enough to tear him out of his lethargy. The good-hearted General unintentionally offends the pride of the sensitive Tentetnikov, and the latter leaves off his visits with the general despite the pain caused him by the separation from Ulinka, who returns his love. One day Chichikov happens to stop at the house of Tentetnikov because his carriage has been damaged. We do not find out what Chichikov has done in the time since his departure from the town of NN., but a considerable period of time must have elapsed since then, even though Chichikov is quite the same. The two like each other, and Chichikov stays with Tentetnikov. He learns of his quarrel with the general, and smelling profit, he wants to reconcile the two. He decides to pay the general a visit. This much, then, makes up the contents of the first chapter.

The second, or rather the fragment of the second, tells how Chichikov managed to please the patriotic general and introduces the idealized Ulinka, who fails to come to life and who was apparently meant to embody the perfect woman. Again Chichikov turns the conversation with the general to dead souls and achieves the greatest success through a rather naive anecdote which very much pleases the simple-minded general. Here the chapter breaks off.

In order to understand the transition to the third chapter, one must turn to the account given by Madame Smirnova's brother, Lev Arnoldi, who was present for part of the reading held in July, 1849: Chichikov succeeds in reconciling Tentetnikov with the general. This is followed by Tentetnikov's engagement to Ulinka, and Chichikov is asked by the general to travel to some of his relatives in the surrounding vicinity to bring them the news. The first one he is to vist is the retired colonel Koshkarev. Here the third chapter begins. Instead of arriving at Koshkarev's house, through Petrushka's stupidity Chichikov arrives at the house of another landowner by the name of Petukh, who engages in a veritable cult of the stomach and whose whole life and ambition is directed at a refined, tasty, and abundant cuisine. He is uninterested in anything outside this sphere. The scenes with Petukh are brilliantly successful; in humor and in sureness of detail, they are not at all inferior to the first volume.

At Petukh's house, Chichikov meets another neighbor, Platonov, who suffers from boredom. He is a type similar to Pushkin's Evgeny Onegin: a rich dandy who can find nothing to do with himself. Presumably, a cardinal philosophical theme of Gogol's—the destructive effect of boredom upon the soul— was to be developed here. We hear from Madame Smirnova that in the further course of the story Platonov was to meet a beautiful woman, a spoiled, coquettish lady of the great world. Both think that they love each other, but their dead souls are incapable of any living emotion. Disillusionment follows, and hopeless boredom finally takes possession of them.

As a remedy against boredom, Chichikov proposes to Platonov that the latter accompany him. He hopes he will be able to profit from the rich gentleman. Platonov agrees, but first wants to take leave of his brother and of his sister, who is married to the landowner Kostanzhoglo. Kostanzhoglo is the incarnation of the capable man. Chichikov, who is seriously considering the idea of acquiring an estate, is extremely interested in Kostanzhoglo, the ideal landowner. The speeches made by the latter are chiefly concerned with the idea that work

The Second Part of Dead Souls

brings money and prosperity, and according to him, money and prosperity are the final end of wisdom. This is very similar to a theory of Gogol's from the *Correspondence*, only without the religious foundation. With Kostanzhoglo everything is well organized; a useful life devoted to acquiring wealth is described, but one believes neither in Kostanzhoglo's real existence—in spite of his gallstones—nor in his theories. It is also not clear how his desire for acquiring wealth, positively judged by Gogol, is different from that of Chichikov, negatively judged.

There is a very funny interlude: Chichikov's visit with Colonel Koshkarev, who has transformed his village into a bureaucratic machine, which by the way functions very badly. Chichikov also presents to him his request for the sale of the dead souls, but after a great deal of paper work, he receives a negative answer. A passage is missing from the middle of the chapter: Here Chichikov obviously resolved to buy the estate of a certain Khlobuyev, a landowner on the brink of bankruptcy due to the poor management of his land, in order to profit from being a neighbor of Kostanzhoglo and to learn from him how to manage this estate.

In the fourth chapter we are told how Chichikov visits Khlobuyev's neglected estate and how the purchase comes about. Khlobuyev is an irresolute but kind-hearted, pious man who does not have the energy to rouse himself into doing any real work, who cannot give up his aristocratic habits, and who does not know how to hold on to the money that sometimes comes to him by a stroke of good fortune. Gogol wanted to show in him that goodness alone, without carefully planned economic organization, can produce only an utterly useless existence that is harmful to men. In the conversation, Khlobuyev tells of his old aunt Khanasarova, who is going to leave an inheritance amounting to millions. A swindle involving this inheritance, a falsification of the will on Chichikov's part, probably makes up the chief contents of the missing sections, as we can discern from the last chapter.

Now a real landowner, Chichikov leaves Khlobuyev and travels with Platonov to visit his brother, who like Kostanzhoglo administers his estate with great success. Chichikov hears of his quarrel with his neighbor Lenitsyn over a piece of land

and offers to serve as mediator. There is a gap here in the manuscript, but obviously not much is missing. When it resumes again, Chichikov is in conversation with Lenitsyn. They are discussing the sale of the dead souls, about which Lenitsyn is quite skeptical. But Chichikov's charming behavior toward his baby, who misbehaves in Chichikov's arms, makes Lenitsyn change his mind. As Chichikov turns the conversation to his role as mediator, the manuscript breaks off.

Besides these four fragmentary chapters, we also possess the rough draft of the chapter that was to conclude the second part and that reveals a clear parallel in many details to the concluding chapter of the first part. Chichikov succeeds with the will. Through trickery he manages to get the lion's share of the inheritance for himself. We meet him again as he is buying some splendid material for a frock coat. Khlobuyev, whom he has somehow deceived, comes along and wants to speak with Chichikov, but is taken in tow by an extraordinarily rich and pious man (his riches are actually the result of this piety and honesty) by the name of Murazov, who proposes that he travel around Russia and collect funds for the building of a church. In this way his senseless, wasted life would acquire a higher significance. Khlobuyev joyfully agrees to it and feels "that freshness and strength are beginning to penetrate into his soul." The religious tendency dominates this chapter.

Chichikov tries on his frock coat and finds himself at the peak of his good fortune. At this very moment, he is arrested. His swindles have been exposed, and the honest governor-general, who only speaks in superlatives ("You have repeatedly defiled yourself with the most dishonorable swindles that a man ever defiled himself with"), is determined to show no mercy. Chichikov is put in prison. Here Murazov visits him and witnesses a terrible outburst of despair on Chichikov's part which deeply shakes his whole being. The threatened loss of all his possessions, the greatest misfortune that could strike Chichikov, paves the way for a conversion and offers an opportunity for spiritual purification. Gogol here illustrates the necessity of suffering for the salvation of one's soul. Murazov furthers this positive development by pointing out to Chichikov that he could have accomplished great things had he directed his

The Second Part of Dead Souls

resourcefulness and endurance to the Good, rather than to the egotistical acquisition of property.

There are mysteries of the soul. However far the one who has lost his way may have strayed from the right path, however much the irrevocable criminal may have hardened his feelings, however fast he may be frozen in his debauched existence; but if he is reproached with his own self, with his own good qualities that he himself has disgraced, then everything in him will begin to quake, and he will be completely shaken.

In Chichikov too something new is stirring, something that his education and environment had buried in him. Murazov calls upon Chichikov, who is lacking in love for the Good, to force himself to do good, even without this love: "This will be reckoned of higher merit for you than for someone who does good out of love for it. Just force yourself a few times—and then love too will be given to you." This salvation by force is very characteristic of Gogol's attitudes. He too lacked love and forced himself to salvation. The whole chapter again and again presents ideas which decisively influenced him and his spiritual development and of which he wrote in his *Correspondence*. Touched by Chichikov's genuine grief over the loss of his money and seeing in him potential for spiritual regeneration, Murazov decides to appeal to the governor-general in Chichikov's behalf.

In the meantime the situation is made so obscure by Chichikov's friends, mostly officers of justice who are involved (partially by very unlikely means, reminiscent of naive adventure novels, e.g., the substitution of the key witness), that Chichikov has excellent prospects of coming away unscathed. Again Chichikov's identification with the Antichrist is alluded to. Murazov succeeds in obtaining Chichikov's release from the governor-general. In the conversation between the two Murazov advocates the Socratic doctrine that virtue can be taught, which Gogol exaggerates in a utopian manner. "Whoever the man may be whom you call scoundrel, he is still a human being. How can one help defending a man when one knows that he does half of his evil deeds out of coarseness and ignorance? For we commit injustices at every step, and at every minute we are the cause of another's misfortune even without evil intent."

The motif of the chain of evil, of the guilt that everyone shares with everyone else, reappears. Murazov reproaches the governor-general with injustice even in the case of Derpennikov. This Derpennikov is identical with the Tentetnikov of the first two chapters; we learn from Madame Smirnova that in the destroyed portions he was arrested and sent to Siberia because of his membership in the "philanthropic society"; Ulinka, his ideal wife, followed him there. The "position" philosophy is illustrated and personified: during the conversation, a young government official appears who belongs among the few who carry out their official duties *con amore*. "Consumed neither by ambition nor by the desire for gain, nor by the wish to imitate others, he worked only because he was convinced that he *had* to be here and not in another position, and that life was given to him for this purpose." Again there is a gap in the middle of the conversation. We hear only the conclusion. Murazov, the millionaire, has succeeded in obtaining freedom for Chichikov. He suggests to the governor-general that he deliver an enlightening speech before the corrupt officials and show them what is good. "I don't have a single good official: They are all scoundrels," says the governor-general in his superlative manner, and then Murazov goes off to announce to Chichikov that he is free. Although Chichikov is already considerably comforted, above all, by possession of the cash box with his money, he follows Murazov's advice and leaves town. So the second part too ends with his departure. "It was not the old Chichikov. It was a ruin of the old Chichikov. One would compare the inner state of his soul to a building broken down into its component parts; this building was knocked down with the intention of constructing a new one out of it; but the new one had not yet been begun because the architect had not yet sent the definite plan, and the workers stood there perplexed." There is no doubt that the third part was to be concerned with the construction of this building. Even Plyushkin, the old miser from the first part, was evidently to become purified, for in *Selected Passages*, Gogol writes to Yazykov: "Address a strong lyrical appeal to beautiful but sleeping Man. Oh, if you could tell him what my Plyushkin is to say, if I ever get to the third part of *Dead Souls*." While Chichikov is leaving town, the governor-general has the officials assemble and then delivers the enlightening speech, of which there are several versions; the manuscript breaks off with this speech. One of the versions presents a positive program for the renovation of society by means of the "simplification of life." All of the achievements of civilization have contributed only to moral decay. Here Gogol anticipates one of Leo Tolstoy's fundamental, Rousseau-influenced concepts.

One can only make vague conjectures concerning the contents of the missing parts. Gogol was never a master at constructing a plot, so that the whole work probably possessed a mosaiclike character. The real heart of the plot probably lay in the falsification of the will and the corruption of the officials revealed in this connection. Representatives of various classes were introduced, including a priest, in whose character Matthew Konstantinovsky recognized himself, although, as he thought, falsely portrayed, with Catholic traits. (Hence he opposed publication.)

In comparison with the first part, the tone of the narrator is much more serious. This gravity appears to have increased more and more towards the end. Only on a few occasions does the comedy peek through, surprisingly enough. The scandal in connection with the will, for example, expands and spreads over the whole province: "In another part of the province the Old Believers were stirring. Someone circulated among them the rumor that the Antichrist had been born, who would not even leave the dead any peace as he went around buying up some sort of dead souls. They did penance and they sinned, and under the pretext of catching the Antichrist, they did in some non-Antichrists." This is genuine Gogol, but one clearly feels that he is forcibly restraining himself. The writer is a preacher: jokes are out of place in matters of great concern. Gogol succeeded in doing violence to his talent, but only with great difficulty; what could the burnt completed version have been like?

Looking back on Gogol's work we recognize in him a poet who succeeded in finding the only form suitable for *his* statement about the world. It is filled with a profound pessimism in regard to human nature, which, due to the influence of evil powers, is incapable of recalling its real essence, which inclines toward the good. Man is the battleground of good and evil principles, and evil is victorious in most men by means of petty trifles. Instead of recognizing himself in all and instead of bringing about an earthly paradise through love towards his actual, flesh-and-blood neighbor, everyone considers himself the center of the world, indulges in his petty passions, and does not think of the great whole. In the face of this attitude, there is place only for a knowing irony that sees the pettiness of that which deems itself great, portrays it, and smiles at it resignedly. The smaller the motives and results of human actions, the clearer the true nature of this world, which could indeed be so good. Gogol portrays these trifles with such a deep inner truth that one feels touched by the immediacy of it; he knows how to make his reader feel the essence of the real, even in what is most unreal. A wealth of inner human life moves on an extremely narrow foundation of external events, which nevertheless fascinate in spite of their triviality. "The task of the writer of novels," says Schopenhauer, "is not to relate great events, but to make little ones interesting." Gogol performed this task in perfect fashion.

BIBLIOGRAPHICAL NOTE

THE MOST complete and easily available edition of Gogol's works (excluding *Dead Souls*) is: *The Collected Tales and Plays of Nikolai Gogol*, New York: Pantheon Books, 1964. The most recent edition of *Dead Souls* is: New York: The Modern Library, Vr. 40, 1965. *Selected Passages from Correspondence with Friends* was never translated into English. *Meditations on the Divine Liturgy* has been published under the title *The Divine Liturgy of the Eastern Church*; London: Darton, Longman and Todd, 1960.

Some studies of Gogol available in English are:

BOOKS:

Lavrin, Janko. *Gogol*, New York, 1926, and *Nikolai Gogol* (1809–1852). *A Centenary Survey*. London: 1951.
Magarshack, David. *Gogol, A Life*. New York: 1957.
Nabokov, Vladimir. *Gogol*. Norfolk, Connecticut: 1944.

ARTICLES:

Čiževsky, Dmitry. "Gogol: Artist and Thinker," *Annals of the Ukrainian Academy of Arts and Sciences in the U.S.*, IV (1952), 261–78; and "The Unknown Gogol," *Slavonic and Eastern European Review*, XXX (1952), 476–93.
Erlich, Victor. "Gogol and Kafka: a Note on 'Realism' and 'Surrealism,'" *For Roman Jakobson*, The Hague, 1956, 100–108.

Stilman, Leon. "Gogol's Overcoat—Thematic Pattern and Origins," *American Slavic and Eastern European Review,* XI (1952), 138–48.
Wilson, Edmund. "Gogol: the Demon in the Overgrown Garden," *The Nation,* CLXXV (1952), 520–24.
Yurieff, Zoya. "Gogol and the Russian Symbolists," Harvard University, 1954 (Dissertation).

INDEX

Aachen, Germany, 49
Abramovo, Russia, 83
Academy of the Arts, St. Petersburg, 30
Aksakov, Ivan, 69
Aksakov, Konstantin, 69
Aksakov, Sergey, 5, 35, 58, 59, 69, 70, 72, 74, 78, 79, 82, 83, 86, 173, 242, 247
Alexander II, Crown Prince, 55
Alfred (Gogol), 166–67
Annals of the Fatherland (periodical), 31
Annenkov, Pavel, 34, 36, 37, 38, 47, 64–65, 76, 216, 219
Annunziata (Gogol), 64, 227–30
Anselmus, 132
Arabesques (Gogol), 40, 41, 44, 124–35, 139, 230
Arnoldi, Lev, 86, 250

Bad Ems, Germany, 73, 79
Bad Gastein, Germany, 71
Bad Homburg, Germany, 76
Baden-Baden, Germany, 49–50, 53, 73, 74, 79
Balabin, Maria, 50, 68
Balabin family, 49–50
Balzac, Honoré, 138
Basel, Switzerland, 50
Basil the Great, 85, 86
Basili, 80, 81
Beirut, 80, 81

Belinsky, Vissarion, 44, 59, 78, 173, 217, 230, 241
Belousov, Nikolay, 15
Bely, Andrey, 60, 118
Berlin, Germany, 76
Berne, Switzerland, 50
"Bisavryuk, or St. John's Eve" (Gogol), 31, 99
"Bloody Bandura-Player, The" (Gogol), 139–40
Boris Godunov (Pushkin), 166
Bossuet, Jacques, 244
Bremen, Germany, 49
Brothers Tverdislavichi, The (Gogol), 16
Bulgarin, Faddey, 29, 31, 44, 161

"Captive, The" (Gogol), 139
"Carriage, The" (Gogol), 162–65
Carus, Dr., 76
Casimir, King John, 3
Censorship Committees, 68
Cervantes, Miguel de, 183
Chamisso, Adalbert von, 161
Chichikov's Adventures, or Dead Souls. A Poèma (Gogol); see *Dead Souls*
Chizhevsky, Dmitry, 226
"Christmas Eve" (Gogol), 95, 105–10
Clarissa Harlowe (Richardson), 36
"Confession of the Author" (Gogol), 182, 244–46

Contemporary, The (periodical), 33, 155, 162, 230

Danilevsky, Alexander, 19, 26, 39, 49, 50, 52, 55, 66, 82, 183, 203
Dead Souls (Gogol), 50–51, 53, 60, 61, 62, 63, 64, 65–66, 67, 68, 70, 71, 72, 74, 82, 83, 84, 86, 88, 90, 104, 115, 117, 121, 165, 180, 182–215, 222, 230, 232, 235, 244, 245, 246, 247–56
Delvig, Baron Anton, 31–32
"Denouement of *The Inspector General*" (Gogol), 77
De Quincey, Thomas, 132
Derzhavin, Gavrila, 23, 237
"Diary of a Madman, The" (Gogol), 37, 42, 133–35
Dmitriev, Ivan, 44
Dostoyevsky, Fedor Mikhailovich, 17, 113, 147, 154, 224, 235, 239, 242
Dramatic Fragments and Individual Scenes (Gogol), 178
Dresden, Germany, 67, 76
Düsseldorf, Germany, 49, 73

Eikhenbaum, Boris, 222
"Enchanted Spot, The" (Gogol), 95, 117–18
Evenings on the Farm near Dikanka (Gogol), 34–35, 38, 41, 95–119, 136, 144
Evgeny Onegin (Pushkin), 183

F., S. von, 183
"Fair at Sorochincy, The" (Gogol), 95, 96–99
Family Chronicle, The (Aksakov), 35, 70
Ferney, Switzerland, 50
Fielding, Henry, 183
Filippov, Terty, 89
Frankfurt, Germany, 49, 53, 67, 73, 75, 76, 79

Gamblers, The (Gogol), 177, 178–79
"Gants Kyukhelgarten" (Gogol), 21–24, 28
Geneva, Switzerland, 50, 53
Gogol, Andrey, 3
Gogol, Anna (Gogol's sister), 36, 57, 59, 60–61, 62, 81
Gogol, Elizaveta (Gogol's sister), 36, 57, 59, 60–61, 62, 81
Gogol, Maria Kosyarovskaya (Gogol's mother), 5–7, 19, 20–21, 30, 35, 42, 54, 59, 61, 62, 81
Gogol, Nikolay V., academic career, 39–42, 44, 45; *Alfred*, 166–67; ancestors, 3–7; *Arabesques*, 124–35; birth, 7; "Carriage, The," 162–65; childhood, 7–9; "Confession of the Author," 244–46; *Dead Souls*, 182–215, 247–56; death, 90–91; early experiences in St. Petersburg, 19–26; education, 9–18; employment of, 29, 30, 33–34; estate of, 91; *Evenings on the Farm near Dikanka*, 95–119; fragments, 120–24; *Gamblers, The*, 178–79; illnesses, 36, 38, 41, 42, 49, 52, 55, 62, 63, 68–69, 75–76, 83, 84, 87; *Inspector General, The*, 167–72; "Leaving the Theatre After the Performance of a New Comedy," 180–81; *Marriage, The*, 172–77; *Mirgorod*, 136–54; money problems, 20–21, 25, 29–30, 35, 61–62, 72; "Nose, The," 155–62; *Order of Vladimir, Third Class*, 179–80; "Overcoat, The," 216–26; personal appearance, 10–11, 36–37, 46, 58, 87; poetic endeavors, 12, 14, 20, 21–24; "Portrait, The," 230–31; Pushkin and, 34, 35, 40, 44–45, 51–52, 89, 155–57, 165, 167–68, 173, 182, 184, 244; relationship with women, 38–39, 73, 84; "Rome," 227–30; *Selected Passages from Correspondence with Friends*, 232–46; theater pieces, 166–81; theatrical talent, 11, 14–15, 28; travels abroad, 26–28, 49–58, 62–67, 71–81;

Index

turn to religion, 55, 56, 76–77, 86, 88–89; works of, 95–256
Gogol, Olga (Gogol's sister), 62, 81, 82
Gogol, Vasily (Gogol's father), 5–7, 13
Gogol's Spiritual Path (Mochulsky), 88
Gogol-Yanovsky, Afanasy, 4
Gräfenberg, Czechoslovakia, 76

Hallam, Henry, 166
Hamburg, Germany, 49
Hanau, Germany, 67
Herder, J. G., 119
Hetman, The (Gogol), 139–40
Hoffmann, E. T. A., 119, 127, 130, 132–33, 138, 161, 162
Homelife in Russia by a Russian Noble (Anon.), 187
Homer, 141, 142
Hugo, Victor, 218

Innocent, Bishop, 70
Inspector General, The (Gogol), 42, 43, 45–48, 59, 68, 77, 97, 167–72, 173, 177–78, 180, 221
Isaac the Syrian, 85
"Ivan Fedorovich Shponka and his Aunt" (Gogol), 95, 113–17
Ivanov, Alexander, 55, 234, 235
Izmaylov, Alexander, 183

Janin, Jules, 132, 138, 140, 141
Jerusalem, Palestine, 80–81

Kaluga, Russia, 83, 87
Karksbad, Czechoslovakia, 76
Khomyakov, Alexey, 69, 83, 90
Khomyakova, Madame, 90
Kiev, Russia, 43, 82
Kiev University, 39–40
Konstantinovsky, Matthew, 87–89, 90, 255

Kosyarovsky, Ivan, 5–6
Kosyarovsky, Pavel, 17, 20
Kotlyarevsky, Ivan, 119
Küchelbecker, Wilhelm, 22
Kukolnik, Nestor, 15
Kutuzov, Loggin, 19

"Landlady" (Dostoyevsky), 113
Lausanne, Switzerland, 50
"Lawsuit, The" (Gogol), 179
"Leaving the Theatre After the Performance of a New Comedy" (Gogol), 177, 180–81
Lermontov, Mikhail Y., 62
Lesage, Alain René, 183
Literary Gazette, 32, 120
"Little House in Kolomna" (Pushkin), 127, 156, 157
Lizogub, Tatyana, 4
"Lost Letter, The" (Gogol), 95, 104–105
Lübeck, Germany, 26–28, 49

Mainz, Germany, 49
Maksimovich, Professor, 43, 84, 119
Malta, 80
Marienbad, Czechoslovakia, 57
Markov, 248
Marriage, The (Gogol), 42, 43–44, 115, 172–77
Marseilles, France, 57
Maturin, Charles Robert, 127, 138
Matveyevna, Agafya, 31
Matveyevna, Anna, 31
"May Night or the Drowned Woman, The" (Gogol), 95, 101–104
Meditations on the Divine Liturgy (Gogol), 246
Melmoth the Wanderer (Maturin), 127
Metropolitan Filaret, Moscow, 90, 91
Mickiewicz, Adam, 51, 53
Mirgorod (Gogol), 37, 42, 44, 97, 116, 136–54
Mochulsky, Konstantin, 88
Molière, 46, 50, 51, 85, 201

Mont Blanc, 50
"Morning of a Busy Man" (Gogol), 179
Moscow, Russia, 35, 43, 58, 59, 61, 67, 69, 82, 83, 86, 87, 88
Moscow Observer, 155
Moscow Telegraph, The, 23-24
Möser, Justus, 244
Mukhanov, V. A., 79
Mundt, N. P., 28
Munich, Germany, 57
Münster, Germany, 49
Muscovite, The (journal), 227

Naples, Italy, 54-55, 76, 77, 79, 80
Narezhny, Vasily, 119, 184
"Nevsky Prospect" (Gogol), 42, 128-33
Nezhin, Russia, 9
Nice, France, 79
Nicholas I, Czar, 15, 45, 46-47, 53, 233, 234
"Nights at the Villa" (Gogol), 56-57
Nikitenko (censor), 35
Northern Bee, The (periodical), 24, 161
Northern Flowers (almanac), 31, 139, 140
"Nose, The" (Gogol), 42, 46, 127, 155-62
Novalis (Friedrich Leopold von Hardenberg), 122

Obolensky, Prince, 220
Odessa, Ukraine, 81, 85-86
Odyssey, The, 234
"Old-World Landowners" (Gogol), 91, 115, 136-38
"On the Middle Ages" (Gogol), 40
Optina Pustyn monastery, 84, 87
Order of Vladimir, Third Class (Gogol), 37, 133, 177, 179-80
Ostende, Belgium, 75, 76, 79
Ostranitsa, Stepan, 139
"Overcoat, The" (Gogol), 62, 114, 115, 117, 133, 154, 216-26

Paris, France, 50-51, 55, 75, 79
Patriotic Institute, St. Petersburg, 32
Pavlovsk, Russia, 34
Pellico, Silvio, 244
Piskarev, 132
"Plan of Instruction in World History" (Gogol), 40
Pletnev, Peter, 32-33, 51, 59, 73, 77, 82, 84, 232, 233
"Poet and the Mob, The" (Pushkin), 156
Pogodin, Mikhail Petrovich, 38, 42, 43-44, 46, 48, 55, 56, 57, 58, 62, 64, 69, 78, 82, 173, 227, 247
Polevoy, Nikolay, 24
Poltava, Russia, 9, 82
Poor Folk (Dostoyevsky), 224
"Portrait, The" (Gogol), 42, 98, 124-28, 145, 230-31
Priessnitz, Dr., 76
Prokopovich, Feofan, 59, 71, 72
Pushkin, Alexander, 12, 20, 23, 32, 33, 34, 35, 40, 44-45, 51-52, 55, 89, 127, 128, 155-57, 162, 165, 166, 167-68, 173, 174, 182, 183, 184, 234-35, 244

Rapin-Thoyras, Paul de, 166
Realism in Russian literature, 217-19
Repnina, Princess Varvara, 50, 55
"Result of the Errand, The" (Gogol), 120, 121-22
Reutern, Gerhard von, 67
Revolutions of 1848, 85
"Robbers, The" (Gogol), 12
"Rome" (Gogol), 227-30
Rome, Italy, 51-54, 55-56, 57, 63-67, 71-72, 76, 79
Rozanov, Vasily, 218
"Russia under the Yoke of the Tartars" (Gogol), 12

"St. John's Eve" (Gogol), 95, 99-101
St. Petersburg, Russia, 19, 34, 36,

Index

40, 44, 59, 67, 71, 82
Sainte-Beuve, Charles Augustin, 57
Sand, George, 218
"Scenes from the Great World" (Gogol), 180
Schaad, Professor, 15
Schelling, F. W. von, 119, 122
Schiller, Johann von, 132
Schlegel, August Wilhelm von, 122
School for Wives, The (Molière), 85
Schopenhauer, Arthur, 256
Schumann, Robert, 45
Schwalbach, Germany, 76
Scott, Sir Walter, 50, 118, 138, 141
"Sculpture, Painting and Music" (Gogol), 123
Selected Passages From Correspondence with Friends (Gogol), 71, 74, 76–80, 82, 232–46, 247, 253, 254
Servants' Room, The (Gogol), 85, 179–80
Shakespeare, William, 166
Shaved-off Mustache, The (Gogol), 58, 62
Shchepkin, Mikhail, 35, 37, 43, 46, 47, 77, 173, 174
Sheremeteva, Nadezhda, 70, 73
Shevyrev, Professor, 33, 78, 227
Shulgin, I. P., 41
Simpleton, The (Gogol), 6
Singer, Theodor, 16
Slavophile movement, 69–70
Smirnova, Alexandra, 8, 51, 70, 72, 73, 75, 78–79, 83, 86, 247, 250
Sollogub, Count, 73, 75
Sollogub, Countess Sofia, 73, 75
"Something about Nezhin" (Gogol), 14
"Some Thoughts on the Teaching of Geography to Children" (Gogol), 32
Somov, Orest, 119
Son of the Fatherland, The (Gogol), 20
Sorochincy, Ukraine, 7
Sosnitsky (actor), 46
Soulié, Frédéric, 138
State Theater, St. Petersburg, 46
Sterne, Laurence, 114, 132, 138, 156, 157, 183
"Story of How Ivan Ivanovich and Ivan Nikiforovich Quarreled, The" (Gogol), 109, 136, 147–54
Strasbourg, France, 74
Sturdza, Alexander, 85
Sue, Eugène, 138
Suitors, The (Gogol), 43–44, 172
Svinyin, Pavel, 31, 99

Tales of Belkin (Pushkin), 162
"Taras Bulba" (Gogol), 62, 136, 141–43
"Teacher, The" (Gogol), 32, 120–21
Telescope (periodical), 44
"Terrible Boar, The" (Gogol), 32, 120–22
"Terrible Vengeance, The" (Gogol), 95, 97, 100, 110–13, 138, 143
Théâtre Français, Paris, 51
Thierry, Augustin, 166
Thomas a Kempis, St., 74, 244
Tieck, Ludwig, 119, 122, 138
Tolstoy, Count Alexander P., 75, 76, 79, 82–83, 87, 90
Tolstoy, Leo, 255
Travemünde, Germany, 27, 49
Tristram Shandy (Sterne), 156
Troshchinskaya, Anna, 6
Troshchinsky, Andrey, 29, 30
Troshchinsky, Dmitry, 6, 9, 29
Tsarskoye Selo, Russia, 34
Turgenev, Ivan, 41, 87
"Two Little Fishes" (Gogol), 12

Ukraine, 3, 38, 84
Uvarov, Minister of Education, 40

Venetsianov (lithographer), 37
Venice, Italy, 63
Vevey, Switzerland, 50
Vielgorskaya, Countess, 73
Vielgorskaya, Countess Anna Mikhailovna, 73, 82, 83, 84
Vielgorsky, Count Iosif, 45, 56–57, 75

Vienna, Austria, 57–58, 62–63
Vinogradov, Viktor, 132, 157
"Viy" (Gogol), 136, 144–47, 154
Volkonskaya, Princess Zinaida, 54
Voltaire, 50
Voss, Johann Heinrich, 23
Vyazemsky, Prince, 45, 47
Vysotsky, Gerasim, 13–14

Wackenroder, Wilhelm Heinrich, 122

"Washerwoman, The" (Gogol), 36
"Woman" (Gogol), 32, 122–23

Yazykov, Nikolay, 57, 67, 72, 254

Zhukovsky, Vasily, 23, 32, 34, 40, 45, 46, 50, 52, 53, 55, 56, 59, 60, 61–62, 67, 73, 74, 75, 76, 85, 205, 234, 247